NEW SCHOOL ACTING

TAKING IT TO THE NEXT LEVEL

BY

JEREMY WHELAN

WITH THE

DICTIONARY OF THE EMOTIONS
THESAURUS OF THE EMOTIONS

AND

THE MANIFESTO OF NEW SCHOOL ACTING

© 1996

NEW SCHOOL ACTING
A Whelan International Publications Book with Peacock Productions.

For information
Whelan International Publications
701 Grant Avenue   Suite C
West Collingswood, New Jersey 08107

ISBN: 0-9650908-0-9

Includes Index

Cartoon on page 46 by Mena of Madrid, Spain.
Copyright © 1991 Cartoonist & Writers Syndicate

NEW SCHOOL ACTING
Distributed by Samuel French Trade,7623 W. Sunset Blvd., L.A, CA,
(213)876-0570

Cover photo by: James Higgins

OTHER BOOKS BY JEREMY WHELAN

INSTANT ACTING
Better Way Books,1507 Dana Avenue, Cinncinnati, Ohio 45207, (800) 289-0963

THE ABC'S OF ACTING
Grey Heron Books, 290 S.W. Tualatin Loop, West Linn, Oregon 97068

DEDICATION

TO MUSES AND MENTORS
AND ACTORS EVERYWHERE

ACKNOWLEDGMENTS

I have many people to thank for their help, inspiration, and in those cases,financial support, in helping me get this book ready. First, I would like to thank Maura Kelly for her hard work and dedication. She not only put tremendous personal effort in compiling The Dictionary and The Thesaurus of the Emotions, she also lead a team of students who aided her in her research. She will thank them individually in her introduction to the Dictionary, so I won't do that here, but you all know how much I appreciate your efforts. The Dictionary and Thesaurus of The Emotions has been a project of mine for years and with the help of the above, I finally have it.

I would also like to thank Pat Pallies for all of her hard work in proof reading this book and for giving me an English education in the process. While she must get credit for proofing the book, she can not be held responsible for any errors which remained. I have a penchant for awkward constructions at times and it is also possible that some of her corrections were missed in preparing the book for press. My brother Michael again contributed invaluable editorial advise, as well as providing me with information from his vast knowledge of the subject. Michael's wife Linda for artistic contributions along the way. Like Pat, I didn't always take Michael's advise, so if you see editorial errors, they are mine. To Beth Gorhing of The Fireside Theatre Book Club for her support and confidence over the years. To Jim Fox and Gwen Feldman at Samuel French in LA. Others contributing editorial advise are also thanked. Since this is an early version, I'm not sure who they are yet. Many other people deserve thanks. Sharon Andrews of Wake Forest university for support, Stan and Jane Wilson for friendship and support, Bill Pallies for trust and support, Ed Jorden for years of friendship and his company, Spirit Arts for the cover. Bruce Curless, Artistic Director of The Ritz Theatre in Oaklyn, NJ, and his wonderful staff for giving me a place to teach while I worked on this book, and for providing the nurture and support environment that I sometimes make difficult. Bill Brohaugh of Betterway Books for all his help with editing INSTANT ACTING. Bill Roudebush, Head of the Drama School at The Walnut Street Theatre in Philadelphia, for letting me teach there and for his enthusiastic support for the ideas I teach. To Bill's Asst. Frank Licopoli, for his help in organizing my classes there. William Morris, Chair of Theatre at Rowan College, for bringing me over there for a seminar, and the chance to share my ideas with his departments students and teachers. Thanks to Rose Gruber at Gloucester County College for the same opportunity. Gersh and Carolanne Morningstar of The Florida Blue Sheet, for friendship an years of Mentorship. Bruce and Janin Paine and family, Ted and Leslie Demos and family and my brother John for all of their support, they are my LA family, and of course, my daughter L.A. and her family. To Dick Schaal my first teacher in a professional environment. To Liz Power for support. To Sue Shisler for finishing the index. I would also like to thank Lisa Regina, a friend I met here for the help she gave along the way. To Ed Fiscella for giving me the opportunity to work with hundreds of young actors at Summer Stage, a wonderful theatre camp he directs for the Gloucester Township Centre for the Arts. I want to thank the teachers around the country who have taken these ideas into the classroom and the rejuvenating effect it has when I hear from them. Paul Cerra is one of those teachers and he's also a real enthusiast for these ideas. Roseanne Shaker for her help and support and Laura Kelly for help around the office. To Cathy Parker Management and to Cathy in particular for having confidence in me and a very warm personality. Christina Karman of Miami, for the wonderful job of helping me get INSTANT ACTING into the Spanish language and a publisher in Spain to get it to those actors. To Mark Majorian at Cypress College for support and advise. To Matt Garfield and Peacock Productions for getting involved with this project at a crucial time. To Mike Berman for putting a fine final polish on the formatting of this book and hanging in with me until four in the morning at Kinkos in Cherry Hill to get that done. I know I'm leaving out some very important people and I will be very embarrassed when I am made aware of that error. I'll put you on the CD-ROM, when I get to that and I'm sorry I forgot.

The reason I finished this book in Collingswood, New Jersey, was to be able to spend time with the east coast part of my family, I grew up in South Jersey and although I would rather talk about living in Paris, London and Rome, this is home. My mother and father, John and Mary, have been a source of joy as I wrote this, as was my sister Pat and my Uncle Pat and my sister's husband Dick and all their kids, and their kids' kids.

TABLE OF CONTENTS

<u>AUTHORS PREFACE</u>

AN OUTLINE OF MAIN IDEAS IN THIS BOOK

Nobody will ever know how many skeletons are in the closets of directors/teachers who demand that students use their own emotions to portray a character's tragedy. This practice is known in Method Acting terminology as Affective Memory, Emotional Recall, Effective Memory etc.

How many kids, that wanted to be actors, went over the edge from putting themselves through the worst moments in their lives repeatedly in an attempt to meet that directors/teachers expectations? That technique is probably the major reason actors, as a group, are so neurotic. Affective memory is a harmful, intrusive and abusive practice it should be recognized as such and discontinued.

The preceding two paragraphs clearly define one of the major objectives of this book and New School Acting, i.e. to stop the emotional abuse actors suffer at the hands of the Old School acting style. New School Acting is equally concerned with the abuse to actors creativity by that autocratic Russian school. American acting has slavishly followed and doggedly clings to the Method, even though it has clearly outgrown its usefulness. Ninety percent of American acting teachers have bought into the Method, either as it is, or in one of its many disguises; of the remaining ten percent, most are on the fringe or over the edge. Over the edge can't be dealt with; on the fringe is generally interesting work but so hyper-personal to the teacher, that it can't be boiled down to a set of rules and procedures, which would make it accessible for classroom or professional use on any sort of broad base. New School Acting can be taught and used by anyone possessing the knowledge found in this book. The two major innovations of New School are presented in clear, step by step, easy to follow instructions. There are quick tests that will let you prove the potential value of these ideas and techniques, to yourself, in minutes.

The Manifesto of New School Acting, which begins this book, points out some of the abuses actors suffer from Old School style acting. The Manifesto outlines the eleven major differences between Old School and New School Acting.

The Manifesto also exposes a giant failure in actors training; an oversight that must equal the greatest lapse in any training program for any profession ever; that being the failure to educate actors in the use of the number one tool of their trade, the very root of the art form, the emotions. This historical blunder should be addressed immediately and forcefully. The Manifesto calls for a thorough, objective and on going study of the emotions in any acting program that purports to take itself seriously. This book gives a very specific and simple to use technique to get us on that road and heading in the right direction. I must admit that it took me twenty years to see the problem clearly, and guilt, as much as anything else, feeds the adamantcy connected to this proposal.

Going back for a moment, as an actor, I've used that tactic, Affective Memory, myself and even advocated it as a last recourse, in my earlier days of teaching, before I realized there was a better way; a way to give the character an emotional life of his own.

The fault lies in the naivete of the acting world and people in general, about emotions. Most people can't even pronounce the words used to represent what they are feeling, let alone have an in depth knowledge of that emotion. Some of you may be familiar with a book called <u>Emotional Intelligence</u>, it has been on <u>The New York Times</u> bestseller list for months at this writing. This is a book that all actors should read. It clearly points out the emotional ignorance of the world and many of the negative repercussions that that ignorance has and is causing.

I will go deeper into some of the more pertinent (to actors) aspects of that book later in this book, however, if you doubt my ascertation about the emotional ignorance we actors suffer, read <u>Emotional Intelligence</u>. As a Ph.D. from Harvard and a writer for ten years on behavioral and brain sciences for <u>The New York Times</u>, the author Daniel Goleman, has access to all the top level research and researchers. These are some of the best minds in the world and they have been working in the area of the emotions for decades. If you want to understand emotions better, his book should be very useful to you. The goals of <u>NEW SCHOOL ACTING</u> are much different from those of that book. <u>NEW SCHOOL ACTING</u> is aimed at the actor/artist. I knew that this emotional ignorance existed, that is why I have been teaching emotional awareness to actors for twelve years. I believe actors and teachers of acting will accept the obvious, now that it has been pointed out, and we can get to work building our emotional vocabularies.

The greatest failure, in acting, comes in not recognizing the distinct and emphatic difference between the character played and the person playing the part. The intellectual approach to acting, that we have always used, fosters that confusion. The heightened emotional awareness, which is the base of New School Acting, makes the distinction between actor and character clean and simple to achieve. Actors are not afraid of work but they must be given productive work to do; work which brings them closer to their audience. I am asking actors to look at acting in a whole new light, in a way that they have never looked at it before, and it starts with the following basic realization.

<u>Emotions Are To Actors What Colors Are To Painters</u>. Ask any painter how much of his/her studies were concentrated on color. The answer will be, most of them. Color is a lifelong study for painters, yet, to my knowledge, actors have never had to, as a natural part of their education, study emotions. It should be very obvious from the importance emotions play in the acting process that actors should know as much as they can about them. I define the essence of acting as going from emotion to emotion in a theatrical manner. Yet, there is not an acting program in this country, and not in any other that I know of, that offer classes such as, Emotions I, Emotions II, etc. There is no doubt in my mind, and I hope when you've finished this book, yours as well, that this is not only something that should be done, it is something that must be done. An area of study as vital as this, demands a hard look from everyone connected to the acting experience. In the instances where some emotional training was attempted, it was done with actors ruminating on their own subjective emotions rather than a broader, more universal level. This understanding of emotions as they exist in a pure universal state is necessary for the artist to have control of his tools. I don't know of any attempts to do that type of study. I'm told there have been some, although when I challenged that, no names were offered or books mentioned.

Emotions are the primary tool we actors use to tell our stories and we are ignorant of them. This book not only calls for a systematic, thorough and on going study of emotions in actors training; it also provides exercises and techniques for broadening the actor's emotional vocabulary as a means of increasing her emotional mobility. That knowledge will shield the actor from the violent self abuse involved in using her own emotions. Affective Memory, Emotional Recall, Effective Memory etc.; by whatever name it's called, is an ancient and barbaric practice and it should be barred from the classroom.

I am not ignorant of the fact that these boundaries between the character's emotions and the actor's emotions are sometimes blurred. I've been an actor for thirty four years. I know that those boundaries blur as a natural component of the craft. What I will say is that this natural bleeding over is automatic and, within that framework, is manageable. What I condemn is focusing on that area, working to that end, that is where it gets dangerous. You do not need to work to use yourself, it is impossible not to. Working to use yourself is a fool's errand, it's very dangerous and a waste of time. The key is in finding out where you and your character are most different emotionally, that is where the focus of the work must be placed.

It may be that the Method was the best we had at the time and as such was an improvement over what went before. As a stage in the evolution of acting, that danger is past. It is no longer necessary, a better way is now available.

When actors are ignorant of emotions, they have no choice but to use their own, on whatever instinctual level they access them. A systematic study of emotions will allow actors to make creative choices from a much broader artistic palette, without dragging themselves through some potentially harmful psycho-drama.

The color analogy should make this concept easy for most people to understand, but I'm afraid, not to all. In order to get this idea across, with the urgency it demands, I'm looking for any analogies I can find which will make the concept clear. One such analogy comes from the Art of Music; think of scales and the endless hours that any good musician spends on them. "No scales; no music", is the way one musician answered my question about the importance of scales. I am not talking about four chord rock and roll which is the musical equivalent of a Schwarzenegger action adventure movie. Don't get me wrong, I love Arnold and Sly, and especially Zena, but occasionally I need more subtlety. The painter's colors are the greatest part of his creative vocabulary, the musician's scales are the greatest part of her creative vocabulary, the chef's spices are the greatest part of his creative vocabulary, the actor's emotions must be the greatest part of her creative vocabulary and actors are virtually bankrupt in this area, mainly because acting teachers have never bothered to teach them. If you wanted to be a four star chef you would be trained to have a thorough knowledge of the taste of <u>all</u> the spices available. Every art and every profession has it's vocabulary and it's basics. Lawyers have torts, doctors have anatomy. Would you want some doctor, who failed anatomy, cutting into your body. No, you'd want her to know every thing about the body. It would not be enough for that doctor to know everything about her own liver, you want her to know everything about livers in general and your liver in particular, before she cuts. You have to know your character's liver, I don't know for a fact, but I would guess that no two livers are alike. Actors would fail any emotions test given them, because emotions have never been part of the curriculum.

If you have any doubt about how inadequate actors emotional vocabularies are, go to the quick test of emotional awareness and give it to any group of actors. Actually, there are two quick tests; one might be called the super quick test, it examples the thesaurus technique, it's on page 9. The other, although not taking much longer, points out very rapidly actors' emotional ignorance, it's on page 7.

Though I've been teaching emotions for 12 years, I have only begun to develop a range of exercises for this systematic study of emotions. I present them here with the certainty that others will recognize this obvious need and create a broad range of techniques and exercises to fill this virtual vacuum. To facilitate this study I have created <u>The Dictionary of the Emotions</u> and <u>The Thesaurus of Emotions</u>. They will prove to be a great help as teachers, directors, actors and students adjust to a new and more creatively satisfying approach.

It is very important to realize that by understanding emotions and having a broad emotional vocabulary, I am not, in anyway, suggesting that actors use this knowledge to score the script from emotion to emotion. That would be as uncreative as going from intellectualized objective to intellectualized objective, as is done in the Method. I am suggesting something much more subtle. I will go into detail later in the book, but the basic idea is that of a very elevated ensemble style of acting. While this definition may echo the goal of ensemble since the concept originated, the tools to achieve that goal where not available, until now. For centuries, man dreamed of going to the moon, but that goal could not be achieved until the tools were available. The type of emotions studies I propose, an objective knowledge of all the emotions, as universals, is the tool necessary before the ideal of a true ensemble performance can be achieved. With that knowledge, every theatrical performance, on stage or film, has an equal opportunity to reach the highest goals of ensemble.

In a discussion, someone said that a play such as Cyrano could never be ensemble, because it is such a star vehicle. I argued that it is not the audiences perception of a performance that makes it ensemble, it is how the cast conceives and executes the piece that makes it a star vehicle or a perfect example of true ensemble acting. To use a sports analogy, while the fans at a football game may focus on and give credit to the quarterback, the quarterback and everyone on that team knows, were it not for every player on the team doing their job, in deep communication with each other, the star quarterback is dogmeat.

The point is, that after the initial emotion of a piece is played, everything that follows is a reaction. It is similar to a landslide; the first emotion being the boulder at the top of the mountain, which, once started on its downhill movement causes all that follows to happen. The actor is the little Dutch boy who sticks his finger in the dike, when the dam goes, the actors are carried along on the current. There is no time for an actor to think as a theatrical piece moves along on it's current of emotion. Only an actor schooled in the emotions can keep up with that current and still seem natural. In less time than it takes the heart to beat, emotions change dynamically. I call the actors response to that change, "the moment of creation." An actor schooled in emotions can trust that at "the moment of creation", her instrument will provide the exact degree of the emotion the moment calls for. The actors emotions studies gives her this highly broadened pool of possible choices, and her instrument will choose the most appropriate one. There is nothing premeditated about it, it is simply providing inspiration with the greatest array of possibilities.

The need for emotional truth in contemporary audiences should be evident, if it isn't I will make points throughout this book in an attempt to establish that fact. In the past, with limited tools, we must have had to abuse ourselves emotionally, we don't have to do that anymore. Aside from the humanistic concerns, looking at it in a purely practical light, Old School doesn't work anymore, not on the audience. The Russian school starts at the head; the audience wants emotion. Watch talk shows for a week. Watch reality shows for a week. Watch the news shows, look into the faces of the Bosnian people. Watch audiences run to these shows to fulfill the need for emotional stimuli. Audiences are running away from bad acting, not even bad acting, just old fashioned acting, that seems bad because it is out of synch with the audiences need for real emotion. The book I mentioned before, Emotional Intelligence was the cover story of Time Magazine in October, 1995, it has sold millions of copies. The author has been on Oprah and every other talk show, as well as Internet chat sessions; even Cosmopolitan Magazine interviewed him in the January 1996 issue. Time Magazine, Oprah, Cosmo and the Internet, if that's not a cross section of American audiences, what is? All of this is really a giant cue from the audience as to what they want. People are hungry for this new awareness. The seed of the new audience is reflected in the public's response to that book, the TV shows they chose to watch and other indicators discussed in this book. An emotionally aware actor can deliver what that audience wants, on cue. The increase in sensitivity to, and curiosity about emotions is reflected in many areas of contemporary culture.

The work I've been doing with emotions is very much a part of that, however, whereas others are trying to satisfy this audience's curiosity about their own emotions, I am trying to give actors the tools to meet their demands and esthetic needs. Make no mistake, this audience is demanding a new acting style to suit their special needs, with the same fervor that the emerging middle class of the industrial revolution demanded theirs. One point, that everyone working in this area of emotions agrees upon, people (actors) are uneducated when it comes to emotions. I learned that along the way, from observation and intuition, and since it was obviously true, I started working on teaching emotions as part of the artistic discipline of acting. We must forget how they used to do it in Russia in the old days. It is USA, Nineteen Ninety-Six; not Russia, Eighteen Ninety-Six; it was more than a century ago that those ideas bloomed. We hop off to the moon now, anytime we want. They didn't even have radio when those ideas were born. If the acting technique defines the style of a piece, then everything we're doing is Retro. I know of the wrinkles that have been put on the Method and I know about the face lifts it has gotten, but it's still a hundred years old. Acting, as a living art form, must be vibrant and speak in the language of the day.

• Aside from the sections on broadening the actors emotional vocabulary, this book contains an overview of American acting. You will see that I think American acting is something that has never really existed to date. We have had Americans who act, but they were Americans, who at the inception, acted in the European style and as soon as they stopped doing that they started acting in the Russian style, and we've been stuck there ever since. While I credit Viola Spolin with the breakthrough that showed the light at the end of that dusty tunnel, we have a lot of work to do before we arrive there. Spolin is part of the answer but this is not a book about improvisation. The professional actors first obligation is to the text. Improvisation, properly used, can be helpful in exploring character relationships, improperly used, it can destroy the integrity of the script.

• The Whelan Tape Technique is a remarkable tool for directors, teachers and actors working on their own. This chapter is a complete step by step guide to using the basic tape technique. Everything you need to know to use the technique successfully is in those pages. The emotions work and the tape technique are powerful tools when used individually but, used together, they take acting to new levels. You can test them both in less than half an hour; although you will start to see some of the advantages immediately, it becomes more interesting as you go. The thesaurus idea can be proven in the time it takes to run a short scene (three minutes) twice. The tape technique hits a big payoff at the fourth time through a short scene. There are other ways to use the tape technique in training actors and in audition situations. There are 14 other applications of the technique and various other support techniques, but for those you will have to refer to my book, <u>INSTANT ACTING</u> .

• Another section of this book deals with the changing relationship in New School Acting of the actor to the director. Once again, I have had to put this into some sort of historical perspective. The autocratic style of Old School directors is not compatible with the level of creativity and commitment demanded of actors by contemporary audiences. It points out audience needs and leads to a discussion of ways and means for the actor, working with and without the director, to meet those needs.

• The section called The New Elite deals with the increasingly international and increasingly sophisticated nature of contemporary audiences, and how new socio-economic conditions are creating an audience unlike any other in history.

• In theory and in the development of techniques, education has taken giant strides. Learning Styles is a general heading under which most of these advances fall. Decades of research, by some of the best minds in education, have come up with answers to the question of, "How do we improve the ability of teachers to teach and students to learn?" The fact that the institutions of American education; universities, high schools and elementarys schools, have largely ignored these advances is something that must be looked at, and I do that in the chapter on Education. It also looks at the educational system as it takes half steps and faux pas in an attempt to deal with an emerging one world reality. Actors are students and suffer as much from this crime as any other student. Old School rules acting education in academia and in professional and private schools as well. This is a warning to actors seeking instruction as to what to avoid and what they have a right to demand from the institutions they attend.

• I've been spending time on the Internet and have gotten into discussions with directors, actors and educators regarding my work in the area of emotions. This work is as new as the popular Internet and on the net there is a section called FAQ's, which stands for Frequently Asked Questions, since some of you may have the same questions that my on-line companions had, I've borrowed that device from the net and included a chapter called, FAQ's. I won't use their letters, but I will use as much of my answers as I can, so the format is the same as JEOPARDY, from my answers you will be able to guess the questions. It isn't a true question and answer session because some of the ideas came to me while editing, but the format serves a purpose.

• In the final chapter, I play with some theories why the subjective attempt to objectify emotions works, and why it has such a profound effect on the power of an actors performance.

• I hate skimpy indexes. I might just remember a phrase or a few words that key me to something I want to reread, and if the index is meager, I'm in trouble. I find myself endlessly flipping pages to see if I can stumble across what I want to look at again. I tried to make sure that wouldn't happen to you by having a big fat index, hopefully, whatever you might want to find again, is in there.

This book may seem to contradict everything you have been taught about acting and in most ways, it will. That radical a change can be hard to adjust to; but I've packed enough facts, ideas, information and exercises in these pages that, if you follow them, you shouldn't have a problem letting go of what you were taught and entering wholeheartedly into this new work. The rewards come quickly, so the first step you take will provide the energy for those that must follow.

I think the best way to approach this book would be to just read the whole thing without worrying about remembering anything or doing any of the exercises. Just read it and take whatever you get from it. One thing about that, those of you who bought it, should freely mark it up, write notes in margins and highlight anything, anywhere. Many people have a reverence for books, they love the crisp immaculate pages, with the words all stacked nice and neat. The idea of scribbling in margins or slashing big bold bright highlighter marks on its pages is not within their normal thought process. Forget it, this book is a tool and all tools pick up nicks and scratches in normal usage. So as you're doing your casual read, keep a pen and some different colored markers near by. One color could be things you want to try right away, another color could be things you want to research, another could be things to reread, etc.

you're doing your casual read, keep a pen and some different colored markers near by. One color could be things you want to try right away, another color could be things you want to research, another could be things to reread, etc.

If you follow that advice, I'm sure your copy of <u>NEW SCHOOL ACTING</u> will be brightly colored and enough notes in the margins that you will know exactly where to start applying these ideas and exercises to your own work and study programs.

Sometimes in the course of writing this book, I refered to the Whelan Tape Technique as the WTT, I think the reasons are obvious. I also use New School Acting as a book title, these should be in caps and underlined, the other occasions represent the contemporary movement in acting.

I recognize the difference between the Stanislavski System, the American Method, the work of Stella Adler and Sandy Meisner, etc., but it is the physco-intellectual root of the work, not the branches that I argue against. As these are all psycho-intellectually based styles, they are virtually the same in relation to New School Acting. The Method was the easiest generic to use most often when referring to that general old school concept.

As a final word, some of the chapters in this book were written as essays. Although I've gone over and over them in an attempt to remove redundancies, I missed some, others I felt could be heard more than once at no annoyance to the reader and removing them would make the original seem choppy and incomplete.

Welcome to New School Acting
Jeremy Whelan

NEW SCHOOL ACTING

CHAPTER I

THE NEW AUDIENCE AND THE ENSEMBLE

Without an audience there is no such thing as acting. Actors could get together and do shows, but without anyone to watch, it would just be kids playing a game. Whatever anyone says; when it comes to what kind of shows get produced, the audience is who decides what those shows will be. Occasionally, in history, this audience has a massive change of taste. The last time it occurred on a scale such as the one we are seeing today began in 1864, with the appearance of the first director on the theatrical scene. Up to that point, actors basically directed themselves. The advent of the director established the power structure that would later allow Stanislavski to organize the very disparate world of actors training. As Stanislavski's authority grew, he was able to bring the psychoanalytical work of Freud to the forefront of actors' training, and that is where we still are today. The psycho-intellectual style of acting created by Stanislavski has finally run its course. Audiences are abandoning it and that is forcing a change in the way actors are trained.

Separating a cause from a symptom is not always easy, but one thing is obvious, the immense popularity of talk shows, as well as a host of other reality based shows, has caused a real shift in audience awareness, and in their wants and needs. The latest television survey (April 1996) showed three news shows in the top twenty for the first time in the history of the medium. Today's audiences are being exposed to greater and greater doses of real life-real people, both ordinary and extraordinary; how they act, walk, and talk and how they feel. The emotional pull of talk shows is very powerful and their popularity is a testament to the tastes of contemporary audiences; not necessarily in the low brow sort of programming many of these shows generate, but at the core, at the very heart of them, you find genuine emotion. As a result of endless displays of real people exposing their deepest feelings, today's audiences know the difference between acting and truth better than any audience in history. This emotionally educated audience demands a deeper level of emotional commitment and greater emotional variety.

Before the boom of talk shows, on television and radio, most people only knew a few other people with any sort of intimacy. Usually, the people they knew had some common ground; neighbors, church groups, somebody from work. This was known as a social circle; a closed end system. Those few people were what we had for a frame of reference, and only a few of those people were personal friends, people about whom we had some insight into their private lives, what they were really like. These ordinary people were what and who we knew, some were a little wild, but in an ordinary way, anybody too extreme gets shunned. People who are too extreme are bad for business; the kind of person you don't want around the kids.

So, since actors portray extreme types of some sort: i.e., extraordinary people in extraordinary circumstance, extraordinary people in ordinary circumstance, ordinary people in extraordinary circumstance; actors were the audiences only frame of reference for these types.

The public's knowledge of the type of people seen in movies, plays, TV, was confined to an actor's interpretation of that type. Now along come talk shows and reality shows and every kind of freak in the world, the real thing is in your living room, on ten channels, six times a day. People you sat next to on a bus are up there spilling their guts, telling every dirty little secret they, and everybody they know has ever had, to anybody that will listen. They tell things that would embarrass you to know about anybody. They break your heart with run away kids and raped children, abused spouses etc. You see your neighbor on Oprah in a Gestapo uniform. You see the waitress from your local restaurant talking about tricking the neighborhood men and boys. These ordinary people tell you everything; they tell you that they have and will sell themselves for a sniff of cocaine; the bus driver who, even though you thought he was a man all these years, is really a woman, her wife's a tri-sexual and his kids are really midgets working a welfare scam.

Extraordinary people, and the extraordinary aspects of seemingly ordinary people lives, their most personal hopes, dreams, memories, and secrets are lined up and paraded in front of millions of people on Oprah, Geraldo, Montel, Jenny Jones, Jerry Springer; and dozens of others, all day every day. Talk radio has shot up in popularity; something to do with your car phone, a chance to let people know how you really feel. Then of course, we have the biggest talk show of all, the Internet.

Only the internet is different, you don't have to get on their show, because there is no "they", and nobody can censor what you say. The Internet represents a change in communication that will easily transform the world as much, or more, than the industrial revolution, and it was the industrial revolution that ushered in the last major change in acting style well over two hundred years ago; now acting is changing again. Over thirty million people are already members of the Internet and you can send a message to all of them in one click of a mouse. Kids in five different nations are having video conferences, live from schools across the world; third graders are mentoring first graders in computer usage. When anybody in the world can talk to anybody else in the world, as long as they want, about anything they want, for twenty dollars a month, well, as you might guess, everything is about to change.

It isn't all good, but it is a form of freedom of communication, on a scale that the world has never known. These people are talking about how they feel, about everything and anything. While there are some things that are a concern, as yet, the Internet is uncensored. The extent that people are talking about their feelings can be seen in the fact that someone can talk honestly and openly about his desire for children, to people who understand and who feel as they do, they trade pictures. Someone talks about how she plans to kill all the blacks and Jews. Hey, say what you feel, and thirty million people, from every country in the world, are free to say what they feel, about what you feel. These are extreme examples; there are pedophiles and kiddie porn on the Internet, rampant racist are on the Internet and any one of thirty million people can get it, with video, at the click of a mouse button. The thing to look at, is that these types have always been a part of society and they have always found a way to communicate with each other. What is important about the Internet, is that people who would never have had a chance to talk to each other, from all parts of the world, are in daily communication. Especially the children, who, with live video, are meeting kids from all over the world, in open dialogue. The natural optimism of the young, communicated on an international basis, daily, is a bright spot on the world horizon.

The point I'm trying to make is that audiences today don't rely on actors to give them a peep show on the abnormal, or insights into the deepest secrets of "normal" people. Audiences today compare actors' performances to the real thing. They compare actors performances to a person they saw, live on Oprah, Richard Bey, etc., that very afternoon. The reason they watch these shows is because they see heavy doses of real emotion. The actors can't compare to that, they can't compete with "Cops", as they drag a crack mother out of her house, her kid hanging onto her ankle. Actors can't compete with skin heads busting Heraldo's nose, or black militants talking about killing the white devil. Emotional honesty is extremely compelling to watch, people get caught up in it, regardless of whether you watch in shock or with sympathy, you feel something from watching them, feel something with honesty and intensity, this emotional honesty is what is missing in acting. Today's audiences, having always been denied their own emotional freedom, crave these displays with a passion once know by Roman audiences craving the gladiators blood.

The reason it is missing in acting and why today's acting is not as satisfying to today's audiences is that ninety percent of that acting comes from a Psycho-Intellectually based acting style; the Stanislavski system or some variation of that Method. Today's audience wants raw emotion and actors are not trained to give that to them, except from their own very limited experience with specific emotions. The audience has already seen actors do those emotions in other parts; with reality shows they get huge gobs of fresh meat every day; hundreds of guests with hundreds of unique twists on an emotion. They get an extremely wide based variety of anger, joy, love, hate. etc. A quick observation, that is a clue to the desire for variety in contemporary audiences, can be found on the shelf of your local market. When I grew up, there were maybe 10 kinds of breakfast cereal, today there are fifty to sixty, we drank orange or grapefruit juice with the occasional grape or pineapple, not kiwi-mango and papaya-guava. So, when it comes to watching actors, who cares if here comes what's his name, playing his own puny emotions, in the guise of yet another gangster; so who cares that he's got a different name and a different haircut. I can see four live Mafia hit men sit in front of a camera and tell me, so I can see, hear, feel, what it's really like to beat somebody to death with a baseball bat. I can watch a panel of them have a discussion about it, arguing over technique and describing how it makes them feel; Channel 3 at four; right after Montel. Emotion based acting, New School Acting, is the only chance we have of getting these audiences back. Actors must learn a much more universal language of emotion. We do have an advantage over talk shows and reality shows, primarily because our stories are much tighter and also because we're generally better looking and in better shape then most of these real people, or we can be lit and dressed to seem so. But we do need to build our emotional vocabularies, expand our emotional mobility and use those tools to create a true ensemble acting style.

ENSEMBLE

Ensemble acting is usually considered the most artful form of acting and generally the most enjoyable for actors and audiences alike. While small groups of gifted actors could pull this off on occasion, the limitations of psycho-intellectual old school style acting, made it very difficult. In new school acting, the goal is that every performance will be, by nature, ensemble.

Intellectualism has, as a natural by product, elitism. The old saying, knowledge is power, is true in an intellectual age. The fact that woman and minorities were denied education in effect denied them power. The fact that more woman and minorities are rising to power today, is another signal that the emotional age I speak about, is here. Education can be bought, therefore power can be bought. Elitism, in acting, meant an ego based acting style. In that environment, a director represented designated power. In an ego based atmosphere, someone must have power, or, all would be striving to subdue the others, to turn the spotlight on themselves. The type of creative co-operation I'm talking about is an impossibility in that type of environment, however, as we are already at the edge of the age of emotion, we can start working in a new and exciting way.

The difference between intellectualism and emotionalism, is that emotion can't be bought, we are all born with a full range of them; that equality, when recognized, is the basis for the first broad based, truly ensemble acting style. There are many definitions of ensemble, but the purest one would start with character. The key word, is of course, character; a character can change from moment to moment because that is what people do every day. At any given moment, there are many possible ways to act or react to that moment. We can try to write the script of our lives, so that it would go the way we want, but anyone who has tried to do that usually fails miserably. Anyone who could succeed at that, is either not in the real world, or they are so boring no one would want to talk to them, let alone write about them.

That same element of unpredictability, the unexpected, that is in every human's life, must be in your character's life. In the same way people must respond to a situation as it happens, characters must too.

Example: You are feeling good, heading into Seven Eleven to get a soda, got your girlfriend in the car, you are going to a movie, everything is great. Suddenly the guy in line behind you pulls a gun, jumps the counter, blows the head off the cashier and then points the gun at you. You are not going to get psychological about it and you can't say,"No, I don't want to play this scene." Fear is going to force you to do something, something that probably involves movement, even if it's only your bladder. In theatrical terms, it is called the illusion of the first time and that is what you're paid for, so create it. Actually, if you are working moment to moment, it will happen automatically.

That unexpected aspect of life will be in every part you ever play and the emotional mobility to respond to such moments is something actors have to train to achieve. Since you can't memorize every possible situation you will encounter in your acting career, and then plan for them, you must train your emotional awareness the way an athlete trains for an event. For example, a baseball player learns how to hit the genre "fast ball", because no two fast balls are going to be alike. One is: higher, lower, faster, slower, inside, outside and anywhere in between, sometimes they come straight at your head at over 100 MPH. The "Fast ball" that the actor deals with, is the reality that you and the people you are acting with are changing emotionally, moment to moment, and you don't know into what, until you get to "the moment of creation." Nothing can ever go outside of the circumstances of the script, so we are not talking about wild, completely off the wall deviations. However, an actor may have been so affected by something that happened in his own life that day, that a choice he had played with some basic consistency, suddenly makes a choice that pushes the limits of the extreme part of the soft edge of the given circumstance. I'll give you an example: I was doing a play; an actor had always kept a line he delivered to me, in a low controlled contempt and I had generally been moved to scream my response. One night, out of nowhere, he screamed his line at the top of his lungs. I had nowhere to go, except to take my line way under him in response. Something had happened to him that day and he released it in that line, there were two hundred people on three sides of me, in a very small theatre. I had a nano second to adjust, without ever showing my surprise, as an actor, at his delivery that night. I did it and in that second, our onstage relationship was changed for the rest of the play. Sometimes the differences in performance aren't that drastic, usually they are much more subtle. It could just be the placement of a hand on your arm, or a much deeper warmth in the look you are given, perhaps it's a more broken, beaten aspect of another character's posture which moves you to a richer response. You don't have time to think about the response, it has to be immediate and emotional, to the exact degree called for, that takes a rich emotional vocabulary and a lightning fast emotional mobility.

We are paid to create the illusion of the first time. The fact is it is always the first time. It may be "take two,"or "take three," but it's the first time you're doing "take six." You're different, so are other actors. Fluctuations in performance will be less extreme than life, because the script sets up boundaries that have to be respected. The fact remains, no matter how skillful an actor is, she can not repeat exactly what she did the night before in a play, or even after lunch in a film. People (actors) are always changing, hopefully growing. Subtlety is the goal, ensemble playing, working moment to moment in synch and sympathy with the other actors.

Extreme examples are the easiest to give and I'll give a few, but great performances need not be in the extreme, none the less, extreme examples help communicate a concept. Once a concept is grasped, it is much easier to recognize the much more subtle situations where that concept applies; so here are a few extremes.

I was doing a play, in which a certain actor and I had a lot of scenes together, one night, twenty minutes before curtain, he got a call that his father had died. He was a fine and disciplined actor. He got through the show and stayed on the script, but you don't need much sense to realize that his performance was significantly different than it had been the night before, and I could obviously not play it as I had the night before. Show business is rife with stories of actors surmounting personal tragedy to keep the dictum; the show must go on. It isn't always tragedy, sometimes it's elation. One actor got a call, just before curtain, that his wife had just delivered twins. These are extreme examples that required adjustments by every member of the cast. The fact is, an actor could just be reacting to a bad lunch or finding out the car got towed, that alters her emotional balance in playing a scene shot in the morning and the same one re-shot in the afternoon. This isn't unprofessionalism, it's human.

The key is to be in the moment and sensitive to those that you're working with. If another actor gives you something different than they gave you before, obviously, you can't play it the way you did. Anyone who has ever heard a symphony orchestra play the same piece on two different occasions noticed variations in the playing. Same orchestra, same score, same conductor, different sound, why? Individually they felt differently and so collectively they sounded different. Despite all the seeming similarities in life, nothing human ever duplicates itself with any absolute precision, that is the province of the mechanical.

If you're working from a limited emotional vocabulary, you'll be limited in your ability to respond to these subtle shifts in emotional balance that occur moment to moment, hour by hour, day by day. Some will say that actors do that, it's part of the job. I'm not saying they don't. What I'm talking about is how well they do it, and the obvious truth is, that an actor with a very thorough objective knowledge of the emotions, will have a greater emotional mobility and make these shifts quicker, smoother, and more uniquely than an actor working solely from his own emotions. Certainly, the emotionally aware actor is in less danger of resorting to cliché responses. Some of you will be familiar with the Internet term, hyper text. Actors could look at this enhanced emotional mobility/ability as hyper subtext. Reading in hyper text is different from reading in normal text because it is not linear, it floats with the moment to moment curiosity of the reader. Actors, working in old school fashion, will work from a, more or less, fixed subtext; they may even have it scripted. In any event, their subtext will have a continuity that could more easily be disrupted by a deviation in response from the other character, much more so than a new school actor. Actors schooled in emotions are more capable of recognizing and responding to subtle shifts in emotional tone coming from the other character. It boils down to the new school actor being a better ensemble player.

Everybody uses the term "ensemble," and many think that means a bunch of actors living in the same house, eating out of the same pot. Others confuse it with a Company, a group of actors that works on many shows together over long periods of time. True ensemble acting is what I just described above. It is playing together with absolute sensitivity to each other's delicately shifting emotions; having the training and skills to respond, from an instinct honed by training, fortified with a long and deep emotional vocabulary, with just the right shade of the precisely appropriate emotion.

It should be obvious that an old school actor, wallowing in the depths of her private hell, would have less energy left over to be properly attuned to those with whom she is playing. Many critics today confuse this self absorbed display of personal intensity with good acting; to me it is a high level of self indulgence, that prevents that self absorbed actor from communicating with the high degree of empathy necessary to keep the play in emotional balance. True, this ego based acting may blow the other actor off the screen or off the stage, but if that's the goal, I missed the point. I'm not being an art snob. I subtitled this book, Taking It To The Next Level, and true ensemble, created by emotionally aware actors, is that next level. I think the way audiences are running away from that, "Hey, look at me" kind of acting is proof that they are really tired of watching such boring cliché. "Everybody back up, here I come," that kind of acting is the masturbation/flagellation, conceit based school of acting. I really don't need to see you drag your dead mother out of her grave again, so you can wow me with your power as an actor. I don't care if you have a mustache this time, and you're talking with a German accent, all you're showing me is your limited ability to create a fully developed character. I don't know if he actually said it, but I have no trouble believing he did; Marlon Brando was doing a movie with Jack Nickleson and a reporter asked Brando what he thought of Nicklesons acting and Marlon is said to have replied, "He's like a guy that plays piano with two fingers, what he does, he does very well." I'm not putting down Nickleson or Brando, but the quote would seem to fit many of today's stars.

The delicacy of performance, that I am of demanding of actors, may not be as obvious as the same changes demanded of winners in other areas of society. The world of sports offers a fertile ground for investigating this cross-societal heightening of sensibility. There is very little similarity in the physical appearance of a modern football player as compared to one of fifty years ago. I know that some of those guys were six-six and weighted 350 lbs., but not nearly as many of them, and that three fifty was shifting around on the frame a lot more. One of the commentators from Monday night football said, "These guys today have arms bigger than most of the guys had legs when I was playing." If any decent college team of today were to play the best professional team of fifty years ago, there would not be enough ambulances or hearses to take those pros of yore to the nearest hospital or graveyard. They would all be dead or severely busted up before the game reached the half way mark. The college kids would be standing around drinking Gatorade, telling jokes and maybe bench pressing three hundred and fifty pound guards just to keep busy. That professional football team did have strong men and talented men, but there were a much smaller percentage of them than a team of today. Even those with strength and skills did not work as hard to develop them because it was not demanded by the times in which they lived and worked.

In his book Emotional Intelligence, Daniel Goleman quotes Anders Ericsson, "Studies of Olympic athletes, world class musicians, and chess grand masters find their unifying trait is the ability to motivate themselves to pursue relentless training routines. And with a steady rise in the degree of excellence required to be a world class performer, these rigorous training routines now increasingly must begin in childhood." Anyone who has competed in any area, be it business, academia, sports or the arts, should have noticed that every real winner got there because she worked harder. While sometimes in show business, jobs go to relatives or for sexual favors, it is still essentially the professional and talented that get most of the work.

This is slightly off track, but it is an important note. One of the reasons that so many jobs go to relatives, is because people coming from show business families learn the rules of professionalism with their ABC'S. Talent without professionalism will never work; lesser talents with professional habits will win every time. As I've said elsewhere, it's a thirty thousand dollar a minute business, sometimes much more. Professionalism is easy to learn.

On the talent side, fortunately for actors, old school training has been focused on intellectual procedures; intellectually analyzing the script, intellectual motivation for movement, intellectual exercises to generate the actors emotions, etc. While some of it does still serve a useful purpose, much of that intellectual work is no longer necessary. So, basically, we are all starting over. It is the actors who start this emotional training now and who work hard at it, that will be on top.

A Story: I was in college and I was studying French; it was a struggle. While walking to class, I met a classmate who asked me how I was doing in there. I told her that I really wanted to speak French, but I didn't want to memorize all the rules of grammar. She said "Yeh, I know what you mean. I don't want to learn how to use the Dewey Decimal System so I'm memorizing every book in the library."

The moral being; there are no short cuts to excellence.

CHAPTER II

NEW SCHOOL ACTING MANIFESTO

New School Acting is coming; actors, directors and audiences are restless. I call it New School Acting to differentiate between the approach I'm advocating and Old School, that being the Russian school which has dominated American acting almost since it's inception. Born over a hundred years ago, the Stanislavski system no longer serves the needs of contemporary actors. This goes for all its variations, from Stella Adler to Lee Strasberg and all the disciples that have come along and have put some wrinkle or twist on Stanislavski, including the Miesner approach. I think it must be recognized and it is certainly to his credit that Sandy Meisner acknowledged the danger to actors from using their own emotions, as was demanded by the Stanislavski system and its followers. Miesner took responsibility for that and created a system which let actors avoid that perilous trap. Unfortunately, he did it by doubling the actors cerebral process, trapping them in their heads much more than the Method, distancing them even further from the character. Actors trained in the Meisner approach did learn something very valuable. They have highly developed imaginations; the nature of that work demanded it. The fact is, many actors do not work on developing their imaginations to the degree necessary for the finest acting. However, it seems to me, that if you're working Meisner's way, somebody could hit you on the toe with a hammer and you wouldn't have enough energy below the neck to feel it. If those were the only choices, I'd rather abuse myself emotionally and go with the Method. At least there are emotions in it, even if they are inappropriate to the character and dangerous to me, the actor. While I strongly disagree with the basics of the Method approach, actors who studied the Method also learned many valuable lessons. Stanislavski created an entire system for approaching actors training; in the process of doing that, he took much of what has always been part of the actors craft throughout time, and organized these elements, labeled them, and put them in one place. So in many ways, studying the Method was studying the history of what had worked for actors; where Stanislavski runs counter to the needs of contemporary actors is in the priority he gave to hyper psycho-intellectualization of character and situation. Historically, at the turn of the century, that was, in the evolutionary sense, the appropriate approach; but it's a hundred years later and we are turning another century now.

It is a tribute to actors that even approaches as dangerous as the Method and as clumsy as Meisner were made to work. In light of what I've just said, it may be hard to believe it when I say that I respect the accomplishments of the teachers I mention and others who have dedicated their lives to better acting. I do respect it. My first book was dedicated to Lee Strasberg and Viola Spolin. The Method made a great contribution to acting, it made it human and passionate. Meisner worked hard to develop a system that would spare actors great pain and he did it, and as I just said, he demanded his actors to develop a fantastic imagination. Viola Spolin broke the chain of director dependence and opened the door for actors to reclaim their birthright as creative artist and all actors owe her a deep debt of gratitude for doing that.

The Method itself replaced a style that had reached the end of its usefulness. The change really started earlier in the century with Zola and the movement in art and literature know as Naturalism, which will be talked about in the section on the birth of the director. The greatest impact in this country came with the importation of the Stanislavski system. Certainly, Naturalism as it was applied, and some might say perfected, in the Russian School was a vast improvement over what went before, which I will call The European School. The European style was where actors stood facing the audience and declaimed their words, outlining them with very broad gestures in many cases. Like the style of acting it replaced, the Method is now used up.

I'm offering superior, intelligent alternatives, in some cases they may be subtle but they are hardly complicated. I would also point out that in those places where I am critical, I am as harsh on myself as I might seem to others. As far as Old School is concerned, I do not blame those conditioned to follow a certain path. I blame the conditioner, and since, in this case, it is history itself that dictated the road, as it is doing again now, the ideas I present should be recognized as evolutionary not revolutionary.

I've said Old School doesn't serve the needs of the contemporary actor. So what are the needs of the contemporary actor? They are, to give an honest emotional portrayal of a character. To get lost in a character for the time they contracted to play it, without all the unpleasantries that visit, and sometimes stay with actors forced to use their own emotions in the way dictated by the old school approach. These old techniques are damaging to the actor's emotional well being as well as to their creativity. An actors well being has not been a priority to too many people, unless you have half a film in the can, with that actor in a leading role, but the creative drop off is of concern because it adds up to audience erosion.

Haven't we all seen enough of the drunken actor, the drugged actor, the actor on the psychiatrist couch as a running joke and the type of acting that comes out of that environment. I think audiences have, that is why all the reality shows, talk shows, game shows, news shows, home shopping network and even infomercials have become so popular. Some people would rather watch the weather channel than these "forced" dramas and "by the numbers" comedies. How many times can you watch an actor, in a different disguise/character go through the same emotion? As an actor, you can only play yourself once. In Method terms, going through your own personal angst, drowning in your own sea of personal despair over and over, is known as Affective Memory. Some of you know that means, the practice of having an actor, when he feels he can't reach a character (?I don't understand this, I thought that was my job as an actor), substituting a moment from his own life that has a similar emotional value as that which the character is going through. Since I don't have the space to detail all my objections to Method techniques, I will focus on this one as it is the most offensive and dangerous to the actor.

Ever stop to wonder what this must do to the actor as a person? Going through the death of somebody close to them, or some other intensely painful moment in their lives, so they can appear tragic on stage or screen. Doing it six days a week and twice on Sunday in a play, or months in a film, recalling that personal tragedy in graphic detail each time. Let me see, when I saw Mom get hit by the truck, did her left eyeball pop out first or was it the right? That's not a joke: that's part of the process, if you didn't know it, you know it now. Isn't it quite possible that this is why we (actors) are so neurotic as a group? Whatever it is, it can't be healthy. I've used it quite effectively, except that it got to me a couple of times. I was so destroyed by the personal memory I was using that I just wanted to sit down on the stage and cry. I was so close to not caring about that audience, my fellow actors or anybody, all I knew was that I hurt, and the tears that were falling were really Jeremy's and the pain was all Jeremy's. The fact that I was able to maintain my character does not excuse the fact that I was talked into doing that to myself, in the name of art.

I taught this technique. Affective Memory is a chapter in my first book, THE ABC'S OF ACTING; at next printing I will yank that chapter and burn it. Right here, I would like to apologize to any actor I ever put through that and I would like to forgive myself for using it, if I could. The fact is that many young talents may have run from the profession when they encountered that technique, some may have never recovered. I hate to beat a point over the head like this but I believe that the practice of ignoring emotional awareness, having actors use their own emotions, is so dangerous that it either indirectly killed some actors, by subconsciously driving them to drugs, drink, and ultimate distraction, or even perhaps directly, some kid that walked out of an acting class after being put through that ugliness and blew her brains out. It might have been my class.

There are a lot of fragile kids that are drawn to acting and some actors who have been in the business get so worn down from it that it can overpower them. Nobody cares more about pleasing people than actors. We will do anything, no matter how painful, if it promises to make us better. Being ruthlessly, cruelly abusive to ourselves emotionally was thought and taught to be the best way, so we did it. I know that an art is not supposed to be safe or easy, but nothing ever said it had to be cruel and abusive. I am speaking from over thirty years in the trenches of acting and 14 years as a teacher; I know and love actors. We really have to stop that practice with professionals and we have to stop teaching it to kids. The problem is that it works, or more correctly, gives the appearance of working. Anyone who has ever done a part knows that actors will use anything that lets them survive the terror of creation. That technique has been used for such a long time, only because we all missed what was obviously a better way, a way of giving a character an emotional life of her own.

The way to do that is to build the actors Emotional Vocabulary. Emotions are our primary tool and we are ignorant of them. I didn't see how narrow and restricted our (actors) emotional vocabulary was for over twenty years, and I might never have noticed this astounding incongruity, had it not been for a Viola Spolin game that I've always enjoyed and employed in the classroom. The game is called "Jump Emotion Improv." I think, this test will convince many teachers and students of the seriousness of the need; then, what has to happen, will.

A QUICK TEST OF EMOTIONAL OF AWARENESS

I am a huge fan of Viola Spolin and this exercise, Jump Emotion Improv. As I use it, the game calls for students to write two emotions on two separate pieces of paper and to drop them in a hat/box, whatever. They pair off as teams and set up an improv, using the classic Who, What, Where formula. Just before they start the improv, each is asked to take two of the emotion slips from the hat. Without knowing what emotions each other has, they pick one each to start with and are instructed, at a given signal, (I use a loud clap of the hands) they are to change immediately, without missing a beat, into their second emotion. When I've ended the improv, the class tries to guess actor number one's first emotion and then her second and then we repeat this with the other actor.

It is great fun, but over time I started to notice the absolute and generally across the board, bankruptcy of actors' emotional vocabularies. Try it, you will find it to be the same with your students. I teach all over the country on many different levels, from college to little kids, and pros of all ages. It was always the same; in a class of fourteen, you might get four happies, four sads, four loves, and two hates. A very short range, mostly consisting of primary emotions, and if anyone does get exotic, you will often have to whisper a definition into a student's ear when they come and say, "What does this mean?"

I saw this over and over until the pattern was clear and the problem obvious. We, as a group of artists, had neglected, since the beginning, the systematic and concentrated study of the primary tool of our trade, Emotions. How could that be? How was it possible that we did not even know how to pronounce the names of the emotions we were supposed to be experiencing as characters?

I'm not talking about a class of Yale grad students, whose overall vocabulary has increased through a range of studies. I'm talking about your average beginning acting class; that is where it has to start. If you don't believe me, about the general ignorance in this emotional area, take your class through the test I just outlined above, it will convince you. The Dictionary of The Emotions and The Thesaurus of The Emotions are valuable tools to student and teacher alike.

"Emotions Are To Actors What Colors Are To Painters." Not too many people will argue with that statement, so how is it that we have never really studied them? What would a painter be without her intense and lifelong study of color? Scales are the same source of methodic study to musicians. Musicians spend endless hours practicing scales, so that in performance, they have a solid and broad base that their inspiration can draw from. Painters spend their lives in the study of color. In the art of dance, the basics are called the "syllabus of the barre." Dancers spend much of their lives at the barre, actors spend much of their lives at the bar.

Actors have never been asked to spend one minute on the study of emotions. We have never had, in my awareness, in the entire history of acting, a thorough, systematic and continuing study of the emotions, such as the one I am proposing here. I have been publicly calling for that work since 1990 with the publication of my first book, THE ABC'S OF ACTING (Gray Heron, 1990) and expanded that call in my second book, INSTANT ACTING (Betterway Books, 1994). Actually, I've been teaching emotions since 1984.

I always ask every new class if any students had trained as painters, musicians, dancers. Usually there is at least a few, sometimes more. I ask how long they studied painting, music, dance and usually the answer is, years. How much of that time did you spend studying color, scales, at the Barre?" Almost all of it," is not an uncommon answer. Artists are lifelong students of the basics of their art. Actors must be lifelong students of emotions, as these are the colors we use to paint our stories.

During a weekend intensive one recent Sunday, a young actress, who was still shaking and crying after an intense scene, looked up at me and through her sobs said, "That's the first time I've been able to cry without thinking of something horrible." That is a giant reward for me and hardly an isolated instance. The techniques proved to me again, as they have over the last twelve years of developing them, that they work and that they are better for actors and for acting.

So how did this actress, in such a short time, connect to character so quickly and completely, that the tears were the character's? Her whole being was the character's. We did emotion studies (described below) five hours the first day and the second day I checked their emotions homework, then we worked the Whelan Tape Technique. It was a combination of the two elements that caused this success. The basics of the tape technique are presented in this book, so that you can begin working with it immediately.

The first question I would expect is, "How does an actor get away from using her own emotions, when it would seem that that is all she posses?" I've said, the objective study of the emotions is the way. Some people pointed out that that study contains the seeds of subjective evaluation, which is true. That fact would seem to contradict everything I am saying, but it doesn't. I go into the theory of this phenomena at the end of the book; more important than theory, to most actors, is results, and the results are there.

I do know that from twelve years of doing this emotions work with a thousand plus actors, and seeing it work every time, that it does. I really don't know how an airplane works but it gets me where I want to go and that's good enough for me. Life is full of things that no normal person understands "how they work." I don't know how my radio works; I don't know how my TV works, and I certainly don't know how this computer works, but it makes my life better, so I use it.

I'm not a clinical psychologist; I'm an artist and a teacher and I must admit I grasped this concept intuitively. I then experimented with it extensively. It felt "right" on an intuitive level and it worked on a practical level; basically, that was good enough for me. I can only speculate on how that transference from subjective/private self reference to objective/universal reference occurs. I am stumped when asked about this but I know that some of you won't try it until I can answer that question, so I am seeking that answer, in the last chapter of this book I theorize on how and why it works, but if you have ten minutes, you can prove to yourself that it does work, try this quick test.

QUICK TEST OF THESAURUS TECHNIQUE

If you are a director, next time you are working some actors and you see one find a strong emotional connection to a certain line, have her tell you what she is feeling when she says that line. Then give her a thesaurus, ask her to look up that emotion, read the synonyms of that emotion, using whatever circumlocution necessary to put some form of the first person, "I", in front of each synonym; then immediately replay the scene. Her performance will be noticeably richer. If you are actors working alone and you find that emotional connection to a line; between run throughs, do what I described above. I've been doing this for years and it always works; try it. That is oversimplifying the work that must be done, but if you see such a subtle influence cause an observable improvement, you should be inspired to do the move involved exercises.

Let me say I think the actors job is to lend the character their instrument and then get out of the way. You don't borrow somebody's car and then ask them if they want to go along. So lend the character your emotional apparatus, which, even though you're not conversant with it, possesses a full spectrum of emotional colors, a very rich palette. Lend it to the character and then get out of the way. All the emotions of the world are in there. It is obvious that you don't have to know their names or what they mean to feel them, because life automatically synthesizes them into a harmonious psycho-physical expression, that is you. However, and again, as an actor, you can only play yourself once. The physical, emotional, intellectual and spiritual being that is you the actor; you can play that once. After that, each new character needs a whole new set of these, meaning, you can't use your mother's death again! Where will you get a new source of emotional inspiration? The process is indirect, but many years of close observation have shown me how effective this emotions work can be. By broadening the actor's emotional vocabulary, you increase her emotional mobility; this frees her and opens her up, performances take on very delicate and very subtle nuances that are generally only available to the most exceptional and gifted actors. How do you do it? That question will only be fully answered when more people turn their attention to the problem. I have however a very workable system. A very important tool is this Emotions Chart (below, not actual size, see workbook) and some exercises it supports. In continuing with the color analogy, we break emotions into Primary Emotions and Secondary Emotions.

The first step in using the chart is to read over the list synonyms in column 1; then go to the dictionary of emotions and write their definitions in column 2.

(not actual size—see workbook)

Primary Emotion:	Definition	Emotion (rearrange in order of descending intensity)	Color (descending intensity)	Weight (arbitrary, in order of descending intensity)	Smell	Taste	Sound	Feel (physical texture)	Physical Object
GRIEF									
Secondary Emotions:									
affliction									
agony									
anguish									
bemoaning									
bereavement									
care									
dejection									
depression									
desolation									
despair									
despondency									
discomfort									
disquiet									
distress									
dolor									
gloom									
grievance									
harassment									
heartache									
heartbreak									
infelicity									
lamentation									
lamenting									
malaise									
melancholy									
misery									
mortification									
mournfulness									
pain									
purgatory									
regret									
remorse									
repining									

Primary Emotion:	Definition	Emotion (rearrange in order of descending intensity)	Color (descending intensity)	Weight (arbitrary, in order of descending intensity)	Smell	Taste	Sound	Feel (physical texture)	Physical Object
rue									
sorrow									
suffering									
torture									
trial									
tribulation									
trouble									
unhappiness									
vexation									
woe									
worry									
wretchedness									

In column 3, Intensity, rearrange the secondary emotions from the strongest intensity to the weakest intensity as distinguished by the definition in column 2.

In column 4, select one specific color that represents that emotion to you. Go to a paint store and get those color strips that they give out. Get every shade of your emotion's color possible and then cut them down to size and paste them into column 4 in the appropriate place; remember the strongest to the weakest. You can also go to an artist supply store and get a set of artist pencils that are all that color's intensities and color them in, but that can be expensive.

Column 5 is an arbitrary weight you assign to each level of that emotion, it too is in a highest to lowest mode.

The rest is pure imagination, but imagination is a muscle too little exercised. Artists have to work that muscle the same as body builders work their muscles. It's happened often enough that I should mention a problem that comes up using the chart. It is bizarre that actors, in doing these charts, will go along fine until they have to give the emotions smells, tastes, sounds, etc. I'll find them sitting there, staring at the chart and leaving those things blank. I say, what's the matter, and they say they can't think of anything. I really don't understand it. It smells like gasoline. It tastes like pizza. The object it represents to me is a bowling ball. It feels like a maple leaf; this column causes some problems, so heres a note to clarify the point. Column 9 must be understood to be a specific feel/texture, rough is not a proper entry, sand paper, tree bark, etc. would be correct; that sort of specificity is required throughout. Actors, you can't make a mistake; it's all subjective. What's the problem? The problem is a clogged imagination and that is a terrible thing for an actor to have. You have to open that channel up and this is an excellent exercise to do just that. So you're really solving two actors problems with one exercise; be glad for the opportunity and just get it done.

It is not important that one actor thinks Love is gold and another thinks it's purple. It is important that each actor is very specific about his choice, i.e., it does not feel like a puppy, it feels like a cocker spaniel puppy. It does not smell like a flower, it smells like a Lily. As an actor works his way through the various primary and secondary emotions using the charts, he will immediately see that his performances are becoming more textured and subtle. Those rewards will provide the energy and the impetus to continue this work.

The exercises for expanding the actors emotional vocabulary that you find in this book will take your acting to a level of power and subtly that you could never have experienced without them. The increase in your acting ability will come quickly. There are exercises in my other books that also deal with expanding the actors emotional vocabulary and consequently her/his emotional mobility. You will have to find these exercises, create your own, or both. This is new but vital work and many people will contribute. I'm sure I will grow from the work of others, as I hope some will from mine. If I've connected to some of you who found this area of work on your own, we should share what we have learned. Some others may have read my books and taken the cue from them; I'd be very interested in hearing from anybody involved with this type of work. Maybe, like myself, it took you a long time to see the need for this work and to realize we can make this a better and less abusive art. Perhaps this article started it for you. We do have a job to do. Old School is not going to roll over and play dead; too many of them have serious vested interest in maintaining the status quo. I have this poster I want to make, it is me driving a stake through Stanislavski's heart; the great teacher looks up at me and says, "Thank you." Let the man rest. He's been dead for fifty-eight years. We have picked over his bones and now some still insist on picking at the ashes of his bones; it is time to bury him. Kick some dirt into the grave the Method has richly earned and let's go forward. Stop abusing actors, it is no longer necessary. Dying is no disgrace, when you have served your purpose well; Stanislavski and his system certainly did that.

Stanislavski (1863-1938) and Freud (1856-1939) were born and died at essentially the same time. Stanislavski embraced Freud's ideas and put them, heart and soul, into his work with actors. Psychology has left Freud behind but acting keeps dragging him out of the grave. If you want to bore yourself with some details, there is a book called, <u>Freud and Stanislavski</u>. Those teachers and directors that are crawling into class rooms and onto stages in some Post-Freudian haze; those covered in 100 years of Pre-Revolutionary Russian Psycho-intellectual dust, are probably more to be pitied than censured, because the rest of us are having fun.

This is the most exciting time in the history of acting and those of us who are in the middle of the experience are seeing an art form reborn; we are causing it, doing it daily. New School Acting is open to everyone with an idea, with a sense of adventure, with the openness to try something new.

(This Manifesto was originally written to accompany a package that I would leave on tables and in green rooms of college and professional theatres, that I mailed out to everybody connected to acting that I could get an address for, and that I put onto Internet Bulletin Boards; as is the case with other essays in this book, some redundancy is inevitable.)

The following should clarify some of the major differences between the two; hopefully provoking sufficient curiosity to make you want to read further; to try the ideas contained in this book. New School Acting is just that, new; there are years of growth ahead. Many will contribute, and by the time it is replaced by the next advance, it will have made a important contribution to the art form. Regardless of its newness, New School Acting is sufficiently developed to make a powerful contribution; today; these ideas are cutting edge. Any actor using these tools, even those just beginning, will be propelled past old school actors, many of whom have trained longer, in auditions and in performance. Schools that adopt these techniques will be recognized as leaders in the field, not for what they have done, but for what they are doing. The actors, directors and teachers these schools put into the field will shine with a greater luster than those coming out of Old School Institutions. The quality of work will prove the validity of this approach. This is the beginning of the next step in the evolution of the art form; a tribute to the Muse I have followed since I met her thirty five years ago in the darkened theatre of San Francisco City College.

SIDE BY SIDE COMPARISON OF NEW SCHOOL TO OLD SCHOOL DIFFERENCES	
NEW SCHOOL	OLD SCHOOL
1. EMOTION BASED New School acting is primarily characterized by two innovations; the two are equally important. One is that New School actors are trained to be Masters of Emotion. They study emotion with the diligence of painters studying color. A beginning student of painting has a limited knowledge of color, in much the same way that a beginning student of acting has a limited knowledge of emotions. • New School actors will learn the names of all the emotions. • They will look up the definition of each in dictionaries and write them out. • They will learn how, with the various definitions they encounter, to find the one which most aptly communicates the subtle distinction between seemingly similar emotions. Actors will learn the definition which captures the essence of that distinction; the definition which shows most clearly why that word is different from what seems to be almost the same emotion, in short, why the word was created.	**1. PSYCHO-INTELLECTUAL BASED** In order to understand this primary distinction between Old School and New School, there are a few things about the birth of the old school you must know. Old School, generally, the Method or any one of the many wrinkles put on it by teachers such as Strasberg, Adler, and Meisner, along with many lesser lights, might be said to have been officially born in 1897; the year that Stanislavski founded the Moscow Art Theatre. He was thirty-three years old at the time. Sigmond Freud was forty-one years old at that time and his baby, Psychoanalysis, was 12 years old. Stanislavski leaned heavily on Freudian Psychoanalysis in the work he was doing with actors and in developing the Method. If you want some details, read a book called, <u>Freud and Stanislavski</u>. This was a fresh approach at the time and startled audiences with its intensity, however, after a hundred years of Psycho-Intellectual acting, it's looking pretty dusty. This Ultra-personal approach has lost all vibrancy and it is taking acting with it into the grave reserved for stale acting. It is time for a fresh approach. NEW SCHOOL ACTING is right on time and perfectly in tune with the demands of contemporary audiences.

13

| SIDE BY SIDE COMPARISON OF NEW SCHOOL TO OLD SCHOOL DIFFERENCES ||
NEW SCHOOL	OLD SCHOOL
EMOTION BASED (cont.) • New School actors will give each of these emotions: colors, tastes, sounds, feels, smells, and they will pick a very specific object that embodies that emotion for them. • They will put these all into charts created for the purpose of structuring and facilitating this work. • They will be very specific in doing all of these things. Love does not smell like a flower, it smells like a Lily. Anger does not sound like a mad dog, it sounds like a mad Pit Bull. It will not matter to these actors that love is red for one and blue for another. The goal is not uniformity. The goal is complete awareness of all their creative options. As the painting student watches her palette grow richer and richer as she continues her studies of color, so too will the actor see a dynamic expansion of her creative options. The New School actor will go to schools that offer Emotion Studies as part of her curriculum. Emotions I and II and III and as many as are needed to become a Master Of Emotion. If she cannot find a school near her that offers these studies, she will teach herself. She will do exercises specifically designed to continue broadening her EMOTIONAL VOCABULARY and to increase her EMOTIONAL MOBILITY. THE NEW SCHOOL actor will not be trapped, tricked, bullied or cajoled into using her own emotions, risking all the deleterious repercussions that accompany that vicious self-abusive practice. She will have a viable option because she does not suffer from the bankrupt emotional vocabulary of Old School Actors and the world in general.	

SIDE BY SIDE COMPARISON OF NEW SCHOOL TO OLD SCHOOL DIFFERENCES	
NEW SCHOOL	OLD SCHOOL

2. INTEGRATED, UNIFIED DEVELOPMENT OF CHARACTER

The Second innovation of New School Acting is the Whelan Tape Technique. Using the tape technique the actor's discoveries come off of the moment to moment interaction of the characters, according to the lines and the given circumstances of the script. The actors are 100% on the script without having it weighing heavily in their hands.

When actors are free of the tyranny of the script at the very first reading, when they are unrestricted in their ability to see, hear and touch the other characters, they experience an accelerated creative involvement with their own character, the other characters and the script. The growth is exponential rather than linear. This happens for many reasons but primarily because the actors are using all three networks at once. The Physical, Intellectual and Emotional Networks (PIE for ease of remembering), are all working at once and the effect is synergistic, as opposed to the fractured approach of Old School. One obvious effect is that lines are learned in one-half to one-third of the time usually necessary, but that is only an elemental aspect of the benefits to the actor. The truly amazing results are in the unprecedented depth of character penetration and the evolvement of a natural organic movement that is esthetically superior to any blocking ever devised/designed by a director in a naturalistic production.

All of this happens so quickly that it is as if you were given double the time normally allotted a production. The extra time can be used any way you want, perhaps to polish the work to a brilliant sheen, to save the money that would have been spent rehearsing, or to allocate it to production values.

2. FRAGMENTED APPROACH TO CHARACTER DEVELOPMENT

Old School style is to break up a script and a character and then attempt to integrate them later. Various terms such as, Super Objective, Objectives, Actions, Beats, Intentions, Motivations etc. are used to define these fragments. Everyone of these terms represents an elaborate intellectual process and has a restricting, if not paralyzing effect, on any sort of spontaneity. This is the work of a technocrat not an artist. This approach seemed to work for years only because actors exhausted themselves to make it work. There is nothing wrong with work but technology has eliminated unnecessary work and increased creative options in all other art forms. Why are actors still toiling away with turn of the century tools?

In the end, the Method was weighted toward the intellectual actor. I know that may make some people laugh, especially producers and, admit it or not, most directors, but it is none the less true. Recent advances in education have recognized that not everyone learns the same way. Three distinct learning modalities have been recognized. In kids they call them, Seeing, Feeling, Hearing, or Audial, Visual, Tactile /Kinesthetic. These correspond to the Physical, Intellectual and Emotional networks that the actor uses in discovering and playing a character.

Right now, education is in a massive restructuring to meet the needs of students who do not respond to traditional one-mode teaching styles. The results are startling. Students who were thought dumb by those old standards are doing exceptional work and proving that the only thing really dumb was the educational system itself.

SIDE BY SIDE COMPARISON OF NEW SCHOOL TO OLD SCHOOL DIFFERENCES	
NEW SCHOOL	OLD SCHOOL
INTEGRATED, UNIFIED DEVELOPMENT OF CHARACTER (cont.)	FRAGMENTED APPROACH TO CHARACTER DEVELOPMENT (cont.)
This technique is ideal for allowing the actor to explore her creative growth through her study of emotions. This technique is foolproof in its ability to develop intelligent, independent actors; actors who have absolute confidence in their creative choices and the professionalism to make them fit into the demands of the medium in which they are working. In professional situations it devolves much of the creative responsibility, formally held by the director, back onto the actor, most notably in the early stages of rehearsal. The director is not eliminated, however the Actor-Director relationship is greatly modified, this is discussed later.	Many actors who were having trouble connecting to character using old school techniques, have amazing breakthroughs using the tape technique and through working with the emotional expansion exercises. New School Acting in its tools, rules, and reasons, anticipated some of these discoveries, contributed to others and incorporates all of them in a natural organic manner. It makes sense to try it. I might add, that despite decades of research proving the benefits of the Learning Styles approach to educating children, the educational system is resisting implementing them. Old school once again is fighting for its life, and students pay the price.
3. ACTOR USES CHARACTER'S EMOTIONS	3. ACTOR USES OWN EMOTIONS:
Because of the emotional work mentioned above, the actor has immediate and complete access to the characters emotions. He avoids the very real danger of using his own emotions, as well of the cliché acting that quickly comes from that device. All the baggage, physical and intellectual that he attaches to his own emotions are left behind and a fresh and interesting interpretation is possible.	Probably the single biggest fault of the Method is that it has actors using their own emotions. The process is intellectual. The actor is to sort through her own real life experiences to determine which one is appropriate for that moment in her characters life. Next, she coaxes the emotion out of her memory by intellectually re-creating the moment in the minutest of detail, until the cumulative weight of the details brings the event to the actors emotional side. A breakthrough occurs and the actor is inside the emotion. The same one she felt the moment of the actual event, in effect, past and present blur. Now the actor's job is to use her character's disguise/costume and the author's words to fool the audience into thinking it is the character's emotion. When this doesn't work there are other Method techniques that are equally tedious, dangerous and which also dodge the issue of actually creating the characters emotion. There is now a more effective approach and a safer one for those who pay the price, the actors. Build the actors emotional vocabulary.

SIDE BY SIDE COMPARISON OF NEW SCHOOL TO OLD SCHOOL DIFFERENCES	
NEW SCHOOL	OLD SCHOOL
4. LINES SECONDARY TO EMOTIONAL CONTENT Learning lines is the last concern of the NEW SCHOOL actor. One of the benefits of the Whelan Tape Technique is that that happens automatically. The tape technique creates a situation where the actor uses all three memories, integrating character penetration, natural movement, and absorption of the lines into one organic process. The New School actor focuses on the emotional content of the line and everything else falls into place. Absolutely no conscious attempt to memorize the lines is ever made and yet they are learned in one- half to one-third of the time that this process normally takes.	**4. LINES ARE PRIMARY** In old school, characters are developed in isolation, which is a result of the heavy emphasis placed on learning lines. Actors are often requested to memorize lines before the first rehearsal or are urged to get off book as quickly as possible.
5. CHARACTER DEVELOPED IN ENSEMBLE In using the tape technique, actors/characters are forced to adjust to the other actors/characters actual responses, to a line, or more precisely, the emotional content of the line. This constant interaction allows for a smooth and rapid growth of relationships between characters. Since it is a response to all the elements which go to make up a human being/character, i.e. their Physical, Intellectual, and Emotional response, it is integrated and complete. It arises from that actual moment in their characters life. There can be no second guessing about what another actor/character might do in that situation because she is standing in front of you. No preconceived idea of how it will be played can take root in the actors mind. She can't lock on to a choice and attempt to force it unnaturally upon another actor/character.	**5. CHARACTER IS DEVELOPED IN ISOLATION** As stated above, actors spend a great deal of time learning lines on their own. This is a really bad idea for many reasons. Firstly, while memorizing lines in this isolation, alone in their room, whatever, each actor will envision how the other actors are going to respond. The way they are going to look and how they are going to sound. These preconceived, intellectual imaginings seldom match the same intellectually conceived ideas of the other actors/characters. Consequently, when they all show up for rehearsal, a power struggle goes on as actors try to manipulate each other into following their own idea of how it should play. That was one of the main reasons the director was invented, to act as a referee between warring actors egos. Beyond that, script in hand rehearsal isolates the characters in a more subtle way. The script acts as a shield that actors can hide behind should they become uncomfortable with the intensity of a moment. It also isolates, in that it only permits the actor to make contact with the other characters, during those brief moments when their noses are not buried in the script, trying to find their next line.

SIDE BY SIDE COMPARISON OF NEW SCHOOL TO OLD SCHOOL DIFFERENCES	
NEW SCHOOL	OLD SCHOOL
6. COMPLETE EMOTIONAL AWARENESS A wide and deep emotional vocabulary will give the New School Actor full knowledge of creative options producing very textured performances. This full range of emotions is virtually free of the actor's "baggage" related to that emotion, this stimulates unique, <u>from character</u>, physical expression.	**6. LIMITED EMOTIONAL VOCABULARY** Most people can't spell half the emotions they feel and they certainly could not make the subtle distinctions implicit in the definitions of similar emotions. This is by no means limited to actors, but real people don't have the obligation to be anybody but themselves and so their ignorance in this area is no more than a personal and social handicap. The actor/artist has, as his/her job requirement, to be somebody else. A limited emotional vocabulary is a serious career disadvantage, one which forces actors into very limited / narrow choices. Another serious negative, the limited emotions available are heavily colored by the actors personal relationship (baggage) to that emotion. The "baggage" is often reflected in the physical expression of that emotion. This is the reason some actors become identified with certain repeated physical gestures regardless of the character they are playing.
7. FULL EMOTIONAL MOBILITY Objective knowledge of all existing emotions allows the actor to move with spontaneous ease, quickly and confidently through the entire spectrum of potentially appropriate emotional choices.	**7. LIMITED EMOTIONAL MOBILITY** When an actor is working from her own emotions she is limited by the choices she can make, because life has conditioned her to a personal, therefore insufficient perception of those emotions. It is mostly like the difference between Checkers and Chess. It is quite possible that the character has been conditioned to react differently to the same emotion. This can happen in many ways. As a simple cultural example, go to an Italian wake and then go to an Irish wake. In business, Bosses react differently to anger at workers, than workers to bosses. There is an old Chinese saying,"If the Prince is indiscreet he loses his servant, if the servant is indiscreet he loses his head." Actors can learn to "play" these differences but with a limited emotional vocabulary; that is the best they will ever be able to do.

SIDE BY SIDE COMPARISON OF NEW SCHOOL TO OLD SCHOOL DIFFERENCES	
NEW SCHOOL	OLD SCHOOL
8. REDUCES DIRECTOR DEPENDENCE. It might surprise some actors to learn that there was no such thing as a director until 1864. Somehow the Greeks, Shakespeare and the rest, were able to get their plays mounted without the aid of this modern day wonder. In New School the director becomes an ensemble member, without authority to dictate actor's choices, a friendly - artistic third eye; more in the vein of creative consultant, not absolute dictator. This would be the ideal, and while a few directors do and have worked this way, and other directors are allowing actors more freedom, we are a long way from this goal. The importance of reaching that ideal, insures that we will achieve it. The ways and means are discussed below.	**8. DIRECTOR DEPENDENT** Actors training, as it is practiced in this country and many others, seems to have as it's goal to make actors director dependent. It is something inherent in the Old School style. This is not surprising as the founders of that school were Autocratic in their personal style, most probably as a result of the social and political influences of their time. The problem is that while this may satisfy the teachers, it does little for the student approaching acting as a profession. It should be understood that almost everyone who auditions for a play or takes an acting class has a dream that someone is going to see her and she will be swept up into the spotlight. The dream may dim, but it never dies. This may be the single greatest thing about show biz; as long as that person is alive, the dream survives. That was a bit of a diversion but it sets up why it is important that actors be trained as if they wanted what they want, a career. The fact is that some schools are starting to put acting programs on a more professional level. I love the theater and have spent many years "on the boards" but most actors that stay alive from acting do so by working in television, films and commercials. In those mediums, the director is more concerned with the myriad technical considerations than with the actors, and they have every right to be. If you are a plumber, you don't ask the people that called you how to do your job. The mediums I mentioned are very expensive and at fifteen to thirty thousand dollars a minute and higher, the director is not there to give you an acting lesson. If you put yourself out there as a professional actor, they expect you to know how to do your job. If you don't, they are very quickly going to replace you with someone who does. So, the long discussions about motivation etc. are generally nonexistent. This Hollywood story comes to mind, an actor walks up to the director and says "What's my motivation!" The director says, "Your pay check."

SIDE BY SIDE COMPARISON OF NEW SCHOOL TO OLD SCHOOL DIFFERENCES	
NEW SCHOOL	OLD SCHOOL
9. ORGANIC MOVEMENT FROM THE CHARACTER'S SINCEREST EMOTIONAL NEED RIC's, (Repels, Impels, Compels), These three are the only moves actors can make, actually they are the only moves anybody can make . The emotional content of the line will Repel you, make you want to move away from someone, Impel you to move toward her, or Compel you to stay where you are. In using the Whelan Tape Technique, actors are free to receive this stimulus from each other on every level. It is Emotional Surfing ; a natural result of actors, in character, responding to the deepest emotional needs of that character. In responding to those emotional demands, the actor can never look clumsy or find herself in an unnatural position. The stage picture will always have a sense of truth about it and will therefore be beautiful, in the sense that it is appropriate.	9. TABLEAU OBSESSED BLOCKING IMPOSED MAP-LIKE ON THE ACTOR It would seem that many so called directors wanted to be painters. They move actors around like a photographer posing people from picture to picture. The result comes off as stilted; actors are forced out of character as they try to remember where they are supposed to be. Nobody has to tell you to sit down when you are so emotionally drained or physically exhausted that you can no longer stand. This happens naturally in life and if the character is alive it will happen to him, yet a director will say, "Sit on the couch when you say that line." How can the character be alive, when the actor is trying to remember whether he is sitting or standing or if he is supposed to be over here when he says this and over there when he says that? He can't!
10. RESEARCH WITH INTEGRATED APPROACH All but the most viable choices are eliminated because possibilities are selected by the whole character, in full interaction with all the other characters. This saves time and eliminates possible/probable complicated intellectual justification of choices.	10. RESEARCH POSSIBILITIES ARE ALMOST INFINITE FROM INTELLECTUAL PERSPECTIVE The most neglected word in the amateur actors vocabulary is research, but its importance is never lost on a pro. The problem is actors can intellectually construct almost any scenario to justify almost any choice they want to make regarding a character's actions. Some of these scenarios can get seriously convoluted as actors strain to justify a choice they want to play. Each of these scenarios will present different research demands. Actors are running all over the place swamped by a plethora of possible choices. This wastes a great deal of time as well as muddying the water when a choice is finally made.

| SIDE BY SIDE COMPARISON OF NEW SCHOOL TO OLD SCHOOL DIFFERENCES ||
NEW SCHOOL	OLD SCHOOL
11. NEW SCHOOL NEVER REHEARSES SCRIPT IN HAND Actors are free of the tyranny of the script but are always 100% true to the script. Since the professional actors first obligation is to the text, the New School actor is never in danger of violating that cardinal rule.	11. OLD-SCHOOL REHEARSES SCRIPT IN HAND Scripts in hand during rehearsal is the greatest single block to creativity that an actor faces when beginning work on a new part. It is not only clumsy physically, but the very act of holding a script is the same as holding a big sign that says, I'm not the character, I'm an actor. Some avoid the script by doing improvisation, which is a big mistake. The professional actor's first obligation is to the text. Letting actors run wild at this point is almost like having them use their own emotions. Actors will be, without the script to guide them, tempted, if not forced to play subjectively. They must, since they are unfamiliar with the script, deviate from it. In leaving the script; actors establish some, if not many, bad associations with the character. Later when they know the direction of the character and the script, they will have to work very hard to undo those associations and many never succeed.

CHAPTER III

THE SYSTEMATIC STUDY OF EMOTIONS IN ACTORS' TRAINING

EMOTIONS ARE TO ACTORS WHAT COLORS ARE TO PAINTERS

Just as nouns, verbs, adjectives etc. are the cornerstones of the writers art, colors are the cornerstones of painting, scales are the cornerstones of music, the syllabus of the barre is the cornerstone of the art of dance, emotions are the cornerstones of acting. All art forms must have a basics, to which the artist can constantly return to refresh herself and extend her creative options.

As an art form evloves, the artists in that discipline are met with new demands. These new demands require new tools to meet them. For instance, computers now offer the painter new tools and millions of new colors to learn. Electronic music has provided as many new challenges to the dancer as it has to the musician and the internationalization of our taste buds has redefined the combination of spices available to the art of cooking. These new tools become the foundation on which the basics of an art form are redefined. We must redefine the basics of acting before we can take this art to the next level.

Why is the objective study of emotions the next logical step in the evolution of the art of acting? As you may have noticed by now, this entire book is an attempt to convince actors, directors and teachers that it is important, so any attempt to wrap that up in a few sentences here doesn't feel comfortable. If I had to, I suppose the single most important reason to me, is the emotional health of actors, also as an artist, I am excited by the greater degree of creative accomplishment it allows the actor.

Emotions have always been part of acting and they have followed a very natural progression. The tradition of emotion going from actor to audience evolved into the tradition of emotion going from actor to actor. While that had started many years before Stanislavski, it was he who, through the influence of Freud, developed an intellectually based system for actors to access their personal emotions and substitute them for the characters. The next step, taking emotions from that narrow personal realm into a universal conception, will make them easier for a character to embrace.

Describe a feeling. How close do you think you really came to describing what you felt? This isn't a trick question. We have all been frustrated at times because we could not explain what we were feeling. The truth is you couldn't do it is because it can't be done! Explaining is an intellectual activity and feeling is an emotional activity; it's the old comparing apples to oranges routine, so what's an actor to do?

The first thing actors have to do, is stop trying to get to the character's heart from the actor's head. Actors trained that way invariably discover the impossibility and substitute their own emotions for the characters. Using your own emotions is a form of cheating and if you've got nothing else to work with, use them, which is what most actors are taught to do. This, however, puts actors in the unworkable position of trying to get to the character's emotions through an actor's brain. Emotions can only be simulated at that point, because the actor has established a separation between self and character.

I have never been comfortable with training in which I was asked to use my own emotions. It seemed intrusive and I knew it distracted me from getting into character, which even early in my career, I felt was the challenge of acting. Anybody could be/PLAY themselves, but to actually make a full blown commitment to being somebody else, seemed to me the highest level of achievement for an actor, even knowing it was virtually impossible, didn't detract from the loftiness of the goal.

Actors have always used their own emotions; a subjective viewpoint that forces them to look at the characters needs, wants and fears, trapped inside their own perspective; filtered through their own experience with any particular emotion. As dramatic artists, we must have an objective viewpoint of emotions so that we can feel the characters needs, wants and fears, from a perspective other than our own; one unique to the character. Actors emotions are either decorated or stained by their life experience with that emotion. The advantages to a universal awareness of emotions in helping character development should be apparent.

PRACTICAL TECHNIQUES AND EXERCISES FOR THE SYSTEMATIC STUDY OF EMOTIONS

It doesn't matter what your (the actors) emotions are; it only matters what your character's emotions are. So you have to know emotions as a pure universal, as a concept, not simply as they occur to you in your daily life. This thesaurus type chart should help anyone who might have difficulty making this distinction between your own private emotions, and universal ones.

CHART: SUBJECTIVE VS. OBJECTIVE VIEW OF EMOTIONS

ACTORS AWARENESS CONFINED TO THEIR OWN EMOTIONS	ACTORS AWARENESS EXPANDED BY EMOTIONAL STUDIES
PRIVATE	UNIVERSAL
SUBJECTIVE	OBJECTIVE
Particular-personal-specific-adulterated-restricted-limited-local-singular-confined-colored-individual-introspective-biased-prejudiced-unobjective	Gerenal-whole-unaldulterated-unrestricted-unlimited-global-unconfined-pure-impersonal-nondiscriminatory-openminded-unbiased-uncolored-unprejudiced

The following exercises will take you a long way toward the goal of being emotionally literate, and that will take you closer to the pure acting experience. While the exercises are written as if to a teacher, one is not necessary for actors to do this work. I am constantly urging actors to get together, in groups, on their own, and work on their craft. The worksheets from the Thesaurus of The Emotions will be a valuable aid when doing these exercises.

EMOTIONS EXERCISE I

Write an emotion on the board

After you have placed a primary emotion on the board, have a student write numerous synonyms underneath it. Have students each take one of those synonyms and write it on an index card. Have them write one or two meanings of the word, and a sentence using the word properly. They read these to the class. Put these definitions on the board next to the word. By consensus, assign each a "color" of that emotion: and a number signifying the intensity level of the emotion. Students can see that some of these differences are very subtle, but if there wasn't any difference, the word wouldn't exist. Subtly is what makes good acting. Remember any idiot can get into an anger scene and scream for three minutes.

EMOTION EXERCISE II

Physicalize Emotions

As an exercise to expand emotional awareness, I have each student pick a different emotion. The homework is to then go to the Thesaurus section of the Dictionary of the Emotions and make a list, in descending order of intensity, for that emotion and write the meaning next to each. Use the emotions charts in the workbook for this exercise.

Next class, each student takes a turn going in front of the class and reading his list, after which he gives the list to another student. He returns to the stage (if there is one). He faces the class; at that point, the student with the list, reads the emotions, pausing a few seconds (beats) between each. The student on stage, has to respond instantly upon hearing the emotion, with any physical motion/gesture that comes to him/her. It does not matter what he does, as long as he makes some attempt to physicalize the emotion. Students have only two or three seconds (beats) to do that, but make sure they make some attempt. Go through the entire class like that. You can, if you want to, stack the deck a bit in favor of the class. From day one, exercise one, you can tell which students are the more open types; pick one of them to start the exercise. Their wildness is usually a signal to the rest of them to open up some and go for it. The chance of that backfiring, and intimidating the rest is slight. I've never seen it happen in fourteen years of teaching.

You should have each student, after everyone has done his/hers individually, go back and trade emotions. So that, in the end, every student has done every emotion. You should repeat this exercise, assigning new emotions, until all students have run the gamut. Remember, you don't go into a paint store, walk up to the salesman and say, "Give me a can of blue paint."

Here is something to think about in relation to the painters and colors analogy, in an article in Cosmo about color, The American Color Ass'n., released a catalog of 50,000 colors. Recently, I saw an ad for a color monitor for a computer that had up to "16.7 million colors." Perhaps one day we will have that many emotions; either way, I would take that as a cue, we have work to do.

Note: in a old magazine article I found, Mel Gibson said in doing Hamlet, he went to a dictionary of the period and looked up "melancholy." I had seen the movie and whether it was the genius of the brilliant Italian director Zeffirelli or Gibson, this Hamlet was different.

Any example I give is arbitrary or may not be strictly in line with classic definitions. You may think anger is green and I think it's blue. You might think malice is more intense, while I think rancor deserves a higher rating in the ascending order of intensity in the primary emotion of hate.

EMOTIONS EXERCISE III

Emotional Mobility Exercise

A variation on Jump Emotion Improve would be to have actors start an actual scene that they are working on, instruct them that at any point, you may shout out a new emotion to either one of them. They are to take whatever they are feeling at that moment and change into the new emotion completely in character. They must just "go with it" and see where it takes them. When the scene is finished, it can be evaluated on the basis of, if the character "got away with it" and if so, how many "colors" of that emotion did he hit.

Students could be split into teams, each team is responsible for cueing one of the actors in the scene. No doubt that some of the emotions prompted by the teams will be wildly inappropriate for the situation the characters are in, that is a large part of the fun in playing this game.

When the scene has ended, some elaborate intellectualization of how that character could feel one of those inappropriate emotions, suggested during the scene, at that moment in his/her life, could be found by the class with the teacher serving as monitor. Constructing these scenarios would be an exercise in imagination and at the same time, an inadvertent spoof on the bizarre circumstances that actors sometimes create to justify playing certain choices. You could also note, how much time it takes you to reach that explanation of the characters sometimes abrupt mood changes. The actor in the scene, has to keep going, she does not have time for that long drawn out psychological process. She must play that choice of emotion immediately. If the actors concentration is good and they hold firmly to character, they will be able to make the change seem natural, because they are under no obligation to justify what they do; they just do it.

While this exercise has other creative benefits, it can also be used by a teacher/director as a mechanical devise to break an actor away form a choice she had settled into, and force her to investigate another possibility, regardless of how remote. The very act of taking a new perspective on a moment or moments within a scene, can cause an actor to see a potentially better choice.

EMOTION EXERCISE IV

If Love Was A Tree

Anything you can do to make the emotions concrete will heighten your awareness of them. When my daughter was about five, we took a trip to Mexico. It's a long ride and we got bored, so I made up this game; I asked her if she was a tree what kind of tree would she be, and then she'd ask me. We went through just about every category in any book. If you were a bird, a fish, a metal, a musical instrument, a fruit. We played that for about an hour.

It might be a fun investigation for an individual, or a class to use that format for emotions. What kind of a flower is love? What kind of vegetable is love? What kind of soda is love? What kind of surf board, etc. Exhaust every category you can think of and write them out. Make your own catalogue of the emotions. Keep a note book of the emotions. Discount stores have sales with ten note books for two dollars and they're different colors. You could have a different color note book for each of the primary emotions. Don't get corny, like, love is a warm puppy, keep it concrete and objective. Share you new observations with your classmates or actors in your workshop. If they come up with something that also works for you, add that to your list.

EMOTION EXERCISE V

Emotional Words And Phrases

There are two ways to do this; one would be that the teacher/director compiles a list of 50 emotions and records them, with a few seconds between each. Put class/cast ensemble on stage and instruct them to respond instantaneously/instinctively with any physical gesture that suggests itself upon hearing the word. They can work alone, in pairs, or in a circle as a group.

Isolate non-context emotional phrases, record 50 of them and follow the procedure above. Phrases could be anything that contain the word representing the emotion, or phrases that would normally evoke a strong emotional reaction. Chart of Emotional Words and Phrases

1. You make me sad.	2. You make me angry.
3. You make me happy.	4. You get me hot.
5. You make me furious.	6. I'm disappointed in you.
7. I'm pleased with you.	8. I'm going to kill you.
9. I'm going to bury you alive.	10. I'm going to give you 20 million dollars to star in this movie.
11. I'm going to rape you.	12. We are going to hang you by the neck until dead.
13. The child you hit died.	14. She was killed in the attack.
15. You won the lottery.	16. You should be ashamed.
17. You should be very pleased with yourself.	18. You should be ecstatic.
19. She said she loves you.	20. You're fired.
21. You got the job.	22. Your house burned down.
23. Kiss me right now.	24. The dog ate your kid.
25. New York is under nuclear attack.	26. I don't have any underwear on.
27. Dad just died.	28. Micheal Jackson is on the phone, he wants to talk to your little brother.
29. Your record went Platinum today.	30. Do you take this woman to be your lawful wedded wife.

You get the idea. Don't evaluate the correctness of the response, only the commitment to, and richness of the response. Power words or power phrases, try them both; as a group or with individual actors.

Another way would be, to have actors, as they fill out the emotion charts; read just their list of emotions into the recorder; then as a group/individuals they respond to the playback, as described above. You could place actors in pairs across from each other and have them alternate responding as if the phrase or word came from the other actor, taking the appropriate Repel, Impel or Compel. Do any thing you can think of, just keep experimenting with ways to increase emotional awareness.

EMOTION EXERCISE VI

Write A Monologue

As presented above, writing sample sentences for each color/degree of that emotion will further clarify this concept. You could extend that idea to having students try to write a speech that starts at the lowest level of that emotion, works through each level and leads up to its most powerful level of expression, and then act it out. Use the Whelan Tape Technique for monologues in this exercise; that way the student need not waste time memorizing this monologue, but he must act it out. This technique allows actors to make real emotional connections to material they have only read once, so using it with a monologue that the actor wrote, should allow a very rich exploration of the material.

More Ideas On Emotions

Many people have made an attempt to understand their minds; school does that to all of us. Most people, as a survival instinct, try to understand their bodies, at least enough not to eat poison. However, few have ever studied the emotions in a systematic, detached way that would give them a concrete knowledge of what emotions are, even though emotions can be just as lethal as poison. While it is obvious that the emotions are the root of mental illness, the book I've mentioned many times, Emotional Intelligence, has a great deal of documentation on the very strong correlation between physical health and the emotional state of the patient.

It seems sort of strange, that as a world, we are just catching up with this overwhelming aspect of our human personalities. Basically, emotions, more than anything else, define who we are, and they are the source of almost all of our physical movement and human interactions.

Emotions are a large and generally unstudied part of what goes to make up a human being. How can we make these abstract symbols called words, which are used to describe the even more abstract concepts called feelings, easier to perceive in a physical and sensual fashion. With all the imperfections that words have in the area of abstractions, we should start by giving them as many physical qualities as possible, such as color. The idea is to make them physical and understandable to each individual person. Giving them Colors, Weights, Smells, Tastes, Sound, Touch, etc. will take them out of the abstract and help you to differentiate between their many often very delicate variations.

This work will help actors understand the nature of each emotion. This sort of objective view of emotions is essential to their study, and it makes them accessible to the artist. The possibilities, for the actor, possessing this knowledge are creatively vast. A concrete and complete catalogue of the emotions is an artistic arsenal few possess. With this knowledge, emotions are no longer a threat to the actor; since actors are in command, with a total awareness of what's happening to them, they can go anywhere on the emotional spectrum without fear or negative side effects.

Emotion is being studied more seriously, by more people, than at anytime in history. Books such as Emotional Intelligence and The Emotional Hostage, and many others are bringing these decades of research into popular awareness. Neuro-Linguistics, Learning Styles, Whole Language and other buzz words are shaking up academia in a very healthy way. Armies have always known the importance, in an effective fighting force, of the troops moral, i.e. how they feel. They appealed to the soldiers deepest emotions to stimulate them to shoot-stab-bomb-strangle and bludgeon millions to death.

Norman Vincent Peele said, "In order to get anybody to do anything, you have to make him want to do it." i.e. create the emotion of desire.

Emotional Cerebral Cross Purposes

I realize that I seem to be talking at cross proposes here. On the one hand, I am advocating a direct emotional approach to character and on the other recommending extremely cerebral exercises. Two current schools of thought explain why this has to be. In brain research and in the Learning Styles approach to education, an awareness of the existence and the function of the two hemispheres of the brain is central. Research has proven that we have two parts of our brain, the left side which deals with business/logic and the right which deals with art/emotions. While the functions are more complex, for the purpose of this discussion, that truncated definition will suffice. The fact is that educators have, since the time of Freud (1856-1939) and before, always taught to the business/logic side of the brain. We have been very heavily conditioned since pre-school, to favor that side of the brain at the expense of our emotions. We have not only been deprived of our education in the area of emotions, we have been discouraged from and often punished for expressing them. A sign of the times and an affirmation of what I'm saying is that, when I was in school, a simple emotional outburst brought a beating at the hands of the teacher. That is correct, a really good, make your knuckles bleed kind of beating. The same emotionality would frequently get the same beating at home. Today, a teacher would be fired and sued for beating a student and many a parent has found themselves in jail for child abuse. I had to laugh as I wrote that; my father didn't have any problem taking off his belt and whipping my butt until I couldn't sit down, and all the kids I knew were not strangers to the same treatment. It's OK, I was a brat and almost every time I got my whipping, I deserved it, although I never did or will believe the, "This is going to hurt me more than it hurts you" line that came before each one.

We were taught to hide emotion. The lesson was that, if we could attain a state where we put everything in a psycho-intellectual framework; where we interpreted all stimuli from the perspective of the intellect, we were good and were highly praised. If we couldn't do that, we were considered inferior. So while it is a paradox, it is true, that we have been so long removed from our emotions, that the only possible road back; the only bridge available back to the emotions, is the mind.

Actors can lead the way back to pure emotion; in order to do that we must see emotions as "universals. We must really know, really understand emotions as pure "universals." We can't feel the emotion of love as our particular emotion of love, but as the universal emotion of love, before our character has a chance of having an emotional life of his/her own. This is a slightly crude analogy, but if it helps one actor understand, call me rude. For instance, I'm sitting in a chair right now and it is "my" chair. If somebody else sits in this chair, they will not be as comfortable. Over time, this chair has molded itself to my derriere and unless your derriere is exactly, in every detail, like my derrière, it won't feel as good. This chair however, also represents the "idea" of chair, the "universal" chair. If you've ever gone shopping for a chair, you know that there are millions of kinds of chairs, millions of them. One of them is your chair and it fits you as mine fits me; our character has his chair which fits him perfectly. It is something like that with emotions. I have my kind of "love;" you have yours; and our characters have theirs. So if we can take this analogy to it's logical conclusion; there is a universal "love, "made up of all the kinds there are, and one of them fits our character perfectly, but it is not ours.

It is important that the actor is reacting to the character's emotions and not his own. It is true that the character is, in a manner of speaking, "borrowing" the actors emotions. However, the actor, as is the case with most people, is probably not that sophisticated in his/her awareness of the human emotional apparatus. You don't have to know how the internal combustion engine works to drive a car, but if you want to be a professional race car driver, you do. In old school acting, where the actor used his own emotions, this was an unnecessary tool, you don't need a book to tell you about your arm, your leg or any other part of you, including your emotions. New school actors, working strictly from character, need this knowledge. There is a place in acting for intellectual/psychological and physical research. People have these three types of memories/modes of experience and expression; each has its place in a complete character/person. However, they should be de-emphasized and entered at a much later part of the process. Although, as the brain and body are two of the three human networks, they can never be abandoned.

This work is an attempt to penetrate an essence, to add a dimension, one that is always present in great actor's work, and make it accessible to those of us who may be less gifted or without that highly tuned intuitive accessibility to emotions. Not every actor can immediately grasp the myriad subtleties of a character's emotions and interpret them in perfect harmony with the character's physical and intellectual abilities and limitations.

Some of us, most all of us, have to work at that and be satisfied with what ever proximity we achieve. What I am saying is that the systematic study of emotions will allow, even the least gifted, to get much closer than was previously possible, to that desired state of performance.

CHAPTER IV

WHELAN TAPE TECHNIQUE

Introduction

The emotions studies used alone are a great benefit to actors. The other major innovation of New School Acting is The Whelan Tape Technique. The Whelan Tape Technique used alone is also a great benefit to actors, but when used together with the emotions studies, the results are truly astounding. The Tape Technique is the perfect vehicle for this new emotional awareness. It gives the actor immediate access to the characters emotional responses to his/her changing circumstances as dictated by the script. There are many other advantages to the tape technique; most of which you will notice within the first hour of working with it.

Between each of my books, I think of things I would like to have said in the one, or in this case, the ones before. I know that most people reading this book will find the tape technique startling. The approach will be so radical that many of you will not try it until a colleague insists you try it. It is, however, so fruitful that I can't imagine it not becoming at least a part of standard rehearsal and classroom procedure. When approaching it for the first time, even those enthusiastic from the description, are insecure. As one director/teacher told me. "I know it works. I used it and got great results but I've been teaching the exact opposite for over twenty years. I have to see how you use it." That lead to a seminar in Winston Salem, NC. Sharon Andrews, visiting professor at NC. School of the Arts and Wake Forest University, along with another acting teacher from NC School of the Arts got together with the Little Theatre there and invited me down. It was a very interesting two days and these teachers were much more comfortable with the technique afterward and students were comfortable using it on their own. In my own work with the technique, which is over ten years now, I've noticed that it gets easier every time.

The difference with actors who have worked with the technique before and those just approaching it for the first time is astounding. Generally, any first rehearsal is a mixture of enthusiasm and fear. Actors, who have already worked the tape technique, come to a first rehearsal so completely relaxed you would think that the play they were just approaching, had been running for 10 years. Anxiety levels are zero. This happens because they know that the rehearsal environment is completely non-judgmental; that they will be completely free to explore and experiment. That I, as director, am going to leave them alone and not get in the way of this first attempt to find character. I am not going to impose any technical demands on them or try to control or question their creative choices. I guess the keyword here is, trust actors; that may send shivers up the spines of traditional directors, but I feel sorry for them. Giving actors blocking, or going into long winded intellectual discussions of character at a first rehearsal would make me physically ill.

So, the next few paragraphs are directed to the director. Those directors, who have used the tape technique, have been thrilled with the results, and their actors, equally or more so. One question I've gotten from these directors, in the early stages of the work, is, "It works so well, what do I do? " That concern is an important one, because in the early stages of the work actors are very independent. Something that directors used to traditional techniques will find very foreign. Recently, I've been doing a great deal of research into Learning Styles. I mention this fascinating innovation in education other places in this book. One research paper I read addressed that question,"What do I do?" It was written by Jane Baskwill, who has co-written several books about whole language. The title was "Your Role During Independent Practice." Since the tape technique is almost a perfect example of a Whole Language learning technique, the comments extracted from that article are apropos. Baskwill says,"I think the hardest thing about Independent Practice in a whole language classroom is that there is no specific way to train or plan for it. Independent practice changes daily, yet remains the same. The predictability of the structure and the open-endedness of the materials give children the safe, predictable environment in which to take the risks so necessary to learning." Since I can't quote the whole article, although I would love to; at the end of the paper she sums up, "The key is to establish an environment for learning which encourages, expects, and enables learners to take control of their learning, but which also very much includes the teacher as an indispensable part of the learning process." The combination she mentioned of predictability (in our case, the script) and open-endedness (the actors absolute freedom to explore) are the essence of the tape technique. I've used the analogy of a child's playpen. Once placed inside the playpen the child is safe, if you put some toys in with her, she will use them creatively. The script is the playpen, using the tape technique, the actors are firmly inside the script at all times. The child's toys are the actors props and set pieces, which they will use in a creative fashion.

An Important Note

The director's job initially, is to sit back and observe, to look for moments when actors loose concentration, and when that happens, to guide them back into character with gentle side coaching. Another aspect of the directors job at this point, is to watch for actors negating creative impulses, generally these are the moments where they loose concentration.

Negation consists of the actor having a strong impulse to stand, sit, walk, hit, kiss, etc. and not taking it. Negating a creative impulse is so awkward anyone looking for those moments will notice them. While discussed below; Repels-Impels-Compels are simply the only three moves an actor can make in any situation. The emotional content of the line will make the actor want to move away from i.e. Repel them; move toward i.e. Impel them, or force them to stay where they are i.e. Compel them.

Starting with the first run through, the teacher/director could have an assistant with her, and at any point she feels the actor failed to take an obvious impulse: repel, impel, or compel, the director whispers one of those words to the assistant, who will put a R-I-or C next to that line. The point, as you will see below, is not to bring, or very sparingly bring these to the actors attention at this early stage of rehearsal.

Whatever happens, this exchange between director and asst. can never be done where an actor can hear the comment, or see a director lean over and speak to the assistant; It must be done absolutely inconspicuously. If actors see or hear anything, they get paranoid, thinking that the director was displeased with them. In other words the actor believes he/she did it wrong. The directors "take" on a particular moment is established as different from that of the actors, before the actor has had a chance to explore that moment for him/her self.

It is a very delicate situation. Actors have been subjugated to directors, starting in 1864, which could be considered the official birthday of the director; one hundred and thirty-four years of being conditioned to be director dependent. To just say to actors, "You are free, your creativity is not suspect or inferior, it is demanded!" A moment like that would be roughly analogous to Southern blacks getting off a train in Chicago immediately after the Emancipation Proclamation, and being asked by a white man what they thought about an important issue. There is bound to be some fear, some confusion. Anything that looks as if it is displeasing to Massa' could result in panic. Actors must be weaned away from this dependence on the director and reclaim their birthright as creative artists, but the initial process, must be gently introduced. I'm sure Massa' is going to have some problems with this situation too. Not many directors are consistently in the habit of asking for, or of taking actors creative suggestions seriously. Put into a position where they have no choice but to listen, may tempt directors to intimidate where they cannot command. It's sticky business but it must be worked out, so let's get to it.

Actually as director/teacher, you will be amazed how your observations change from run through to run through. You will often be delighted by the creative ways the actors find to solve these problems, without your ever having said a word. The record you make, of moments when actors denied impulse, will serve a few purposes, not the least being to give you confidence that the technique works beyond any expectation you might have had, and that you can relax and enjoy the creativity it inspires. One by one, you will see the actors fix these "problem spots."

If you will pause yourself for a moment and imagine, the long speech you might have given the actor about that problem moment, all the questions the actor might have asked you about it, and then the discussion that ensued, you will breath a deep sigh of relief that that is no longer necessary. You will realize that you are free of that early rehearsal ritual; as you watch the actors organically block themselves, you will realize that you no longer have to play traffic cop. That traffic cop line took me back years; it reminded me of when I was doing a play at Lincoln Center in New York. The cast was very talented and included Robert DeNiro, Verna Bloom, Richard Bright, Kevin O'Connor, Robert Bergoes and others equally talented. We had rehearsed for weeks and were finally allowed, by the union, to use the main stage for rehearsal. We were in full flight when the Centers director, Dory Schary, smoking a giant cigar, accompanied by an assistant, walked from the wings onto the stage. He watched us for a few minutes and then, flicking an ash from his cigar, said to our director," Just make sure they know their lines and keep them from bumping into the furniture, you'll be all right."

Well, with the tape technique, you will never have to worry about the actors bumping into the furniture or forgetting their lines. Any moments that you feel the actors are still missing will probably be solved in the fourth run through, when you are doing the pause technique, and the actors adjust to the deeper penetration of emotion and character that that variation demands.

The technique is simple to use once you know the rules. At first there will seem like there are many rules to remember, but most of them are common sense once you see what the technique does for you. If kids had to learn all the rules of baseball before they were allowed to play, the game would be dead already. "I'll throw ball and you try to hit it with the bat." That's about the way most of us got started. We thought it was fun so we picked up the rest.

If I took that approach with this technique, I could tell you right now, take a three page scene and read it into a tape recorder. Then as you play it back, act it out. Just don't move your lips. It's emotional surfing, ride it. When it's over, tape and run it again, as above. Do that five times and then just get into your first emotion and do the scene, no tape, no script. Take a minute and when you're ready say the first line. The rest should pretty much fall out of your mouth and show up in your movements.

At whatever point you attempt this, you will quickly notice certain elements of the technique. It might be helpful to point them out now in an abbreviated form. I will go into more detail at the appropriate place in the book. A short list would go as follows. To help you remember, I looked for a word that all actors would recognize. If you're new, it means free theatre.

COMPT

C = Contact is constant, which allows/stimulates emotional penetration of character and relationships.

O = Organic blocking is discovered by the characters. They are moved physically by the emotional stimulus of the lines.

M = Memorizes the lines automatically as a natural result of the above.

P = Prevents premature vocal characterization. This is something that always happens when script-in-hand prevents contact.

T = True to the script - 100% ;- The actors are always relating to the exact words of the script. It's not important, if the script is pure poetry or it cost a million dollars, the professional actor's first obligation is to the text.

HEARING

A big reason this technique works so well was commented on by an actress in Florida. After one run through with the technique, she said, "You know, that's the first time I actually heard everything the other actors were saying. With my script in hand, I was using so much energy just in the mechanics of reading. Holding the script, and trying to find where I was, and where they were, that I never really heard what they were saying. This way I heard every word; it was great. I could really feel it."

The sole obligation of the WTT is to listen, to really hear, to discover the emotional truth of the line and let it move you. The famous choreographer, Balanchine, said that, in classical dance, movement begets emotion. In modern dance, emotion begets movement. In acting, the feelings that move us often come out in words, but the words are only the bowl in which the soup is served.

Remember what I said about baseball. Don't try to learn all the rules before you start to play with this idea. Just read them over once and get a sense of what you're doing, then get on your feet and give it a try. When you come back to them, many will have become obvious while working the technique. There is a very strong logic underlying this technique, so following one rule will trigger many others.

THE WHELAN TAPE TECHNIQUE

Central to this idea, is the fact that there are three basic moves an actor can make, and that they are a response to the emotional content of the line. In acting, the emotional content of the line will move you:

1: AWAY FROM-----REPELLED

2: TOWARD-------IMPELLED

3: TO REMAIN---COMPELLED

I call them RIC's and will go into more detail about them later.

To begin using the technique, take a tape recorder, and any number of actors, involved in any script, for any medium. Sit them around a table, and have them read the script to get a sense of it. They must be exposed to all of the major Given Circumstances of their individual characters, i.e. anything the writer wrote about the character that must be played, for example, missing a foot, anorexic, etc., etc. Then they read it again, only this time audio tape the read. Immediately after, without any discussion, the actors get up and act it out to the playback of the tape they just made. That's it. Oh yeah! Tell them not to move their lips.

It is, and it isn't, that simple. Actually, I've spent the better part of the last 12 years developing this technique. What follows is the result of that work.

A writer in Miami subtitled this, "The don't move your lips technique." I wasn't too thrilled with that, but had she called it the, "get out of your head technique, "I wouldn't have minded. The script should be experienced emotionally, physically, and intellectually, from character, immediately. What you are doing with this technique is integrating many aspects of character that traditionally were broken up into little pieces and then put back together later. That method succeeded in spite of itself, only because actors worked so hard. This way, it all develops at once.

From here on I'll be doing a very detailed step by step guide. It may be too detailed for some. Go through it my way this first time, and then play with it any way you want. I don't follow this format all the time, but it will be useful for you to get many of the major points at once. In this example, I will outline a first rehearsal with two actors doing a 3-4 page scene, working for about two hours. OK, It's time for the first taping for run through.

BASIC RULES FOR TAPING

1) Black out stage directions. (Notes in the script, in parenthesis, telling actors when to sit, stand, or smile.)

   That was the past, another director, another actor. It's your part now, do it your way.

2) Put the tape recorder (microphone) close enough to both actors to make a clean recording.

   One that can be heard from any part of the playing area. If you are in a theater that has one, play the tape through the house system.

3) Do a sound check.

   Record three or four lines, and then play it back, to make sure you're recording. Technical mess-ups happen, and too much time gets wasted when you go through the whole thing, only to find that for some reason you weren't recording. Do this every time you tape. I've had it work perfectly three times in a row, and on the fourth, it didn't record; so sound check every time.

4) Only do one take.

   If you mess up a line, no big deal; keep on going. If you stop to fix that line, your partners going to demand a second take on some line of his. On and on, till you waste a great deal of time on something that should not be in your head right now, i.e. performance. This is first day, first time, one take, that's the rule.

5) Don't rush the reading while taping.

   Be emotionally correct, but the natural tendency of an actor approaching a new script, is to rush it. If you walk past an audition, and you see an actor beating his head against the wall, walk up to him and say, "You rushed it, didn't you?" (9 out of 10 times you'll be right)

6) Stay on the script.

   Every word just the way it's written. Don't try to make eye contact; just read what is on the page; stay on the script. By the way, never say a word unless you know what it means. If there's such a word in the script, look it up.

7) Don't try to act.

   Don't force anything. Don't deny anything, but don't work for anything. Just read it and let it happen.

8) Never use the same taping twice.

   Always use a fresh taping because whether blatant or subtle, there was growth. You can't wear the same shoes you wore when you were five.

OK. You have your tape and whatever you've got for set, and props, are in place. It's important that you make some attempt to at least "fake" a set. Three chairs can be a wall, a single plant can be a forest or a garden, a stick can be a gun, etc. You're ready for your first run through, but you must know that there are rules here too.

Don't memorize them or take a test on them before you do it, just read them and go.

BASIC RULES FOR RUN THROUGH

1) Don't perform.

   You are not to consider what you are doing as being important to anyone, except yourself, and your partner. Don't force anything. Don't deny anything, but don't work for anything. Discount performance 100%.

2) Don't move your lips.

   This is so important and it seems to give actors a great deal of trouble when they first encounter the technique. What you must understand is that the whole point of the technique is to have you fully focused on the character and their relationship to the other characters, at that moment in time. Sometimes actors move their lips without even knowing it, a sure sign that they are not in character. They are in their heads, as an actor. They are not only out of character, but they are in the past as an actor, trying to remember what they said so as to lip sink it in the future. How could anything honest or interesting happen when an actor is so far away from what is going on at the moment. Directors must watch for this and stop it quickly. Actors; when you are working without a director and you see your partner moving his lips, realize you're up there by yourself and it makes no sense to continue. It's like playing tennis with yourself. You hit the ball but there is nobody there to hit it back. Gently make the other actor aware of what is happening to him. The best way is to triple your involvement with the moment, usually that's enough to get the other actor back on track.

3) Don't try to remember what you're going to say next. Stay in the moment.

4) Don't negate any impulse unless it will make the other actor bleed, or walk funny.

   Note: I would never want to do or say anything that would restrict an actors spontaneity, but how far that goes is something the actors discuss before they start the work. To put it another way, spontaneity is not an excuse for sexual harassment.

5) Don't put any obligation on yourself, other than responding to the emotional stimulus of the script from as much of the character that you have at that point.

   When I say as much of the character as you have at this point, I mean, when an actor reads a script, she gets some immediate ideas about character. This has to happen, and it is all you have to start with, but beware/be aware that that conception is very superficial. It has to be, you've only had the character a very short time. Once you start acting out to the tape, the contact with the other actor/actors, may change the character's emotions from the way you saw her while reading. In other words, the character you read, may be very different from the character you meet, once you're on your feet.

   Let go of your original intellectual impression, and go with what you're feeling at the exact moment you look at, or touch, that other actor. It's not as obvious as it sounds, or as easy. Guard your concentration. Stay in the moment.

6) Don't stop yourself from eating, drinking, smoking, sucking on a lollipop, or anything that would normally keep you from talking, just because you are talking on the tape.

   Note: During a Miami workshop, a student working the technique, took a long drink of whiskey, while his voice was speaking on the tape. During the discussion, after the scene finished, a student said he couldn't do that. The scene was far enough along, that I knew they could hit most of the dialogue, so I told them do it again right away. When they got to that point in the script, since they were running with dialogue, the actor of course could not drink. However, the tension of a man wanting a drink very badly, was in the actors eyes, hands, back and feet. It had not been there before he had taken the impel/impulse to drink while WTT-ing the scene. Nuf said. The situation went from passive, i.e. not drinking, to active, energetically suppressing the desire to drink.

7) Do maintain contact with your partner: eyes, hands, feet, with props (light a cigarette, pour a drink), with the set (look out the window, throw pebbles in the lake).

8) Don't be literal in expressing the RIC's.

   Let them explode. Impulse is art. Follow it blindly in rehearsal, and discipline it in performance, but never negate it. Negating creative impulse takes so much energy, that you will appear spastic.

   What do I mean by non-literal RIC'S? Let's say you're playing a shy guy, who somehow gets invited into the apartment of the girl of his dreams. All of a sudden he gets the impulse to scream, bounce off the couch, and tackle her. Do it! As long as it doesn't make her bleed or walk funny. The fact that the character's personality would only let him respond to the impel with a few halting steps in her direction, is what makes him, him. If however, you fulfill the impulse, physically and emotionally, letting it fill you completely, when later, the more dominant aspects of character start to control the "style" of the movement, the audience, should see beyond those few halting steps in her direction, to the dynamic tension of denying the desired impulse to bounce off the couch and tackle her.

9) Focus on your emotions.

"How do I feel saying that?" "How do I feel hearing that?" Let the emotion move you. Repel-Impel-Compel.

10) Guard your concentration.

With all this new found freedom, you might get tempted to think about what you did or what is coming next, instead of what you're feeling right at the moment. Don't! No third eyeing!

11) Do make hand and body gestures, verbal sounds without speech.

Feel free to laugh, cry, grunt, stick your tongue out, flip the bird, point, whistle, scream, etc. But be careful, don't get so loud that you can't clearly hear the dialogue coming off the tape.

12) Don't stop for any reason once you start the tape. Stay in character until it's over.

That should be what you need to know for now; so start the tape and dive in. Remember, follow all impulses blindly.

BETWEEN FIRST & SECOND TAPING

A few of the major advantages of this technique became obvious, whether you were acting, or watching that first run through.

C = Contact; which is constant

Eye contact is possible all the way through the scene, play, film. Physical contact is increased because hands are free to caress, fight, handle props, etc. This constant and total contact, causes/allows the emotional flow between characters to constantly build.

Every time actors have used the WTT, they have made at least one (usually more) major connections to the character this first time through; a moment when the character's emotion was very rich inside of the actor. They got a very strong Repel-Impel-Compel, from character. Most important, don't talk it to death. Just do it again, but:

Don't fall in love with the way you said something the first time (a line reading).

Don't fall in love with the way you did something the first time (a piece of business)

YOUR CHARACTER WILL GROW EVERY TIME YOU DO THIS TECHNIQUE

GROWTH MEANS CHANGE!

When you remember what you did, or how you said something, it is because you don't believe you can do it any better. Why? Don't you understand, there is no top, bottom, or sides, on your creativity. Go deeper, there is better in you.

SECOND RUN THROUGH

Remember, be sensitive to the RIC's. "How do I feel when I say that?" "How do I feel when I hear that?" Let the feeling move you any way it wants. It's like emotional surfing, ride it. Remember: Don't Remember.

BETWEEN SECOND AND THIRD TAPING

Some of the emotions you got the first time were stronger this time, and you probably found some new emotions, and business. Even after only two run throughs with the technique, you can see that movement is increasing, and rudimentary blocking has begun. This points out another advantage of the technique.

O = Organic Blocking

The natural movement discovered by the characters as they respond to the emotional stimulus of the line, move the actor, in an extremely ingenuous manner, around the playing area. A roughed out set, and some hand props create homes for these RIC's, a bar down left, might be the home for a repel, etc.

THIRD RUN THROUGH

You may find the variations, that I suggest you use in this third run through, more beneficial if used earlier or later.

I first worked with mirror exercise in the early sixties. It was a workshop using Viola Spolins' Theatre Games at The Committee in San Francisco. I have always found them highly effective and they adapt incredibly to the tape technique. A mirror exercise is simply; actors stand facing each other a few feet apart, and mirror everything the other person does. Stand in front of a full length mirror and move a little, you'll get the idea. Don't get tricky, move in super slow motion. Never move so fast that you can't be comfortably followed. Feet alike, hands alike, eyes alike, backs alike, bend, stretch, sit, lie down, etc., just like a mirror, use the whole body.

For this third time through, you (actors) are to set up in a basic mirror exercise and then start the tape, whomever is speaking is looking in the mirror (leading). Take the RIC's, but don't break the mirror. I've gotten some pretty incredible results using this WTT variation with a five character ensemble piece. As actors get more and more in synch, the speed at which they can move together is very impressive.

WTT - Mirror Exercise I

Actors are to set up a basic mirror, (above) and do it while listening to the playback of the freshly taped scene. Remember, the character speaking, is the person looking in the mirror (i.e. leading). Actors are to work far enough from each other that they can respond to the Repels-Impels- Compels.

The movement can be literal or stylized. Most often, at least in the beginning, since all movements must be slow enough to be mirrored, this means stylized. The taping is at normal speed, but the movement usually is something like the super slow motion replays of professional sporting events; within that framework, RIC'S can be profitably followed. A slow motion punch can be thrown. Just remember you can't go through the mirror. An embrace can be mirrored, but remember it is a mirror image. You cannot touch beyond the ways you can touch a real mirror. Remember, if you are speaking (on the tape) you are leading, but be ready to mirror when your partner starts to speak. As always, stay in character.

Many valuable discoveries are made doing this exercise, RIC'S that were missed in your initial contact with the material, become obvious doing the WTT- Mirror Exercise I.

WTT - Mirror Exercise II

After a fresh taping, this time the person speaking is following. You are to mirror the reaction, of whomever you are speaking to. In WTT Mirror II, you are responding to and mirroring the other characters response to what you are saying.

Take the RIC's as they present themselves. Remember to stylize the movement. Slow it down enough to be followed.

WTT - Mirror Exercise III

Remember to always use a fresh taping of the scene/play/film. This time there won't be a leader, or a follower. Nobody lead, and nobody follow. "Give and take, help each other. Don't always lead, or let yourself be lead." Give and take. Try to get in synch, flow with each other. At first, one will lead, and then the other will lead. It will go back and forth like that, trading leads, but there will be a moment, and you won't remember where it started, that you are just flowing, and it is absolutely effortless. You will love it. The tape is playing , the scene is going on. You hear your characters voice, and the voice of the person you're speaking to answering you. The emotions are flowing through you and you are both absolutely in synch.

Don't get disappointed if this doesn't happen right away, it will. It sounds hard, but if you really try to synch, it will happen for you, and the character discoveries are very rich. You will be very pleased and surprised by your success, and the insights you get from it. You can do WTT/Mirror I, II & III as part of one rehearsal, or spread them out. Break them up with any variation you want to try. Just be sure to do them all at some point

It's obvious that with this technique the actors are locked into the script. It is an advantage to all concerned that the technique has the actors:

$$T = \text{True To The Script - 100\%}$$

The actors are always relating to the exact words of the script. It's not important, if the script is pure poetry, or it cost a million dollars. The professional actor's first obligation is to the text.

It is, in a way, like placing a kid in a play pen. Once in the play pen they are usually safe. If the actors are forced to stay 100% on the script, they should be safe to explore whatever happens. To extend the analogy, put some toys in the play pen and the child is not only safe but happy. By putting some props inside the area defined by the script, the actors should be able to creatively explore the total experience.

I love improvisation, and find it a very useful rehearsal tool, however never inside the script. It is too easy for the actor to take off into subjective areas that undermine the integrity of the script; going into Psycho-drama, such as, playing her own divorce instead of the character's.

I will always have the actors improvise any possible prior (to the script) relationship. I also like to investigate any possible future relationship between the characters by improvising, but, inside the script they must work with the lines.

FOURTH RUN THROUGH

Now tape again and run it on the set, only this time, if you have a director, she will now work the WTT Pause Technique. If not, you are to leave long pauses between speeches or beats. Use that time to penetrate the emotion generated by what you just said, or heard. I will now give a thorough description of how to use the pause technique. Since this idea is so important, I will present it in the directors version, and the actors version. I hope, by so doing, that it will be easy for you to understand the concept, and maximize the benefits.

WTT PAUSE - DIRECTED

This I believe to be a most significant technique. I and others using this idea, have gotten outstanding results, with the by-product of some very fascinating business evolving. I have found that the pause technique works best, when used after the actors have gone through the WTT's at least twice, usually three times. The actors are getting so much more stimuli using the WTT, that they need this time to assimilate the broad outline of the piece, and get a feel for the emotional flow. Without the script to hide behind, and be distracted by, the actors are thrown into a very naked confrontation with, depending on the piece, some pretty overwhelming emotional circumstance. To prolong some of those moments, for unlimited amounts of time, can be a little more gut wrenching than some actors are ready for. Especially since actors have been hiding behind scripts so long, it's almost in their DNA.

Growth during the pause technique is so rapid, it's consistently stimulating to work this way. The pause technique brings explosions of creativity. It is impossible for an actor working correctly, to deny creative impulse during that part of the technique, unless that impulse is abandoned because a truer, purer impulse replaces it.

While you may not want to keep actors, who are just starting to work this way, paused too long, a director still has to be patient during these first explorations, and should initially prolong pauses, sometimes longer than their own creative impulses might demand. The actor must be made comfortable with the fact that there is time to explore, that mistakes and false starts are O.K., that they can solve those problems by a deeper commitment to character and the emotion. There must be time to forget self, to penetrate character and lose all consciousness of performing.

It is almost magical, when left like this, the actors, if they are working properly, are transported into the time, place and person of the text. It can be absolutely trance inducing and as a director or class member watching, you are spell bound. You know beyond a doubt that you do not exist for these people at this time. Used properly, this application of the tape technique is one of the most powerful rehearsal tools you will ever use.

So let them run the WTT, and get used to the idea first. Then, let's say it's the fourth time through, you the director, who is by now aware of moments that are being missed, moments you want them to explore more, find more, do more. When those moments come up, HIT THE PAUSE BUTTON.

With the old script in hand technique, you would have had to talk to them about a "beat", maybe giving them more than you wanted to, or should have. Now all you have to do is hit the pause button on a tape recorder, and watch the actors tear themselves apart until they get it. They will love you for it.

It's fairly simple considering the super results you'll get. As in all this work, patience is the key, don't worry, you're saving so much time with this technique you can afford to be patient. The actors having read the script, and run the tape a few times are now somewhat comfortable working this way, they know the rules:

1) Stay in character no matter what

2) Stay in contact: eyes; hands; props, etc.

3) Follow the RIC's.

If rule 1 is working, 2 and 3 follow automatically. In relation to this, make it perfectly clear to the actors that they are not to freeze when you pause the tape; that they are to move in any way that the deeper involvement with the moment inspires them to move.

Tell the actors, at certain points, you are going to pause the tape. They are to get in touch with, "How they (character) feel when they say that/hear that." To go deeper into the emotion generated by that line; that they are to penetrate that emotion with every fiber of their being. Tell actors that you may leave them there for a long time and to make sure they don't lose their concentration; never to let themselves slip into mere "waiting." Actually you can see that happen, the tension goes, the posture changes. When you see that happening to actors, side coach, "feel it in your back. Feel that emotion in your toes. Does it make you want to move. Feel it in your butt. Go deeper into the emotion." This type of gentle side coaching should get the actors back into the moment.

NOTE: How long you hold them is up to you, but I seldom go over three minutes on any one pause, sometimes much shorter. Again play with it. It's new work. An open door. I don't know what would happen if I left them there a half hour. They might make a whole dynamic play out of that one beat, melt the stage, quit the class. I don't know. The inventiveness here can be overwhelmingly creative. The business the actors invent, while dealing with this tension, is some of the most creative work I've even seen.

NOTE: As a director, I would always pick these big juicy moments to have the actors pause. Once I had to leave the room, so I told a student to take over pausing for the actors. When I returned unnoticed, I stalled at the back of the room to observe this situation, to see how it was going. It turned out to be quite interesting. The student on the pause button was working some moments I would never have chosen. He was working what had seemed to me minor beats, and the results were yielding some very rich little moments. I suppose the point here is to look beyond those bombastic beats. There are little gems in scripts that get missed, but when added, provide a lustrous setting for those big jewels in the crown. Maybe the point is have somebody else pop the button now and then.

That's how the director is suppose to use this idea, but you are actors, on your own, so what do you do? Well, with the knowledge of how the director is to proceed to guide you, this is what I want you to do now.

DON'T RUSH! USE THE EXTRA TIME TO PENETRATE A LIFE TIME OF EMOTIONAL/PHYSICAL COORDINATION.

That's fairly self explanatory, but maybe it deserves a few words. However old your character is, she has had all that time, and been conditioned by her circumstance, to respond to various emotional stimulus in a certain personal individual manner. In other words, she has, over a lifetime, found her own unique way of physically expressing each emotion, and hers is different than yours.

WTT PAUSE - UNDIRECTED

When actors are working alone, but still want to benefit from the advantages of the pause technique, you have three ways to go, whichever one is used, you're going to have to be very focused, very disciplined. That is the goal of this work, but realistically, if you are paused for a long time, it is possible to lose your concentration.

When a director is present she will notice that, and guide you back with some gentle side coaching. However, when you're on you own, be vigilante. If you catch yourself slipping, kick your own butt back into the scene. Get back to the emotion, as soon as you get in touch with that, your concentration will strengthen and the work will go the way it's supposed to.

Okay, as to form,

1) You can agree with your partner that either one of you can press the button at any time.

2) Agree that, whomever paused it must start it again.

3) Leave very long pauses between speeches, or beats within a speech, when you are taping.

Although this means that you know when the pause will pretty much end, you still have a decent amount of time to explore that emotion. You can get a lot using any of the above; certainly more than if you were running the scene, at whatever could be considered normal speed.

It may work out that major vocal changes occur after running the pause technique. You should notice significant changes in line readings, as the emotional involvement grows with each run through because the technique:

P = Prevents Premature Vocal Characterization

This is something that always happens when script-in-hand prevents contact. The script is like a full body Roman battle shield. Nothing gets in, and nothing gets out. So shielded, the actor creates his/her characterization firstly, intellectually, in the voice. Once the scripts are finally out of their hands, and they can make the type of contact, that happens with the WTT immediately, they are left with two choices:

1) The character discoveries, that always flow from direct contact, can be forcibly stuffed into the prematurely formed vocal characterization.

2) The actor can waste a great deal of energy trying to break out of that premature vocal characterization. This is a limited, if not totally false characterization, which in some instances had weeks of script in hand rehearsal to reinforce its negative influence.

BETWEEN FOURTH & FIFTH RUN THROUGH

By now all sorts of interesting things are happening. The problem you face now is that without ever trying to memorize the lines, you know most of them. So you must guard your concentration. Don't let yourself slip into the future. Don't start anticipating a line, or a piece of business, that is death. If even one of you is working properly, it probably won't come the way you remember it. The time it takes you to recover from your partner's doing something totally, spontaneously different, will be absolutely wasted. It will also kill any creativity that could have come out of that moment, and all the moments before, when you were in the future anticipating that moment. Guard your concentration. Stay deeply involved with the emotion that is coming from what you just heard or said; stay in the moment.

AFTER FIFTH RUN THROUGH

By now you will have seen how the other advantages of the WTT apply, but a very significant advantage should now come home with a bang. The actors do not know how much has gone in, but they know almost all the dialogue, and much of the character by now. The technique integrates all these, which:

M = memorizes the lines automatically

A short scene (3 or 4 pages) will be memorized, by the actors, generally after six tapings; without them ever having to consciously work on them. This happens because the actors are using all their memories.

PIE = Physical Memories

Intellectual Memories

Emotional Memories

In the rote memorization process generally employed by actors, only the brain is involved, i.e. intellectual memory. We are, in effect, adding two thirds more memory. The effect is synergistic. The whole is equal to more than the sum of its parts. Learning is much quicker this way because the memories are working as a team.

SIXTH RUN THROUGH

This is not an improve. Do the script !!!

If you have a director, or a good actor to "do book" for you (someone to watch the script and cue actors, if necessary), or even if your on your actors on your own, go ahead and give the scene a shot. Try to do the scene without the tape and without the script. You probably will be somewhat insecure. Don't worry. You know more than you think you do. Take a moment, get deep into your first emotion and when you are ready, start. Just say your first line, and the rest will pretty much fall out of your mouth. Don't panic and start calling for "line." Give yourself a chance. There is no performance aspect to rehearsal, so take your time. The lines come easier as you get deeper into the script/emotion. Here, as in the WTT Normal, your only crime is breaking character before the scene is over. If you remember a section of the scene you forgot, say it was in the beginning, and you're in the middle, just throw your partner the cue line for that section. He will probably pick up the cue, and you will go right through. When you get back to the middle, just keep acting; do that part over. Stay on the script. Don't start improvising; if you're absolutely lost, ask for "line."

You will probably find that you remember 60% to 90% of the dialogue. Not only that, but you have blocked the scene naturally/organically. Your character is very much alive in you, and you have discovered some very interesting business. This whole process took less than two hours. So taking this step by step first rehearsal as a guide, you can figure how to use WTT to your best advantage.

37

Important: Actors, you will make some very interesting discoveries, and invent some great business as you are doing the WTT. You are going to want to use this in performance, but, and this may be the biggest but of your career, the director is still the boss. If the director disagrees with you, and tells you they want it done differently, do it their way. None of the work you did is wasted. Whatever you have to do on the outside, nobody knows what you're doing on the inside. When someone complained to General Patton, "Your troops don't know your plan", he said, "It's not important that they know. It's only important that I know."

Warning: Some directors want your ideas. Some you can get your way with, others don't, and you can't. Learn the difference fast.

THE SET

It would be interesting , if actors had imput into the set, they are the ones who have to live in it. There are times when the actor does have control over the set and that is in class and in showcase situations; when in those situations, there is a variation of the tape technique that will be useful. After actors have all their given circumstance, they do a taping. Then, in a dark place, they lie on their backs, eyes closed, as the scene plays back on the recorder, the actors are to watch it on the movie screen of the mind; being careful to note where they (as characters) go, and also, what's in that place, chairs, windows, color of walls, rugs, pictures, the physical smells and sounds of the place. Afterward, they take paper and pencil, and diagram the place. It is amazing how similar actors' visions of the place usually are.

You always know where you are; a house, an office, a bar, a kitchen, a living room, whether it's in Paris or London. You know because you went there obviously, but specifically by the things, objects, you see there. You know you are in a kitchen because you see pots, pans, stoves, refrigerators, etc. I always ask students to diagram, in color, the place of their scene.

In plays you have a fourth wall; the one between you and the audience. Every actor must know everything about that wall, and what's beyond it. In film there is a wild wall; a wall of an apartment or office that is on rollers, and is moved so that the camera and lights can fit, but for the actor, it is still there. In a film, when you look over your shoulder, to the audience it seems like you're looking at the Grand Canyon, or a speeding Corvette, but in fact you're on a sound stage and all you see is a screen. This will become more important as digital imaging is increasingly used to save money on locations and create effects. The actors in Jurassic Park could not see the dinosaurs; the actors in Twister could not see the twister, they saw a guy waving a stick.

In TV and commercials, there is usually something you have to see that isn't there. You must create that, and if you're working with someone else, you have to create it together. If you are supposed to see somebody, know exactly what they look like, hair, eyes, height, everything. You have to be in the exact same place, the temperature, the sounds, etc.

I had two actors doing a scene in a restaurant, it wasn't selling. I asked each to write on a piece of paper how much the meal was costing, the total bill. He put $14 and she put $107. I asked them how they could be doing a scene together, when they weren't even in the same restaurant.

In films and plays, you have set designers and real props, but in auditions, most showcases, and classes, you don't. In scripts you have a diagram of the set, but the same is true here as in blacking out the stage directions. This is your place now. You might be more comfortable with the sink down left.

Also, you may change the place of the action to fit your needs. For instance, two students picked a scene that had some great dialogue, but it was all to take place in a small car. They never stood up. In a showcase we want to see you move, so we put them in a living room and it worked much better. Don't just do it to do it, but if it makes sense to you, do it.

Discovering The Set In An Actual Production

A more co-operative approach between directors and actors when creating a piece, would have them discovering the set together; that would certainly be a creative plus. The original set is not "set in stone." As actors get up and start moving around, they may discover that their Repels, Impels, and Compels carry them to different parts of the stage. Actors may want to change the set later, but it is a starting point.

While in Miami, I received a case study in how this works. Steve Neal, Instructor of Theatre, at Barry University in Miami, was very quick to see the possibilities of the tape technique, and put it to work immediately. He was three hours away from his first rehearsal as director of the University's production of Steel Magnolias, when I introduced him to the idea. I worked, with Steve and the cast, the first night of rehearsals to help them understand the technique. Although the set was not in place, there were drawings, and it was roughed out. It was a very exciting night, and the openness of his talent, to this new idea, was very gratifying. It didn't seem to take them long to see the advantages, and they approached the work with energy and enthusiasm.

I didn't get back to another rehearsal for about a week. The work was going great, and enthusiasm was high. I noticed that the set had been adjusted somewhat, and asked Steve about it. I was thrilled when he told me that, he had noticed during rehearsals, that the RIC's (repels, impels, compels.) were carrying the actresses differently than would have been accommodated by his original plan, so he changed it. He said he knew he could redirect the actresses to the original plan, but why not just fit it to the natural organic flow/blocking that the actors discovered using the WTT.

While what I've just presented you is only one variation of the tape technique, it is the basic one, and the one you will use most often. It is presented slightly differently than it is in <u>INSTANT ACTING</u>, but I am positive, that with this much information, you can start to investigate the many benefits of the tape technique. I also know that it is a marvelously creative experience and that it is sure to increase your enjoyment of your work.

CHAPTER V
HISTORY OF AMERICAN ACTING

To date, I think that American acting is an oxymoron. We have Americans that act, but there has never been an American style of acting; that said, I will use the term American acting for the sake of ease.

American acting is now entering its third stage and in that stage we will find a style that can truly be said to be American; something that combines the rugged individualism that we are noted for and the high degree of teamwork that we are capable of when the situation demands it. By looking at the first two stages it will be easier to see how this third stage is a natural evolution of them.

THE BIRTH OF AMERICAN ACTING
STAGE I
A Direct Importation Of The European School

The British school in particular. This was a very natural occurrence since that was where most new Americans came from. The vast majority of those who came here were English and some of them were actors. So why should it occur to these British actors, that simply because they were in another country, they should change the way they acted? Weren't their audiences the same audiences that they had played to at home? Some of the material changed but the style of acting stayed the same.

This was a literary oriented style, in which the idea was for the actor to get directly in the audiences face and say the text. This text was usually in verse or some other elevated form of speech, and it was presented loudly and clearly, accompanied by broad physical gestures on almost every line, to make sure that the audience didn't miss the point. If the dialogue said, "This round earth;" after the actor says that line, he will make a big circle with his hands. Some actors preferred to do it during the line; timing of this ritual was to taste, of course. This was also the style in France and in other parts of Europe. Nothing unusual there either; troupes of actors moved around the continent and influenced each other. The British actor, David Garrick, had brought some token of naturalism to the English stage, but declamation still ruled. That overblown type of acting remained the mainstay of American acting until the "naturalistic" revolution in Europe reached into Russia and Stanislavski made his debut on the world stage in the late 1800's. Stanislavski's ideas didn't take long to flow onto the American stage.

The reason for the end of that European period in American acting, was, as in Europe, the emergence of the director. <u>The advent of the director in the 1860's and the creation of the Stanislavski system in the late 19th and early 20th century was the last major change in acting style, it began over a hundred and thirty years ago;</u> For those who like dates, 1929 might be said to be the date when the Method of Stanislavski completed its conquest of American acting. While his ideas had reached America years before, it was the founding of the Group Theatre by Lee Strasberg, Stella Adler, Harold Clurman and others, that established its absolute rule, and for sixty-seven years, it has dominated, uncontested. As I will detail later, Viola Spolin planted the seed of the demise of the Method in the fifties, but while her work has been strong enough to steadily undermine the Method, it has not been strong enough to conquer it.

This new player in the history of acting, the director, changed the game forever; a player whose role is about to change again, and once more the history of acting will change with it. So, the Russian revolution in American acting, which should actually be looked at as evolution, was brought about by the creation of the job we now call the director. Where did these people come from, what are they doing here, will they ever go away? Those answers can all be found by taking a closer look at:

The Birth Of The Director 1864

It is interesting to note that the "director" as such did not enter the theatrical scene until 1864. That happened at The Prince of Wales Theatre, London, in the person of Mr. T.W. Robertson.

I will come back to that, but I think it is important to understand why the post of director was invented. Two major historical events laid the groundwork; The Industrial Revolution, which occurred around the late 18th and early 19th century, and The French Revolution in 1789. This period saw many improvements in medicine, agriculture, sanitation etc. These and other connected factors were the reason for a population explosion, one which saw Great Britain go from 7 million people in 1750 to over 20 million in 1850.

I'm going to paint this in very broad strokes, because this is an acting book not a history book, but some history is called for. Prior to those two world shaking events, people were either rich or poor; there was a very small middle class. As a result of those two events there was an explosion of the middle class. Large population shifts occurred during the industrial revolution, as people following jobs, went from the fields to the factory and from the farm to the city. Basically what happened was that, all of a sudden, we had large groups of people in central locations. They had jobs and money, and they were looking for something to do. The high brow theatre of the very rich and the low brow burlesque of the very poor did not suit the entertainment needs of this newly large and increasingly powerful middle class. A new form of theatre had to be fashioned to take advantage of this potentially extremely lucrative market. This period provided many opportunities to entrepreneurs of every kind. Seeing a virtual vacuum in the area of middle class theatre, these entrepreneurs went to work. Management structures built up around theaters, with the intent of providing the type of plays suited to this audience.

Prior to this time, due to the lack of a large scale audience, the economic advantages of exploiting theatre were not recognized as being worth the trouble, and actors ruled the day. The actors strutted and posed in the grandest of fashions, delivering speeches directly to the audience. The texts were in verse or in a very elevated style of speech, such as would appeal to the aristocrats and upper class members of this type of theatre audience. As writers started to respond to the financial and social realities of the rapidly growing middle class, scripts took on a more naturalistic speech and acting had to adjust to meet the needs of the new plays.

The birth of this new acting style saw many arguments about how it should be accomplished, but one factor was clear; actors had to be broken of the old habits. They had been kings and they were being told that there had to stop being kings; it was a major revolution in acting. In world revolutions, such as the French and Russian, the crowd simply took the King and Czar, and their families out and killed them. I'm sure many of this new group, known as directors, would love to have done the same with actors, but that was not practical; at that time there weren't that many actors and demand for shows was big and growing. As Management installed itself, certain aspects of the actors' anarchistic artistry had to change. It had to be stopped, and so management stepped in to do it, they created the director; a kind of shop floor/middle management position with artistic control. Since art can not be managed, the position was born in conflict.

How powerfully money affected actors and acting and brought about the creation of the director is made, in a way that can't be argued, by this letter sent to the Times of London in 1869 from the management of the Drury Lane Theatre, one of the most important and largest theatres of the day. It announced it's coming attraction, "*Formosa; or The Railroad To Ruin*. "I am neither a literary missionary nor a martyr" explained F.B.Chatterton, "I am simply the manager of a theatre, a vender of intellectual entertainment to the London public and I found that Shakespeare spelt ruin.... In the extremity to which I was lead by my faith in the fine taste of the upper classes for the poetic drama, I turned to the dramatist who has made the fortune of more than one manager in London. I need not say with what result....the amount taken daily at my box office before the doors open....to see *Formosa* exceeds the gross contents of my theatre to see "*Macbeth*." *Formosa* , as you might guess, was a spectacle meant for the middle classes. I think they had a real train onstage.

The problem of getting old school actors of that day to adjust to this new style of acting was not easy then and it won't be easy to get the "new "old school to leave their director dependence. Since up to that time it was the actors themselves that had made the choices as to just how they were going to do a part, it was felt they could not be counted on to change this on their own. The director was invented to serve that purpose; to break actors. Acting had become big business.

So let us get back to our first director. T.W. Robertson, who joined the new owner of the Prince of Wales Theatre, Marie Wilton and her soon to be husband Squire Bancroft and together they brought "Fifteen years of unparalleled prosperity ..." to the theatre. Robertson stated, "I don't want actors; I want people who will do just what I tell them." I think if we looked real close, we could find that phrase tattooed on some body part, not normally seen, of most directors from then until now.

I believe it was no quaint coincidence that the first play presented at the Prince of Wales, written and directed, by Robertson, was a play called "Society." A play about a woman who's advising her daughter to marry a very rich man, because "Money can do everything." Slightly after this idea of a director with complete creative control began in England, The Duke of Saxe Meiningen began Prussianizing the theatre in his country. The Duke exercised complete control of actors performances, he was absolutely dictatorial. The Dukes autocratic style of controlling every aspect of production and every aspect of actors performances was to make quite an impression on Stanislavski, who saw every performance of the Duke's company when it appeared in Moscow in 1890.

Whether the director was born out of artistic or economical reasons is not the concern, how the role developed and ultimately how it affected acting in America is our next step. To understand that, we have to look at what brought about, the very root of, the second stage of American acting.

STAGE II

A Direct Importation Of The Russian School

Stanislavski is certainly one of the most important names in acting history and it was he who, more than anyone, managed to solidify this new trend in acting and make it a movement.

In 1897 with the birth of the Moscow Art Theatre, and the rise of Stanislavski and Freud at almost the same time, the position of Director/teacher took an even more broad based autocratic turn. Saxe Meiningan had a great influence on Stanislavski. The Meininger company played Moscow in 1885 and 1890. Stanislavski attended every performance of the 1890 season. The Moscow Art Theatre was born eight years latter with Stanislavski as Herr Director. The obvious fact that Stanislavski was also heavily influenced by Sigmond Freud shows itself in his approach to actors training and the results gotten by actors who use his Method. The book, Freud and Stanislavski, states that case in every detail. Stanislavski took his autocratic directorial tactics from the Duke and his psychological approach to character from Freud. The director was god and the actors were the director's psychologically controlled and manipulated puppets.

It was pre-revolutionary Russia and Freud had created the mass merchandising of the mind and what might actually be called the culture of the mind. The rise of the Russian school coincided with the ascension of Freud. Stanislavski, having been born seven years before Freud, was well aware of the psychoanalyst's work and corresponded with him. Stanislavski was influenced by these new ideas as he formulated his Method. This "Method"came to America starting in the early 1920's. Principally through the influence of Lee Strasberg and Stella Adler at The Group Theatre.

The Russian School was dominated by a psychological and intellectual orientation. This approach gave a naturalistic air to actors performance as compared with the older declamatory style, which it replaced as the leading American approach. This Russian Method school has dominated American acting for almost seventy years. This is a simple statement of fact that can be verified by even a casual survey of how acting is taught in American high schools, colleges and private professional schools. It is overwhelmingly Stanislavski based, regardless of the wrinkle that has been put on it or the new name it received in the process. A book called The New Acting Teachers came out a few years ago, and although I don't remember the exact numbers, something like 17 out of 20 interviewed had a Method base. This is what they call "new," this is a book published in the 1990's about people teaching ideas born in the 1890's. When an artistic style has become so completely institutionalized, it has lost all its vitality. The signs of deterioration of creative thrust are evident in all areas of acting; in this case, it has gone on for so long, the art form itself is seriously threatened.

Stanislavski and that school of acting were born in that old white intellectual European environment and have all of the values of it built in, so it is not unusual that it is old world elitist by nature, meaning that the director became even more firmly entrenched.

Stanislavski made order out of the chaos of actors training and rehearsal procedures, and introduced an acting style, that for a time, was very exciting, but as William Bourroughs would say, "The rubes are wise." That bag of tricks is used up, outta gas, seen too often. Actors are losing their audience. The finger gets pointed in many directions but the truth is that the actor must point it at himself. He/she must realize that the

41

old training does not provide the tools to satisfy the needs of contemporary audiences; they must seek out a fresh new approach that is in tune with the needs of contemporary audiences.

It's already to the point where most would rather see a traffic accident live on the news than a well written drama, and that is because the acting is so out of synch. The young would rather watch cartoons or play video games, at least the characters there are not pretending to be real.

History has changed the world once again and every other art form went with that change, staying vital and interesting in the process. Acting alone marches to that antiquated pre-revolutionary Russian drum; this has resulted in the stultification of the actor. The tradition of psycho-Intellectual influence on acting is one of elitism. Elitism of wealth and power was the name of the game when Kings and Czars and that monarchistic tradition, the divine right of the king, ruled the world; that was a time when the world consisted of rich and poor and the middle class was tiny and powerless. History has changed all that; look around, do you see that many kings and queens, yet the power structure that maintained them still exists in acting; and director kings and queens rule with the same authority.

A major problem of old school is that power structure, the dictatorial power of the director. The psychological approach, used by old school directors, is an intellectual approach to understanding human behavior and since human behavior has an emotional base, it is unintelligible from that perspective; well it was for awhile, but not any more. It's like this; when Freud mass marketed the cult of the mind, and everybody agreed to play that game, human behavior was able to be interpreted from that perspective. Directors could take the rules of that game and apply them to creative ventures, and so, even though you can't, with any yardstick, intellectualize creativity, creative decisions came down to, whoever had the power was the most creative. Unfortunately for the actor stuck in that system, the audience, the real rulers, have quit that silly game and moved on to a more 1990's mind set; an Internet mind set, a talk show mind set, a news show mind set. Contemporary audiences are keying to their emotions and reality is where they are finding that emotional food.

The Psycho-Intellectual Age is dead; we are moving very quickly into the Age of Emotionalism and audiences aren't going to pay to see intellectual acting. When audiences won't pay to see something, producers won't produce it. This is where we are today. The evolution that felled the actor ruled acting is about to fell the director ruled acting. New school acting is a collaboration based on an expanded awareness of the emotional needs of the audience, executed by emotionally literate actors in cooperation with an emotionally aware consultant (formally known as the director). I detest the word director and all its dictatorial implications, a new name must be found that more suits the duties.

The director came to an historic zenith with Stanislavski and continued that march all the way to the current day "Autour"; a word meant to imply that everything about a particular work was the product of this one person's genius, omnipotent and infallible. By the time of Stanislavski, management was completely ingrained in the theatre. The link of power between management, and the product produced by actors, was the director.

Today many middle management levels are being wiped out in industry because of the intelligent use of technology. I think this quote from the president of Richard Stockton College of New Jersey, Dr. Vera Farris, is typical of forward thinking educators, "Technology gives students the opportunity to teach themselves and our faculty will become more and more mentors and coaches...It's essential that we teach them to learn on their own..."

This is exactly the role that directors must now take, that of mentor and coach, they will have to let go of their dictatorial power. The technology that, "Gives students the opportunity to teach themselves...", in acting, that gap has been filled by the low tech-high impact, Whelan Tape Technique, while not replacing acting's middle manager, the director, it modifies significantly the job he or she does. I will go into more detail on that technique below, and also how it moves the director from dictator to mentor/coach. A clue on how this, changing of the guard, will come about is that while nobody gives up power willingly, it was management that gave the power to the director and it is management that will take it away.

American business is discovering what the Japanese and many Europeans already know, that empowerment of workers increases productivity and the quality of product. Empowerment of actors increases creativity, i.e. quality of product. The truth is that management styles are changing for only one reason, American Companies are getting beaten by countries that have already adopted that management style. If it wasn't for dollars out of pocket, top management would have never have changed the structure, and middle management would still be draining profits from American corporations. Employers in all fields are becoming aware of the under utilization of assets. Actors are certainly underutilized assets and producers, out of need, are going to demand the most from their product. Actors are Maseraties being driven at twenty miles an hour and New School Acting lets them take the brakes off. When allowed more creative freedom, actors will generate the kind of excitement that will bring audiences back to theatres, movie houses and back from the talk show, reality show syndrome. If the old school directors would see and appreciate the resultant creativity that comes from playing the role of co-creator-consultant, they will be a valuable member of the team; if not, management will replace them.

New school directors know how to let the actor run. They find the role of team player very exciting and rewarding. Some old school directors would have loved to give the actor that much room, however, after 130 years of being beaten down, actors had forgotten how to run. Generally, directors are trained in this country, both on the professional and academic level, to be autocratic and actors to be subservient. Let me finish this section by saying, the Russian school has dominated American acting since the 1920's. It must have been good to have lasted that long, however Stanislavski has been dead for almost sixty years, that era is dead. It was a natural and healthy death. "Thank you, next!"

STAGE III

Spolin And The Break With Director Dependence

The emergence of the new school of American acting finds its seeds in the work of Viola Spolin (1906-1994), even though her "Theatre Games" found inspiration in the Commedia Del Arte of the Italian school; she truly went much further and ultimately gave birth to the hundreds of improvisational companies which now proliferate the American theatre scene. She did not create improvisation, nor did she create many of the games she used in her system. Never-the-less, she was the most important person in contemporary American theatre. She set in motion the will to freedom in the actor. She developed the means, and then sold actors on the idea that they could make a multitude of creative decisions all by themselves, without a director. She broke the chain of director dependence which had enslaved actors for over a hundred years. The genius of Spolin and her great contribution to acting has never been fully recognized; hopefully this work will help to bring her more of the credit she deserves.

Despite her work, which started to break the strangle hold of so called Russian realism, a truly American approach to acting never developed until recently.

The Problem With The Spolin Approach

Improvisation for improvisations sake was not capable of penetrating the overwhelming script oriented world of film, TV or commercial theatre. Even so, many of her"Games"have great usefulness as part of the rehearsal process and are invaluable in actors training. Mike Leigh, the British director, has improvised his movies, but it will be many years, if ever, until Hollywood, Broadway or network TV take a full scale improvisational approach to programming.

Building on the sense of play that Theatre Games inspire, and the demand the games make on actors to take responsibility for moment to moment creative decisions, opened the door to spontaneous, often emotional choices, that the actor made without the help of a director. The chain of director dependence was broken and the actor experienced a sense of freedom and power, which until Viola Spolin and the publication of her book, IMPROVISATION FOR THE THEATRE, (1963) was hardly a broad based movement. While Spolin and game training have had a heavy influence on many contemporary actors, the Method still rules and actors are still relegated to the position of second class artists.

This quick overview of American acting, from it's roots in England and Russia to the genius of Spolin brings us up to the recent present, and the work I believe to be the base of the next step in acting, the techniques and ideas that will take acting to the next level. I first presented these ideas in THE ABC'S OF ACTING (1990, Gray Heron). That book was seminal, in that it is where I introduce, in very rudimentary fashion, both the Whelan Tape Technique and the demand for actors to become emotionally literate. INSTANT ACTING (1994, BETTERWAY) presented the tape technique in a highly evolved and expanded form, and it also expanded on the ways and means of emotional literacy. This book presents an evolved and expanded ways and means of emotionally literacy.

This chart outlines various stages in history and how they effected the acting of their day.

Early 1700's Pre-Industrial Revolution		
Most people worked in the fields		
SOCIAL	ECONOMIC	POLITICAL
Rich and poor—A very small middle class	Wealth concentrated in the upper classes.	Monarchies Kings and Dukes etc.
In this atmosphere theatre was for the nobles and the poor had burlesque. Acting style was declamatory and the focus was on voice and literary value of text.		
Industrial revolution		
Most people worked in the factories		
Mid 18th Century - late 19th century		
A rapidly expanding middle class	Wealth spread among a larger group	Emergence of democratic ideas
In this atmosphere theatre and acting changed to accommodate a new class of audience. The evolution of Naturalism and the birth of the director caused the homogenization of acting styles. This period brought the seeds of Russian realism and the incorporation of Freudian Psychoanalysis into the actors technique through Stanislavski.		
Information Revolution		
Most people worked in Offices		
20th Century - Today		
A very large middle class	Wealth still concentrated in the upper classes but more people than ever with disposable income. i.e. money available for entertainment.	Growth of Democracy to many regions of the world. Monarchy virtually extinct.
Russian psycho-intellectual style of acting dominates American acting. Early 1960's Viola Spolin introduces Theatre Games and the first break with the hundred year old tradition of director dependence gives actors back a sense of creative freedom.		
Emotional Revolution		
More and more people working from their homes		
Today-Future		
Middle class continues to expand, with larger and larger numbers of minorities included than ever before.	World based economy	Democracy expanding to include most of the world.
The first stage of a truly informed, emotionally based acting, comes forward to serve the needs of an audience, responding to the emotional imperative created by the break down of psycho-intellectualism as a guiding force in a new world socio-political environment.		

Now that we have an overview of the American acting and an introduction to the development of the director and the impact that had on acting, we can take a closer look at the actor/director-teacher relationship.

The Changing Role Of The Director In New School Acting

The problem starts with the actor-director/teacher relationship. The structure as it exists is not conducive to maximum creativity; this is not the fault of anyone. It simply happens that these were the steps in the evolution of the art form. The key is not to miss the transition. We must recognize the time of change and act on it.

As it stands now, the most helpless people to change this negative situation are the actors themselves. Actors are at a very serious disadvantage. If an actor feels strongly that a particular moment should be played a certain way and tries it that way; if the director disagrees, that is the end of the actors idea. When the person responsible for your paycheck, or someone who can negatively impact your career (a director), says he thinks it looks better "this" way; most pros, if they want to keep working, say yes sir or yes ma'm. In the case of amateurs and students it's worse. A professional can sometimes figure a way around that stultifying influence, but the built in insecurity that goes with the position of amateur or student will tend to make them defer immediately.

It is not just that one moment of inspiration the actor loses. If this rejection happens too often, a pattern of generally distrusting their own creative impulses, drives actors to the point of being director dependent for the rest of their acting lives. This constant rejection is so discouraging to some actors that they never act again.

If we're just business people, that's the way it happens. If however, we are also artist, that relationship is destructive. We are not on equal creative footing and actors are often forced to throw away wonderful, frequently superior, creative choices at the whim of some director. It does not matter if that actor has trained thirty years in his craft, or the actor is a highly gifted and intuitively perfect beginner, she has no control over her performance.

In fairness there are a couple of reasons why the actors choice is rejected.

1) The actors choice may be genuinely bad.

2) The director didn't think of it, or, it didn't fit in with the directors rigid preconceived idea of what he wanted to happen, so he never even considers the possible value. This type of director will never trust actors.

The problem here is that these directors/dictators came out of old school, where the teachers were autocratic, or they came through the ranks and the people they learned from were autocratic. Some reading this will howl about this man or that woman director being wonderful with actors, or "not at my school, we're very progressive."

I'm not talking about the real or perceived exceptions to the rule. I'm talking about creative talents being stepped on in classrooms, theatres and sound stages around the world, today, by Old School directors and teachers carrying on the autocratic tradition of Old School standards. This Russian system has ruled the American approach to acting and consequently directing, from the early thirties through today. It is impossible to take teaching methods out of the social context in which they were created. The Stanislavski system was devised to teach the student base it served at the turn of the century in Czarist Russia, and that is nothing like the student base studying acting today; not politically, socially or economically. Regardless of how creative, the management and artistic teams were then and are now, they are overwhelmingly white bourgeoisie autocrats. There has never been nor will there ever be any confusion about who has the whip in Old School.

This taught obeisance to directors inhibits the actors creativity and in extreme cases, it will actually kill it. It doesn't matter that the actor is right, it only matters that he says "Yes boss" and do it the director's way. The fault doesn't belong to anybody, it was simply the evolution of an art form as it responded to the changes in the society of its day. The fact is, that style of directing; that style of acting, is out of synch with the needs of contemporary audiences. The director was trained to work with this intellectual/psychological type of actor, if he was trained to work with actors at all. Directors have been taught that they are looking down from some celestial creative paradise, and proclaiming from the divine right of kings, when an actor should sit, walk, cry, and how to do each. Teachers and directors create the insecurity that causes director dependence. As the directors power grew, the actor's creativity shrunk. I think this cartoon I found illustrates the idea of director dependence better than anything I've ever seen.

DON'T LET THIS HAPPEN TO YOU
Don't be director dependent
Learn how to direct yourself using the techniques found in this book
In the real world that is not appricated
It is demanded

WHEN WILL IT CHANGE? HOW WILL IT CHANGE? WHAT WILL IT CHANGE INTO?

It already has started, back in the fifties, Viola Spolin opened a window for the resurgence of actors exploring their creativity. Her book, IMPROVISATION FOR THE THEATRE, was published in 1963 and has been the bible of improvisation ever since. The Second City in Chicago is home base for that work since the beginning and still is, initially through Viola herself and increasingly through her son, Paul Sills, by now the influence has been felt on a world wide basis. Viola spent much of her time in Los Angeles and now there is a Spolin Center in LA. I have taught all over the country, and whenever I am about to leave a group of students, they always ask, "Who do we study with now?" I obviously have already told them to stay away from the Method, Meisner or anything that looks or smells like that, which is just about the only type of training out there; I recommend that they try to find somebody teaching Spolin based theatre games. I would love to say, go to Joan or Jim, she/he has been a great student of mine and I trained her/him to teach my techniques, but while some Universities, high schools and private teachers are teaching these new techniques of mine, I'm not sure who they all are, or how well they are doing it.

I do tell all my students that one of the most creative workshops I was ever involved with, was just actors working together and helping each other, we didn't have, or feel we needed a director or a teacher. We checked our egos at the door and concentrated on helping each other get better. I'll talk more on that below, but actors take the cue, get together, group up, even if there is only two of you. The tape technique is the perfect self teach tool and boosted by the emotions work, any group of serious actors could benefit each other by having their own workshop. Face it, you can't be an actor, working one day a week on your craft, but not too many actors can afford a good teacher, five or six days a week. So the ideal situation, is for actors to start grouping up and working with each other to hone their skills. This is, of course, right in line with weaning ourselves away from the director dependence, which we have been conditioned to for the last 130 years. It won't happen overnight; it is going to take serious work, so get started. Find a few actors, or those that want to be, and start meeting on a regular basis. Use the tape technique to explore all sorts of material, do the emotions workbook, and you're on your way to better acting. Remember, leave the egos and competition outside, and it will work.

When I first started doing Viola's Theatre Games, in the early sixties, at a theatre called The Committee in San Francisco, only a few people were authorized by Viola to teach them. Dick Schaal was the guy that spotted me and invited me into his workshop. Dick got a Broadway show shortly after and left, but fortunately for us, a man named John Brent came to the Committee from Second City, and John was one of those that Viola approved to teach the games. With Dick at first, and then John, we worked six plus hours a day for almost a year. I was doing a full load of theatre courses at San Francisco City College in the morning and then busting down to the Committee for the all afternoon games workshops. It was a very trippy situation, in the mornings, my primary teacher at City was James Heron, one of the principle actors at the soon to be famous, American Conservatory Theatre. Heron was a great teacher, but Old School to his socks. I remember an early speech of his to the cast of Playboy of the Western World, which was the first play I ever did. One of our young company tried to impose a suggestion on him, he looked at all of us and said, "If you have the idea that this is a democracy," Heron could flare and as he finished this sentence, he flared,"forget it, it's a dictatorship and that is me!" So here I was, in the heart of old school all morning and in the heart of the very beginnings of new school, all afternoon. Not that Brent was an angel of egalitarianism, like I said, it was the still the very birth of new school, perhaps even the pregnancy of it, but while Brent was a hard teacher, the very structure of the games made it a wildly more individually creative experience than the rigidity of Heron's old school. I am deeply grateful for having had these teachers. I was so excited by the theatre games approach that after a year of this study at the Committee, I took off for Chicago and got into a workshop at Second City. I spent about another year and a half there, doing the six hour a day theatre games workshops with another great teacher, Jo Forsberg; thank you Jo.

This was a very intense training schedule and the reason I bring it up is to illustrate the fact that you can not spend one day a week in an acting class and think you are doing the work. I know that many aspiring actors have to have real jobs and that cuts into the time you would like to spend studying. I also know that teachers can be expensive. The problem is that some people approaching acting, and even some that actually get paid to act sometimes, are so arrogant or stupid that they think they don't have to work hard at it. In fact, acting could have been called, the lazy art. One day at the actors studio, nobody had prepared work to show Lee Strasberg, he exploded, "What is wrong with you people, Heifetz practices twelve hours a day, Pearlman practices twelve hours a day, and you people sit around, drinking coffee and think you're actors? You think your artists?"

While this does not exclude actors in the cities; the problem of dedication seems to get compounded with every mile you get outside of New York City, Los Angeles or any major market. If your out in the sticks or in the burbs of some smaller town and you're really serious about acting, you're going to wind up in a major market at some point, if you haven't worked hard, if you've just been doing one class a week, you're in for a shock. Real actors work at it every day. I'll make a list of some of the things that actors serious about a career do, I know I'll forget some stuff but, here goes.

The everyday life of a real actor consists of doing combinations of these and more:

1) A class	12) A workshop
2) Doing a production; a play, a movie, cable TV	13) Sending out pictures.
3) Making phone calls	14) Going to open calls
4) Dropping by offices	15) Auditioning
5) Reading trade papers	16) Reading acting technique books
6) Searching for material	17) Doing staged readings
7) Doing a showcase	18) Developing a scene with a fellow actor
8) Working on a monologue	19) Working on how they look, the gym, working on your tan, shopping, etc.
9) Going to plays	20) Generating income to pay rent, get a car.
10) Getting out and networking	21) Generating income to get a proper wardrobe
11) Studying the films of great actors	22) Hanging out with other actors

This is only part of the actors life. So, you do what? You take one class a week. Some advice, when you hit the big city, wear a helmet.

I know that many young actors would love to be in a top theatre school, spending all day everyday working on being a better actor, but that is expensive and some of the best are locked out of that opportunity. Well, the good news is, that most of those schools, almost all of them, are locked into old school; stuff you should avoid anyhow. So, get a few other people that want to work on their craft, take the new school tools in this book and get to work with them. These tools were created to break director dependence, so don't be afraid to work them on your own. Once you have a group together, if you are working three or four days a week, you might look around for good teachers in the area, and occasionally chip in to bring one of them in for a night now and then, just to get some imput. In the end, that is how we, along with the progressive institutions that are using these ideas, will change the face of acting into something that contemporary audiences will want to see again.

That is the when and the how, of the change from old school to new school, as to what it will change into; the "what" is a creative cooperation between dedicated and professionally oriented artists, bringing the highest level of true ensemble acting to the broadest based most diverse and most emotionally sophisticated audience in the history of acting.

A word about the new actor and her modern audience is presented in the following chapter, as well as some of the problems we face in this challenge.

CHAPTER VI
THE NEW ELITE-THE NEW ACTING

With acting, we are talking about a very important aspect of world communication; one which is in a very sorry state at the moment. The decay of a major art form does have serious negative societal repercussions. We really can't let this deterioration go unchecked. It will take imagination and courage to stop this slide and raise acting to the next level of its evolution.

The elitism which birthed the method is dead. The Method was born into that old white intellectual European environment and has all the values of it built in, so, it is not unusual that it is old world elitist by nature. Old school acting is the ruling elite and they do it with an iron fist, in the finest Czarist tradition. While being an advance over that which came before, this old school style has now become a burden to the evolution of the art form. It's a different world and acting has to reflect that; acting has to be reborn. In order to do that we are going to have to realize a few things. New School Acting must reflect more honestly the world as it is today. I have no desire to regulate what anyone says, I believe in communication. What I'm saying is that, anyone wanting to communicate, whatever your message, you're going to have to change the way you do it, simply because you have a different audience and a different cast.

The American acting machine is controlled by white males, and they bring all that old world psycho-intellectual baggage to the party. Being white, I can't help but feel a certain sadness at losing privilege, but it's not a white European intellectual world anymore and it is not going to go back to that, no matter how many guns anybody pulls on anybody. People with other skills and other ways of learning are exerting a definite influence on contemporary society and the art of acting must acknowledge them.

The New Elite

The trend to elitism is probably built into the human fabric and as long as someone is willing to work harder, longer than others to join that elite, he deserves to be there. But world values are changing and what was elite yesterday is not elite today. Who are these new elite? They are multi-national, multi-cultural, and more and more, multi-lingual. They have a much more cosmopolitan orientation. They are artists and business people who are responding to the growing international dimension in the marketplace and in the arts. They are relaxing in international recreational arenas. They are those people with the intelligence to recognize a shrinking world and the ability to learn to appreciate, or at least tolerate, what they cannot stop. Some things will be lost but others will be gained. I don't like seeing Mc Donald's on the Champs Elysee, but it's there so, perhaps, I'll have an inexpensive milkshake.

The new elite are socially flexible and diverse in their tastes. They are more sensitive to the emotional needs of others because success and survival depends on it. In many ways they are being trained to this new awareness in the schools. The international and non-traditional student base has exploded. More cultures, races and languages, are rubbing noses on campuses, board rooms and street corners around the world than in all of prior recorded history, as a natural result of the largest scale immigration in history. It's happening all the way down to the preschool groups. In those cases, the new behavior doesn't have to be learned because it is a daily reality to many children. Anyone who has spent time around children has to have noticed two things about them: first and foremost, they are survivors. Children of war are examples; school is a war for many. I think back and in my high school; in my freshman class, we had three African-American students, two Chinese and one or two Latinos; in a freshman class of four hundred. This school was a few miles from downtown Philadelphia not Mobile, Alabama. With busing, integration, affirmative action and growing economic advances gained by minorities, the mixture is much higher. Kids, in this situation, look around their school and they see that there are a lot of _those people_;   and they think "I'd better make friends." Two primary motivations for children are fear and money. Out of this fear and greed, lines of communication are opened. It's like virginity, once those lines are open, that's it for life; you can't go back.

The second thing about kids is, they're curious. What do those people eat? What do those people do when they are not around me? What's that music they're listening to?

Adults had better look around and see what's going on, kids are mixing it up out there in the world. The prejudices of the father are not as easily passed on. Isn't your company doing business with foreign companies? Aren't you buying foreign products? As the world contracts through communication and transportation advances, we must look for a common ground. A place where, for business or personal reasons, we can establish a link. Cultures are wildly divided on points of view, but the one thing common to us all, when we are not acting, is that we cry when we are sad and we smile when we are happy. The emotions are the common ground for all peoples and that is why emotions are at the root of New School Acting.

It's time for those who are more in touch with the rhythms of life to take over. Some of the more astute will take the necessary steps. Most other art forms have already made this adjustment to the new world reality. A big reason acting has lagged in making this adjustment is quite simple; it is the only collaborative art form with words at the absolute core. In the ruling old school intellectual tradition, the semantic window of disinformation is wide open, and that is how they stall the day. We know the old school diehards of acting, in and out of academia, are not going to go without a fight, but they are old and toothless at this point, so they should fall without hurting anybody too badly. They are standing by the grave just waiting for a decent wind to come along and blow them in and guess what, New School Acting is that wind.

Much of what I've been discussing are general observations, but exactly how does all this directly relate to Actors/Directors and their training?

The New Elite In Acting

In acting, there is an elitism of ability, and an elitism of untalented, but well connected actors. That's who works at high financial and creative levels. For every one of them, 10,000 other actors just don't have the proper connections to get into the latter group, and their antiquated training stifles their talent which prevents access to the former. You might argue that it is the same in all arts, and you would probably be right, but I believe there is another factor at work here. In times of social crisis, a general heightening of creativity among all peoples is absolutely necessary for the sake of survival. I think as a world we are becoming more creative. Sophistication, as we've known it, is much broader now, and the language of creativity among audiences is much more persuasive and pervasive. It is in that context, that I say acting has not kept up with the times. Actors speak the old language of great grandfather Stanislavski; a language that was used to address a white upper middle to upper class old world audience. A language designed to address the joy, sorrow, and anger of that world in intellectual terms.

The student base at the Moscow Art Theatre, at the time of that languages development, was trained to respond and interpret it. I hate to be the bearer of shocking news, but if anyone hasn't noticed, that world is as dead as that of ancient Rome, and like Latin, so is its language. True, some people still teach and speak Latin, but I think trying to make a living as an actor, doing Latin theatre would be tough. Actors might as well be speaking Latin, as speaking Stanislavski, to audiences made up of multi-cultural, class crossed, computer oriented cyber-kinder. Looking at the student base of modern universities, high schools and elementary schools, should give you a clue. The Method is a Eurocentric elitist model trying to impose itself on a society of actors that resembles that turn of the century one, only in the nostalgic haze of WASP educators and artists who have, and are determined to keep power, until they are finally overrun by history. I don't blame them. I would too, except that my job as an actor is to communicate, not to dominate. My choices would seem to be:

1) To communicate with a tiny group of Eurocentric elitist, who will allow me to amuse them, if I speak their language.

2) To, as an artist, speak in modern language and place myself upon the world stage.

I think an actor looking at his career would do well to spend some time on the World Wide Web. A quick jaunt through cyberspace might wake her up. We live in a world where information and communication are available to almost every single person on the planet, if not through home PC's, then through the ones at school. What are these audiences saying? What is the language of cyberspace? To what does this brilliant new anarchy of communication filter down? Once solely the domain of Academics and the Military, this global intercourse is now truly egalitarian, and if you look hard you will see that what these thirty plus millions are talking about, is how they feel about everything and anything. It is not the language of psycho-intellectualism. It is people talking about how they feel. It is the language of talk shows, reality shows. It is not theory, it is the language of feelings; they are not canned or acted, but real feelings. These feelings are not filtered through the newer outer layer of the brain, they come straight from the gut. The Method based training that an actor receives, is that feelings start in the brain. It is a regional joke, but someone in New Hampshire once actually said, in response to my asking for directions, "You can't get there from here." When you translate that fine piece of Yankee jargon, you get the idea that what you're being told is that, you are a long and complicated way from where you are going and the opportunities to get lost are multiple. It is the same thing that happens when you try to get to the emotions from the brain.

So the big question is; we have the tools to catch up to our audience, so why aren't we using them? Why aren't they being taught to us?

What Is Keeping The Educational System From Adjusting To The New World Reality

While many teachers recognize the need for change, most of those lack the power to act, and those with the power are lacking the will to act. American educational institutions are downsizing like all corporations of our day. Teachers live in fear of losing their jobs and nobody wants to appear a trouble maker; some fool who wants to improve the efficiency of education. School districts will get grants to send teachers to workshops on the new teaching techniques. Schools will snap a grant like an alcoholic snatching a drink, but when it comes to implementing whatever might have been learned, that's a different story. The administration says, "Tomorrow we shall use these better ideas." It reminds me of a phrase of Camus',"The future is the only thing the master willingly bequeaths the slave."

Here we must go off the track for a moment to look at a broader but very important issue; the way we learn.

Every age brings new challenges and "new" is a frightening word to many people. The longer something has been the norm, the more frightening the idea of change. There is a major new trend in education. This powerful movement is generally referred to as Learning Styles. While my research into this trend is just beginning, I've investigated it enough to be in complete agreement as to the advantages.

I was happy to see that The Whelan Tape Technique, and the accent on emotions that I teach, have been, for the most part, paralleling this movement for over 12 years. It is very easy, when you're blazing new trails, to start to question the authenticity of what you're doing. Finding many decades of research, done by very intelligent people, which validated everything I was doing, was a great comfort and a source of renewed energy.

After decades of research and many attempts at getting recognition, a new approach to the teacher-student relationship and to education in general, is slowly gaining acceptance. The trend, broadly called Learning Styles Studies, recognizes that not every student learns in the traditional, lecture/test way.

While some research includes other categories, three major types of learners have been proven to exist. Students favor one of these three learning forms; the visual learner; the audial learner; and the tactile/kinesthetic learner. Each of these has intelligence of value but the audial learners have been favored by the educational system forever. New class room procedures and design are, where ever they are utilized, bringing equal opportunity to those visual and tactile/kinesthetic learners. It seems very odd to me, that anyone could still think that standing up in front of a bunch of kids and talking for hours and then giving a test, is the way to teach. These kids have been bombarded with thousands of pieces of visual information a second, coming off a TV screen, since they were born. The audial approach is radio format, while still useful, it should hardly be as dominant as it is, and never again as exclusive as it was for at least the last century.

Many of us already possess a major key to understanding the value of this new approach. Talk about left brain/right brain has been in the popular press long enough, that most people have heard of that idea. I'll go more into this in a moment.

The 30 years of brain research and the way it blends with Learning Styles has been a benefit to hundreds of thousands of students and is a well known fact among forward looking educators and researchers alike. Many millions could have gotten better grades, if their teachers cared enough to find out about, and use superior teaching techniques. The fact that the educational system has retarded the advance of these exciting discoveries is not surprising. In the February 19th, 1996, NEWSWEEK , the cover story was, "Your Child's Brain." In one article on the topic Sharon Begley says, "... at school, there's what's obvious and there's tradition." "Why is this body of research rarely used in American classrooms?" She then cites Linda Darling Hammond, professor of education at Columbia University's Teachers College, who feels not many administrators or school board members know it exists. In most states, neither teachers nor administrators are required to know much about how children learn to be certified. "Our school system was invented in the 1800's, and little has changed." In an accompanying article, "Why Do Schools Flunk Biology", LynNell Hancock states "Biology is a staple at most American high schools. Yet when it comes to biology of the students themselves-how their brains develop and retrain knowledge-school officials would rather not pay attention to the lessons... Biologists have some important evidence to offer. But not only are they ignored, their finding are often turned upside down. Force of habit rules the hallways and classrooms. Neither brain science nor education research has been able to free the majority of American schools from their 19th-century roots." He quotes Frank Vellutino, a professor of educational psychology at State University of New York as saying, "We do more education research than anyone else in the world and we ignore more as well."

Many educators are upset that this ignorance is being perpetuated, but until major adjustments are made in the hierarchy of the American school system, it will continue. Why?

Outdated approaches to education in general, and in relation to acting, survive for four reasons; none of which compliment those who perpetuate them. These people must ask themselves one or a combination of these questions.

1) Egoism: If whoever thought of this isn't dead or me, how could it be that good an idea?

2) Fear: Can I grasp these new ideas?

3) Laziness: I get by OK on what I know and I just don't want to bother learning something new. Why should I have to?

4) Stupidity: Learn something new? Don't they understand, I don't even know what I'm suppose to in order to have this job?

This foot dragging will change because:

Education Is Big Business

Education is changing in the same way that all businesses are changing as they jockey for position in the international marketplace. If you somehow missed the fact that education is big business, you have never looked at the numbers. According to Dr. Vance Grant, a specialist in educational statistics with the Dept. of Education in Washington DC., Colleges and Universities took in $45.346 Billion in Tuition and Fees in fiscal year 1992-93; another $16.663 Billion in auxiliary services i.e. bookstores, residence halls etc. This is over sixty-two Billion Dollars for colleges and Universities alone. On the high school and elementary side you can throw in another $17 plus Billion. It does as they say, start to add up to real money. The numbers for the year 1993-94 from some large US companies will serve as a comparison.

ATT - $64.71 Billion

IBM - $64 Billion

This should give you an idea of how big the business of education really is and the problems that poses for change. The University system in the United States is as big a business as IBM, however, it has the disadvantage of not being one big company; a company which can establish a single policy for all its units to follow. There are over thirty five hundred Universities and Colleges in the US and most are privately run. While this makes any sort of uniform adaptation of advanced teaching techniques a nightmare, there is hope that these techniques will find their way into all of these schools, without too great a time lag, because education is a very competitive business and the hustle to attract students is endless. Advertising budgets for schools are way up, universities are advertising with the zeal of used car dealers.

Like any other business, Education hates to re-tool. Re-tooling is an expensive and time consuming process. The American car industry almost went under because it failed to recognize the trend toward smaller cars. It did not want to have to spend all that money setting up new factories and re-tooling older factories as well as retraining its work force to build smaller cars. By the time they realized that they were going to have to do that to stay in business, they had already lost massive amounts of market share to the Japanese and the Germans.

Educational institutions hate to change for the same reason. They don't want to have to re-tool their faculty, and for the most part, that faculty has no desire to be re-tooled. They have settled in long ago to their teaching style and life style. They do not want it interrupted by anything as mundane as keeping up with contemporary educational discoveries. They resist with all of their strength and the university faced with this inertia is caught in a classic Labor-Management dispute. Students are looking for the most progressive learning institutions and they and their money flow in that direction. Increasingly international and non-traditional in make up, this student base is what is forcing the change in the American educational system.

In finding out how to treat all these new customers/consumers of American education, as well as dealing with the changing attitudes of the traditional student base, educational institutions are realizing that some accommodation is going to be necessary, if they want to court this jackpot of business opportunity. Alternate learning modalities and with them, new techniques were developed to take advantage of each modalities unique teaching requirement. Adapting curricula to utilize these new techniques takes more time. This is only happening on certain campuses and only to the degree thought necessary to keep the bucks rolling in. The auto industry tried to do it that piece meal way and lost. I hope that the education industry in America is a little quicker on the pick-up or the University of Korea could be the next Harvard.

More on learning how you learn

Why as an actor/acting teacher, would I want you to know about how you learn? Why is that important to you? Well there is an old saying that states, "It's a wise man that knows himself." As an acting teacher, I would say, it's a wise actor that knows him/her self. Many discoveries have been made about the way people learn;

for centuries nobody even thought about the fact that we might not all learn the same way. Teachers just taught one way and it was up to the students to learn as best they could. Today we have proof that the old style of teaching favored one particular group of learners and made life more difficult for all the other students.

Decades of brain research has proven that we have two spheres of influence, these were once called the, left brain and right brain, though they are now referred to as the left and right hemispheres. Very basically, left hemisphere rules business type functions and controls the right side of the face, ears etc. Right hemisphere rules creative type functions and the left side of the face, ears, etc. It was funny to watch actors, who learned about this, as they jockeyed to get the left side of their faces into camera or downstage.

Most people have heard about the idea of our having a left brain and a right brain, and that they have different responsibilities relating to how we approach life on a day to day basis. Education has forever taught to the left or practical side of our brains. The fact is that some people have a stronger right brain and some have a stronger left brain; so that old teaching style basically left right brain creative types out in the cold. So what's this got to do with acting? Well actors have to learn parts, they have to learn the craft, they have to learn the art. If you know how you learn best, you'll learn these things quicker and better.

Actually, I have many reasons for wanting you to understand your learning process. One is, so that you recognize the limitations of instruction you may have already received, or instruction you might be considering, and the value of the one I am offering you. I have to precede this with the fact that it is important for actors to be familiar with all styles of acting, since you may work with a director who came out of one of those schools. A director will feel more comfortable hiring you if she knows that you have had some training in the approach she uses when directing actors. It doesn't mean you have to be a devotee of that school, it just means that you have to be familiar with the vocabulary that type of director uses, so that he doesn't feel he is going to have to learn a new language to get what he wants from you. As an actor you can translate that old school stuff to new school, but you can't do that unless you know both languages. There is an ease of communication that people who speak the same language find when working together, and remember, you're the one looking for a job.

Learning Styles is a broad generic term for the many new approaches to teaching and learning. Thirty years of research, by some of the finest minds in education, have gone into this subject and the results are causing a very real revolution in schools everywhere. Ask any teachers you have now about Learning Styles and they will tell you about learning styles. If they don't recognize the name, or they say it's unimportant, you're are looking at somebody who should only be in a classroom as a student, not teaching you.

I'm not going to go deeply into this, but the most basic idea is that there are three ways in which people learn, they are the visual learner, the audial learner and the tactile/kinesthetic learner. In other words, some of us learn best by seeing something, others of us learn best by listening to something, and the rest learn best by touching or moving around something; these are called learning modalities. One of those modalities is your favorite way to learn and if you are taught by a teacher, who uses that approach, you will get much higher grades/learn more than you did before.

Good teachers, realizing that a class is composed of people from each of these groups, try to use each modality at some point in every lesson they present. One thing for sure, before this work, when we were all taught the same way, some of us got the feeling that maybe we weren't as bright as those other kids. This was only because traditional educational practices were teaching right into one particular group of kid's strength, letting everybody else sink or swim. Learning Styles, research and experiments, boots that old idea of who's bright, right out the window. When teachers approach kids from their favorite learning modality, scores on test jump up; often 50 % or higher. If you think about the classes you most enjoyed and the times you had the most fun learning something, you can probably figure out which one of these modalities works best for you. Knowing something, is different from just letting things happen. I mean, if you know your best way to learn something, and somebody is giving you information in some other modality, you can translate it and make it easier to understand. In the process of doing that translation you are also increasing your understanding of that other learning modality and strengthening your ability to learn that way too.

Some of the learning styles advocate that there are six modalities; some say there are eight, whatever makes the most sense to you is what you use. Here are the names of some leaders in this movement; you can check them out for yourselves. Rita Dunn is a big name here. She started doing this work in the 1960's and with Kenneth Dunn, they created, The Learning Styles Inventory. She is at Learning Styles Network, St. Johns U. in Jamaica, NY.

Bernice McCarthy created the 4-MAT System. She puts out four types of learners. She has a company called Excel in Barrington, IL. Meyers-Briggs created the Meyers-Briggs Type Indicator. They break it into introverts and extroverts and then into Sensing, Intuitive, Thinking, Feeling, Judging and Perceptive types. You can get more on that from The Center for Applications of Psychological Type in Gainesville, Fl. Then we have the Gregorc Mindstyles, which also has four learning types: concrete sequential, abstract sequential, abstract random, concrete random. For more on that: The Learners Dimension in Columbia, CT.

You might also check out Gardner's Theory of Multiple Intelligence's. Another area of study that ties into Learning Styles and one which is also affecting education in a big way is called Neuro-Linguistics.

There are many other theories of Learning Styles, but the one thing that's obvious, is that humans definitely learn in different ways. You have to understand that these are not so recent discoveries and that they are still being rejected by old school types. The other thing you should understand is that Methods of instruction that are older, and this includes approaches to acting, did not have the advantage of this research and the knowledge it produced. In other words, those styles were prejudiced to the intellectual (left) side of your brain and as actors our most important tool, the emotions, are located in the other side of the brain (right). Now, one of the advantages of knowing we have a split brain, is that we can now work to create whole brain functioning, in the same way that knowing we have preferred learning modalities, is that we can work toward a balance, where all learning modalities function harmoniously and effectively. BUT, we must realize that the centuries of bias toward the left brain, have made it imperative that we concentrate on strengthening the right brain so that this balance can be achieved. In other words, we have to indulge our creativity and revel in our emotions until they feel natural again. It is wildly paradoxical that we have to start this party in our brains.

WHO GETS THE JOB OF DIRECTING THE SCHOOL PLAY—AN ESSAY

It is unfortunate that top level professional training is not available to every child with an interest in drama. It is also unfortunate that the first place they confront this trembling desire is at a level where they are least likely to get expert guidance; the school play. Tens-of-thousands of grammar and high school teachers who get the job of directing the school play, seldom if ever have the professional training necessary to meet the needs of the children who bring this dream with them; sometimes this job just gets dumped on a teacher.

I could be wrong, but I would guess most of you have degrees in English and may have done a few plays as an undergraduate. I think you would agree that your expertise is not in dealing with a budding and passionate creativity looking to express itself through acting. Now how much could you mess up doing Sondheim or Rogers and Hart? Not too much, but I think this is the reason high school drama usually never gets past the musical and that is truly tragic.

Kids today live in the most dramatic time in history and you only give them singing and dancing. I love it I really do. I was involved with a theatre camp for kids this summer and they did a production of "Joseph" that knocked my socks off, but there is so much more room for young actors to express themselves and aspiring actors know it and hunger for it. Those that don't, should be taught to appreciate it. I think doing plays with a contemporary focus, on the things that kids today are forced to deal with, would blow a very energizing wind through some very stale school acting programs. They don't need a birds and bee's story to find out about sex, they have Aids to think about. They don't need Conrad to tell them about mans inhumanity to man, they are blowing each other away on street corners or getting caught in the cross fire; it is no longer simply an urban problem. Whatever it is, they have seen it on TV, read it in a magazine, tried it or had it done to them. They live in the real world more so than any generation before them; young actors want to be challenged with making that tragic or funny.

As far as directing that kind of material, I think it is good that people recognize their limitations and don't take kids into tricky areas without having the right tools to do it. It is a fact that, when dealing in heavy drama, with young actors, serious harm could be done to them, if the director does not have a firm grasp on the acting process. I am in no way trying to infer that you lack the desire to help these kids; I am saying that you have not had the proper training to give them all the help they need. Many of the high school teachers that I've talked to were very quick to admit that; these kids would get mangled by the general inadequacy. Guiding young actors through deeply emotional gut wrenching drama takes a very experienced hand. Even if your school brought in a professional to direct, such a failure would result. It would stem from a legacy of training that is based on the false concept of the actors necessary dependence on a director's vision to reach a correct interpretation of character, or to correctly understand their character's relationship to the other characters and the piece as a whole. With actors trained in Old School techniques this is true in the vast majority of cases, any exceptions would come from actors whose natural gifts survived the outdated and abusive practices of that school. Director Dependence was implicit in that training; from the framework of its psychoanalytical base, the Actor - Director relationship in Old School most often resembles group therapy with the actors as patients and the Director as good old Sigmond himself. *It could never under any circumstance be considered an equal creative exchange between artists. There is never any doubt in Old School about who has the whip; ask any actor who tried to get too creative to show you their back.*

Acting has changed from when many of you went to school. I know because I am one of the people changing it. I want to offer you a technique that will let you provide professional level direction, one that will allow the student actor to experience the full range of their creativity while giving you the fun and satisfaction that your hard work deserves. This technique is useful to you whether your school does one big production a year, has a drama club, or a full theatre program. It is easy to use for students and director alike. I offer you two tools that will make your life much easier, more productive and greatly enhance the creative satisfaction that is potential in any such endeavor.

I guess the two tools are like toys at Christmas. One is completely set up and ready to go; the other is what's laughingly called "some assembly necessary." The first is The Whelan Tape Technique (page 28) and it is infallibly simple. You will see very quickly that you can trust it to deliver on its promises. The second tool is much more subtle and requires work prior to production. All the tools you need to do it are in this book, and it is actors work anyhow, although some supervision is necessary. The actors have to do the work, but someone should check to see that they actually do it. So what is it? It is the emotion work which is the core of this book; it is so important that I want to take a moment and go into it here.

I started teaching emotions to actors over twelve years ago. My first book, <u>THE ABC'S OF ACTING</u>, published in 1990 offers some exercises to broaden the actors emotional vocabulary. In it I coined the phrase,

"Emotions are to actors what colors are to painters." I talked about the importance of actors studying emotions with the same diligence as painters studying color; that section of that book was written years before THE ABC'S was published, as was much of it. In my second book, INSTANT ACTING, begun in 1990 and published in 1994, I expanded that area of study and added some new exercises and insights on the subject of Emotion Studies. NEW SCHOOL ACTING, which has as its central focus Emotions, was begun within a week after INSTANT ACTING reached book stores. In reality I had begun making notes on it as soon as my editor cut me off from making anymore additions to INSTANT ACTING. NEW SCHOOL ACTING is a result of my growing awareness of how critical it was to make actors Masters of Emotion. I starting playing with the idea of the emotions charts featured in this book and creating additional exercises and techniques to accomplish that task. I hope you spend some quality time with your actors in this important area.

Now here is the real key, when the emotion studies are combined with the Whelan Tape Technique, even a high school English teacher, who gets the school play dropped on them, can attack the most difficult of dramatic pieces. You will get the overwhelming reward of watching the kids your working with explode with creativity. The Whelan Tape Technique takes away the heavy mechanical/technical demands as well as inappropriately early "creative" demands of directing. It lets you, the teacher-director, function on a level you are quite capable of, sensitizing the kids to a specific form of learning. The emotions work takes away the danger that the young actor will be forced into using their own emotions, and suffering the consequences that plague much older and much more sophisticated actors, grounded in Old School, when they follow that path.

The emotion work can be taught to actors at a very early age. Even in this early stage of development, that work has proved exceptionally effective and is well worth the effort. I have used the Tape Technique with actors from 5 to 80, and it works for all of them. It is especially successful with kids because they have not been exposed to "bad" teachers or good teachers working off of old and, in so many cases, totally outdated or misconceived ideas. I have had kids that couldn't read yet memorize and perform, with conviction, emotionally complicated and demanding material. The way to do this is simply to have a kid that is as close to the actors age read his/her part into the tape. The two kids bond quickly and a very creative symbiotic relationship forms, which results in some remarkable performances. You will find that they will amaze you with the level of creativity they bring, and as a player in the game, you will have a lot more fun than you would being a traffic cop or dictator director.

Emotion Study: How does it work? Why does it work?—an essay

I put this last because I knew that some people would ask this question and although I know this technique works, I really don't understand why. I can theorize, but since most people are concerned with the fact that something works, and really don't care how or why it works, I didn't want to burden them with these hypothesis. The fact is, that somewhere in clinical psychology, there is probably already a name for this phenomenon. Some psych student might read this and go,"that's Finklestein's Law of Subjective-Objective Transference", or some such axiom of contemporary psychiatry, but then of course, that is only conjecture as well; if you're curious, read on.

When it gets down to the very detailed work of filling out the charts, the question I've been asked is why does it work? If you want theory, if you like to spin gossamer webs of thought, you can follow on with me. I'm not a clinical psychologist; I'm an artist and a teacher, and I must admit I grasped this concept intuitively. I then experimented with it extensively, expanding the concept over a twelve year period, working with over a thousand actors and it worked every time. It felt "right" on an intuitive level, and it worked on a practical level; basically that was good enough for me. I can only speculate on how that transference from subjective/private self reference, to objective/universal reference occurs. Somebody I'm sure, has already figured this out and might giggle as I struggle with it, but just in case nobody has, these musings might ignite an insight.

When actors sit down to fill out the emotion charts, they go inside themselves to find a sound, a smell, a taste, a feel, a color, a weight and an object to symbolize an emotion; it is a personal subjective exercise. They use their own life inventory and their imagination to pick these sensory devices. So how, when this is a subjective exercise, does it objectify the emotion? Why does pulling the emotion apart make it objective and universal; or does something else happen?

This exercise is designed to be used with a class or in individual actors work. Since ideas on how it works in a group dynamic are coming easier, I'll start there. The actors, as a group, are exposed to each others individual efforts, and while certain elements might match in this group environment, such as five out of fourteen class members might think anger is red, it would be highly unlikely that they would ever match across the board; smells sounds taste etc. So, as actors compare charts; they are subjected to such divergent stimuli; all the smells etc. that their classmates assign the same emotion, that the individual's concept of the emotion are stretched beyond her own personal frame of reference. This allows each student to take a less personal view of that emotion, thereby opening a door for a universal concept to form.

That same effect could be caused by the individuals work with different emotions; as her emotions workbook starts to fill up, the barrage of sensory stimuli it contains alters the students perspective about particular emotions and emotions in general. As students flip through their workbooks, seeing hundreds of colors, hearing hundreds of sounds, experiencing hundreds of tastes, smelling hundreds of odors etc., the tiny personal conception of emotion, one rooted primarily in the past, takes on a larger more, "in the present"/immediate reality.

Quite possibly, it is as simple as the influence of the imagination that breaks the personal bond and lifts an emotion from private to universal.

One thought I had was that, perhaps by becoming so familiar with the emotion on an intellectual imaginative level, it expands it to a point of reference so general that it can no longer be anchored to a specific point of reference, i.e. the actors own personal history with that emotion. In other words, when we meet that emotion as character, a sensory explosion occurs and engulfs us in the moment; distracted from our baggage with that emotion, the more fragile network of the character's memories, which we have built, can exert the creative influence necessary to allow its expression from this fresher perspective.

Another idea is, that in the actor's own life, the event which became the symbolic moment that framed, what we knew of that emotion in the abstract, crystallized that emotion into a concrete reality. The event which provoked the emotion and the emotion itself became inseparable. The physical reality, and the circumstance around that moment, combined with the emotion it provoked, become so deeply bound together that they fuse, creating a new and un-named emotion. Once categorized in this manner, the general qualities of the emotion are released back into a pure state. It becomes hyper-individual, unique in the circumstance that created it, too specific to apply to any other situation except the one singular moment it defines.

Perhaps by applying so much imagination to a particular emotion, seeing how specific it is to me, and how differently specific it is to somebody else, isolates it from; detaches it from the moment that framed it. Maybe the process of breaking it up into so many imaginative components, displays it to be a piece of a bigger more universal experience. Conceivably, when you look at all the emotions in a stack of 200 work sheets, surrounded by thousands of smells, feels, sounds, colors, tastes, objects etc., it creates such a gestalt that it depersonalizes emotions and brings their universal qualities into a very sharp relief.

I really don't know if these speculations constitute an answer to the question, but I do know that studying emotions this way is both a quick fix and a long term growth vehicle. You can start beefing up moments in your playing today. Then, through daily emotion exercises, you start tying more and more of those moments together with a progressive regularity. Start today on the work book and you will immediately begin to feel a greater involvement each time you work on a part. Your fellow performers, directors, and audiences will comment on your improvement.

The goal is to take the emotion out of the ether, where it is defined by subliminal memories of specific events. An emotion might be said to be the combined sum of our experience with that emotion. "I thought I was in love, but it was only lust. I thought I was sad, but now I know what it is to be really sad."As we mature, our growth in personal emotional awareness keeps expanding, and so, when we go to fill out the charts, we take a smell from that one, a taste from this other one, and a feel from another. By automatically deriving stimuli across a broad field of experience, a specific emotion moves beyond the hyper personalized connection to the cathartic moment which so rooted it to a particular event—framed it; and releases it into a more general/universal form that can be investigated as phenomenon opposed to event.

That is enough speculation, if you know how and why it works, write or call me. I don't know how the phone works either, but I would be lost without one, and yes, I am saying an actor is lost without a real hard objective study of the emotions and a telephone.

CHAPTER VII

CAPSULE REVIEW:

The Great Acting Teachers And Their Methods by Richard Brestoff

As I was getting ready to go to press, a new book came out and I want to say something about it. The book is <u>The Great Acting Teachers and Their Methods,</u> it is an important book for actors to read; all actors but for new actors especially. To many actors approaching the field, the importance of the history of acting often gets lost in the excitement of just wanting to do it. But as all actors learn, getting a job as an actor is hard work. <u>The Great Acting Teachers</u> is a book that could very well make the difference between whether or not you get a job.

The chapter on Stanislavski is justifiably long, the rest are short and concise. Brestoff introduces you to the major approaches to acting used by actors and directors today. He covers acting from the Greeks on, but focuses on the last 100 years. These approaches or schools of acting are like countries. They each have their own customs and languages. Most directors come from one of these schools and as an actor, you should at least be conversant with the language of your director. These directors are most comfortable with actors from that school, actors who speak the directors language. You don't have to come from that school, if you have knowledge of the vocabulary of that school.

Brestoff will give you insights into Stanislavski, Strasberg, Meisner, Adler, Spolin, Brecht, Growtowski and others. You will understand how these teachers worked and the terminology that they used to communicate their ideas to their students, and that directors from that school will use in directing you. As a director, if an actor gives me what I want, I really don't care where it came from. What does matter is that I can tell the actor, in words I'm used to using, what I want, and that the actor understand me. How the actor translates that, into something he can use, is not my problem. But, if I use a term and then have to explain it to him, I might as well get an actor that speaks my language.

Aside from the practical benefits, helping you get work, <u>The Great Acting Teachers</u> has other benefits. I would hope that from reading of the hard work and dedication of these important teachers in acting history, you would find greater pride in being an actor, and more respect for the art of acting.

While my approach to acting is breaking with all these traditions, and despite how heavily I condemn some old school practices; I have great respect for all those who came before and dedicated a lifetime to this art.

I was shocked and thrilled when I read on page forty-one of <u>Great Acting Teachers</u>; in talking about directors frustrated in attempts to communicate what emotion they wanted from and actor. Brestoff states the problem exists, "... because we do not have the words for the thousand subtle emotions that pass through us each day. We simply do not have a rich enough emotional vocabulary to communicate nuance to each other. Why is this so? Maybe it says something about our society's fear of emotional expression..." As I read that, I looked at my copy of <u>NEW SCHOOL ACTING</u> and said to myself, "We have those tools now."

CHAPTER VIII

LETTERS FROM THE INTERNET: FAQ's

I spent a few months in a dialogue on the net talking to actors and directors. I have tried to capture the essence of their questions and statements without quoting anyone directly. While I won't use their letters to me, I will use my answers, it will be like Jeopardy. I give the answer and you guess the question. If I was a bit redundant in the formal section of this book, this correspondence may be even more so; because many of these people had the same question. I'll give a hint as to each question in italics; some will be actual answers, some will be statements and some will be things I thought of while preparing this section; so, while not being a true question and answer session, it's may answer one of yours.

Q) This was a response to a discussion about ensemble. It was suggested that, actors who work together all the time, as a company, have an advantage over actors cast by the show. One point was that when gathering a new group of actors, it takes longer to get the rehearsals up to speed as actors adjust to each other and the director.

A) There is, in these situations i.e., a company, the subtle effect of team, but......The idea of process, actors getting slowly or lethargically into the rehearsal process can be solved by changing the process. They are probably bored with the dead pace it takes to actually get on their feet and get to the work when working old school methods. While working with the same actors all the time seems like a nice idea, actors who make a living at it seldom wind up in this situation. Actors are traveling around the country or from one film studio or TV station to the next. The odds of having the same people in each shows all the time are astronomical. Even a TV show like <u>Friends</u>, where there is a core group of actors, hasn't that consistency; guest artists, day players and extras are always involved. Altman and Cassavetes are two directors who worked in a limited form of ensemble, similar to a theatrical company. Generally, acting careers are less like a musician staying with a band, and more like the life of a studio musician; a top professional player who comes in, does his job and goes on to the next one. Studio musicians might record with five bands or more in one day.

Q) There is so much more to be said in this regard, like, old school rehearsal style has a built in boredom factor. It goes back to ensemble, another director mentioned that directors and actors working together over and over creates a situation where actors feel free to take risk.

A) Classic directorial arrogance or ignorance. Actors trust each other; it is not each other they don't trust, it is you, the director. The director is somebody that can hire or fire actors; recommend them or bad mouth them to other people in the business. The actor's creativity is constrained by fear of having her choices interpreted as being, so far off the mark, that her instincts come into serious questioning. We should also include the factor that actors have been trained to be director dependent; that taking chances in front of a director might meet with rejection. This ingrained intimidation factor is very big, it goes back to the slave analogy I used before. I want daddy director to like me so I'd better not get too wild. <u>Actors will never be able to fully explore their creative impulses until the director is taken out of the position of being able to terminate their immediate employment; and perhaps even destroy their careers.</u>

In these cases of extended involvement, the trust factor is usually the other way around, the director, after repeatedly working with certain actors, finally, actually does trust them. The director must then find a way to communicate that, to the actors, clearly enough to where these actors feel they can take risks, without worrying about losing their jobs.

Those are very serious problems with the old school setup. New School, both in technique and in attitude, creates a zero anxiety level immediately. Actors get the signal loud and clear, that when working The Whelan Tape Technique, they are not only permitted to explore any impulse, they are demanded to investigate their creative impulses vigorously without regard to "correctness" or conformity, to any suggested plan or direction. All that freedom is built into the dynamics and mechanics of the New School approach. The only defining factors being the given circumstances of the script; and these often have some very soft edges, that an actor can explore without fear of breaking character.

The high level risk taking intrinsic to new school is due to the non judgmental attitude of the director/coordinator, coupled with actor's deep involvement with the text and trust in their fellow actors. The Whelan Tape Technique creates that involvement, and it establishes an environment that fosters and demands that trust.

Q) A director was complaining about an actor not making a cross as he had been directed to do it. Well he did make the cross, but he didn't motivate it as much, or in the way that the director wanted.

A) I'd feel comfortable guessing, that the reason the actor had trouble motivating the cross, was because it did not come from himself/character; that that movement, at that time, was instinctively recognized as inappropriate and a violation of the actors creative impulse. A director gets a bright idea that someone should make a certain move; forget that the actors instincts (RIC's) are totally opposed to that move. Don't ask actors what they would rather do; just tell them to do it your way. Some directors like to pose as being sensitive to actors creativity; if you dare disagree with one of their choices, they will listen to your idea and then say something like, "Well that's a good idea Bill, but it doesn't work here; just do it my way."

Q) How to put some extra pop into early rehearsals.

A1) I've always thought it was crazy to wait to give actors props and costumes. You may not be able to get the real thing, but you can get many of the props (or close to it), and some aspect of costume from day one. Go for it. Saxe Meinigan Meinigan, whom I mentioned earlier, had every costume, prop and set piece in place by the first day of rehearsal.

This had to do with a "problem actor." I think this is where someone used the term, Opening Night Actor. It comes up again.

A2) May be the actor is the problem, and maybe it's the director. It is worth the director's time to discuss, with the actor, how the actor approaches a role; then it is much easier to evaluate the problem. Find out if the actor is the product of bad teachers, or if he is lazy or perhaps he just has a style that is different from the directors. The director should explain to the actor the way he works and ask him point blank if he is comfortable with that. If the actor seems hesitant, simply explain that he will be fired, if after taking the role, he doesn't make the commitment. No actor likes to get fired, and yes, you can fire a kid in a high school play. You can fire any actor anytime. Unless he is bone dumb, he will realize that others might be hesitant to cast an actor who has been fired.

Q) More on the "problem actor"

A) The ensemble is the whole reason for doing this. If they can't play that way, as I just said in another note. FIRE THEM! That's what happens in the real world. Fire them and fire them quickly. Of course it is much smarter to smell them out in the audition process and never hire them to begin with. Hiring and firing has nothing to do with money or age. Forget "artistic differences", if his ego/attitude is damaging the show, simply say, "Get out of here you bum." It may be the lesson that a talented actor needs to wake him up to why acting is a gift.

Q) Some young director was getting close to opening night, and the classic concern about time was crashing in.

A) This is another case where the Whelan Tape Technique changes the rules and rituals of old school. It has always been a tradition that as we get close to opening night, rehearsals get longer. All niters are not uncommon; very romantic, coffee and cigs and hanging out in the theatre, waiting for your scenes to come up. Staggering out into a rising sun, exhausted and knowing you have to be back at the theatre in the afternoon because you open that night. It is really stupid to do that today. The best way to do this is to use the tape technique and to put those inevitable long rehearsals on the first two days of rehearsal, instead of the last two days. The intense involvement with character, quick and easy familiarity with lines, and a good awareness of the flow of the piece will result. The energy that comes out of that situation will drive the show to levels of intensity usually not seen for weeks.

The excitement level of all involved will be so high all the way through the rehearsal schedule that you will not have to whip yourselves like dogs the week before you open. This is a time when actors should be rested and ready for the show; even if you don't use the tape technique, put the long rehearsals in front. I can't imagine any reason for not using the tape technique, unless you've only got one tape recorder and it's broken.

Q) Someone thought I was being insensitive toward actors because I recommended firing them at any serious sign of attitude.

A) Please understand, my sympathy is always with the actor, always. When somebody uses the phrase Opening Night Actor, two thoughts come to mind. One, I'm dealing with a prima donna, shoot him. Two, I'm dealing with a hard working actor whose creative style is such that it all comes together when the lights go on. If every member of that cast already knows that this actor is the hardest working actor in the cast, when she has difficulties in rehearsal, the cast will support her, run lines with her, do anything they can to help her along. It is not a question of how an actor's instrument functions, I cast them for a reason and I will stick by them to the end. When however, it is a question of ATTITUDE, one that hid itself in the audition and starts to come out right away in rehearsal; they are fired and out the door quickly and replaced with an actor who cares about the work. Rather than upset a cast, this will quiet rumblings about someone getting away with something, or getting special treatment. The cast will be glad it has a director who does the hard thing for the good of the show.

Q) A director thought that I wanted actors to be mechanical and associate every line with a specific emotion, and then look it, up give it a color etc.

A) First of all, you can't be emotional and mechanical at the same time. I can see why, Method trained directors and actors, would misinterpret what I'm saying. It all has to do with their frame of reference. The Method has actors intellectually break scripts down into objectives, beats, intentions, motivations, super objectives, etc.; they carve it up like a Christmas turkey. The organic development of character, that comes from the tape technique and emotion studies, is hard for them to grasp, to trust. The fact is that musicians don't think of scales when they are playing and painters don't think about the days they spent in the study of color of while painting. It is at "the moment of inspiration," "the moment of creation," when these artist get their payoff for the hours of study and preparation. They are not remembering, they are responding intuitively to the moment. They have built a bank of creative choices and they can trust it to provide anything that their inspiration is looking for; because they did the work. As I get deeper into this work, I've had to ask myself, what have actors learned to do. I've been a student of acting all my life and I tried to think about what it was that I actually studied, what was I working on all those years? A giant part of that was how to intellectualize a part into the ground, and then abuse myself emotionally trying to duplicate a planned event, one that I was capable of imagining. The fact is, I can imagine anything but that does not mean I can get it. So I learned intellectually, to see places where I would be expected to feel certain emotions; however I was never taught anything about those emotions I was supposed to feel.

Q) Someone also missed my point in relation to emotion studies. He thought that I was scoring the script from Big, smaller, smallest emotion. He said, among other things, that friends who were visual artists had said that when creating, they let the colors select themselves.

A) Perhaps, a simple example will clarify the distinction I am trying to make. Your visual artist associates, who said they let the colors select themselves, were able to do so because their studies had given them a very rich base from which these inspirations could arise. If I get hungry and I go to the refrigerator; I can only select from the foods I have put in there. I had to go to the store, select from all that was in that store, pay for it, bring it home and then place it into that refrigerator. In other words, I did the work so that I could have a variety of choices. If I do my emotions studies, when as an actor, I reach the "Moment of creation," I have a full fridge, lots to choose from and instinctively, I pick the most satisfying.

Let's not get semantic about the word "studies", it means:

1) Open up the book and read the pages

2) Pick up the pen and answer the questions

3) Ask my teacher

4) Put a glob of color on my palette and mix it with some other stuff.

Proceeding from there, this director also says, that each situation of anger has nuances which make that anger a bit different. It is not surprising that he goes from, situation = emotion. I say, imagine if you will, that it is the Nuance of the Anger that makes the situation different, rather than the other way around.

He says that the circumstance and the character should be the main focus. That those then lead to emotions, action, etc., He argues that "Death of a Salesman" isn't about anger or despair, it's about a man being used and discarded by society and "Fiddler on the Roof" isn't about love or frustration, it's about the maintaining and adjusting of tradition. My reply was; I can't see myself walking up to an actor and saying, could you give me a little more, being used and discarded by society, or I'm missing the, maintaining and adjusting to society in that section. Actors play emotions, not ideas.

The old school would look at a situation as static, an intellectual frame of time, one that could be measured and then played; this really doesn't allow for the human element in acting. New school looks at the situation as dynamic and within the confines of the situation, a constantly fluctuating dynamic. Actors in character, respond to the moment and the intensity of communication at that precise moment, a moment that has never existed in time, and which will have something unique about it to which the character has to respond.

This may sound like splitting hairs but that is the nature of art, making subtle distinctions. That hair has to be in exactly the right place or it throws the entire composition off balance. Allow that, and I think my point might come clear. If I'm painting your portrait, and you, my living model, have a slightly different look in your eye today than when you posed for me yesterday, and this different look engages me, I will change what I painted yesterday. If I change the look in your eye, I will also repaint that hair that hangs so delicately across your bosom, to match. It all comes down to old school actors working from their own emotions and the cliché responses available within that limited framework. Hopefully, the following paragraphs will open this concept up to some who might still be having trouble with it.

The emotions listed below are the nuances. Using the color analogy, Anger is the Primary Emotion/color and those that follow are the secondary emotions/colors, or as you will, nuances. The visual artist did not intuit the knowledge of subtle differences between colors. They learned them empirically and then aided by their creativity, blended them or put them in juxtaposition in an esthetic manner. Actors arrogance, or lack of proper instruction, has them believing they can intuit the subtle differences between similar emotions. This would be true if you use your own emotions for each character you play, but I fail to see the art in that approach. However, without an objective knowledge of emotions, you are trapped into that very limited and tedious redundancy. Please pick a color for Anger and then as you read the list, try to see each nuance as a degree of that color.

anger	acerbate	affront	agitate	acrimony	animosity	annoyance	antagonism
asperity	bile	bridle	bristle	chafe	chagrin	choler	conniption
dander	displeasure	distemper	ebullition	embitter	enmity	envenom	exacerbate
exasperate	fret	fury	gall	goad	hatred	huff	ill humor
ill temper	impatience	indignation	incense	inflame	infuriation	irascibility	ire
irritability	irritation	mad	miff	nettle	offend	outrage	passion
peevish	pet peeve	petulance	pique	provoke	rage	rankling	resentment
rattle	rile	ruffle	seethe	slow burn	soreness	spleen	stew
storm	tantrum	temper	tiff	umbrage	vexation	violence	virulence
wrath	wroth						

I hope you indulged me by trying what I suggested, and that it gave you a moment of insight or a least a pause for thought. My question would be how many actors/directors do you think could give you a definition of each of those emotions with the subtlety to make the very fine distinctions that would be necessary in many cases?

Q) A director outlined a work procedure that sounded very intellectually based to me; he used the term layering. He too, felt I was trying to mechanically score a script with moment by moment choices of specific emotions to play, instead of recognizing my insistence on honoring the improvisational element that comes into play in any human interaction and the need for the actor to respond to that moment instinctively.

A) "Layering" sounds very intellectual. Motivation comes from emotion and emotion is what gives the impetus to any physical action. New School Directors are not providing precision choices to the actor. They are presenting actors with the richness of an emotion, a richness that directors can be sure actors don't possess. In doing that, they are expanding the possible creative choices that the actor can make. The fact that actors don't know this richness, comes only from a lack of study. New School Directors are not making the choice for the actors. New School Directors would never tell actors to play this or that shade of the emotion, and the actors would never consciously decide to play it either. All you are doing is presenting actors with all the possibilities within that emotion. The actors instrument, will at the time of need, present the best possible choice based on the "at the moment" interaction with the other characters. It will be stimulated by the given circumstance and the look(s) on the face(s) of, the body language of the other character(s), and the sound of their voice(s). The process is automatic. I think that that moment is what is generally referred to as "a creative experience."

Q) Here again, and I don't know how, after having explained, what to me is quite a simple idea, I am misunderstood. I really got the feeling that this misunderstanding was a refusal to understand; a deliberate attempt by old school defenders to confuse others who might be following this discussion. I really wanted to say "Disagree if you must but please stop playing dumb.

A) I really feel it is important for people to understand these ideas, but this, on line time, costs money. If you honestly can't even see the simple concept I've been giving you over and over, in as many different ways as possible... It makes me think of the story about the guy that gets a flat tire in front of the mental hospital. As he is changing the tire, one of the inmates watches him through the fence. Just as the guy is about finished, his foot slips and he kicks all the lug nuts into the sewer. He's all pissed off and now he starts walking away. The inmate says "Hey where are you going." The guy answers " I've got to walk to the gas station and get some more lug nuts." The inmate says, "Why don't you just take one from each of the other tires and then you can drive there." The guy looks surprised and says to the inmate, " How did you ever think of that?"; to which the inmate replies, "Hey, I'm in here for being crazy not for being stupid."

In my final edit, when I reread this, I don't know how the joke works in this contest. I checked back months to find the cut that would bring this into perspective but it must have come long before. I believe it had to do with disinformation; a deliberate attempt to obfuscate the intelligence of my techniques. That doesn't really help but it does present the opportunity to make a point. It's a dogfight with the well installed powers of old school. It's like pretending to be stupid when your stupid already, or in other words, they are not that smart. They cling to it because it is worth millions to them. I'm not saying millions of dollars is such a bad idea, but I wonder what I would say if I was offered a million dollars cash but I had to make a pack with the devil to never have a forward thinking experience again. Like Sisyphus, rolling that dumb boulder up that hill for eternity. Turn over my mind to nostalgia; to sell my right to the joy of creativity, forever. I don't think so, it must be horrible, to only teach history, never to speculate and experiment with the future, never to be involved, never to be fully alive. The implications are too frightening; I like walking up straight and looking at whatever is coming at me or whatever and/or whomever I'm bringing to the party.

Q) Again on emotions.

A) Having an actor wallow in the abyss of her own emotions is both arrogant and ignorant. It is arrogant, if one were to convince oneself that audiences would care to watch that sort of personal display over and over in a series of disguises/characters. By which I mean, repeating that self defining emotional rupture over and over in every part. All that sort of actor does is change her hat, put on other costumes, memorize other scripts, but she continually exhibits the same pitiful self adoring flagellatory and masturbatory sides of her limited emotional experience. To that type of actor, those actions represent Hate and Love respectively.

This comment on the Muses was part of something else but if you think your an artist, you should know the Muses. Artists generally relate strongly to the Muses, those goddesses, patrons of all the arts, daughters of Zeus and attendants of Apollo. Thalia and Melpomene, are two ladies it would do you good to meet.

Working professionals, and those that aspire to that cherished position, are the actors and directors I want to talk to, and to whom I offer whatever knowledge I've gained from being a professional actor for the last thirty-five years.

Last year in LA, I was cast in a play, only to find out in rehearsal that everybody else was devoted to Meisner. When I would talk about my character, they would keep interrupting with "Yes but what does Jeremy feel, how does Jeremy feel about that." I kept telling them that was none of their business, that I did not become an actor to play myself. Where's the challenge in that? Where's the Art in that? I became an actor to try to meet the impossible challenge of being somebody else, if even for a second. I am willing to go along on craft and technique, if I can occasionally get lifted into that sublime area of creation. It is only fair to say it was a fee free play. If it had been a job, I would have played along, after all I am an actor and actors have to know all the styles. You never can tell what school your director is going to be from and you're not there to get into an adversarial discussion on theories of acting, not if you want to keep your job. You're there to make a movie, do a play, whatever. Film, television and contemporary commercial theatre are very expensive mediums, which can cost fifteen to thirty thousand dollars and up a minute. Start talking about approaches to acting and you'll be discussing it in the unemployment line, with some other actor who had the same penchant. We should all know that Old School has as a dictum, "The director is always right." Sometimes directors will throw the actor a bone, as long as they feel it was actually their own idea, or small enough not to stand out.

I think I addressed the arrogant part of the actor using her own emotions, and I would like to take a moment to address the ignorant part of it. I ask, how can a director dare ask an actor to go deeply and repeatedly into the most painful moment of her existence, so that "they" can have a good show? I am offering a way around that and if someone doesn't like my way, then find one that works for you, but please stop doing that. Realize that you are practicing psychological torture, justifying it with outdated concepts and techniques. Directors, stop ennobling this by wrapping yourself in the cloak of Pseudo-art. If you wish to do that to yourself that is your right. Van Gogh had a right to cut off his ear. If however, from a position of authority, teachers lead others into that Psycho-Intellectual jungle, they should realize, were it not for that cloak of pseudo-art, they would be prosecuted in a court of law for emotional and mental abuse. We have learned some things over the years and one of them was that a person does not have to have blood pouring from open wounds to be the victim of abuse. I am not saying I have the only way to avoid that deplorable practice, but I do have one very good way.

Q) As an answer to this charge of abuse, a director said that some people did that, but really, hardly anybody any good did that kind of thing. He said this, in spite of defending the practice of having actors use their own emotions.

A) I agree that no director, who is any good, abuses actors, but there was an old cartoon series called Pogo; in one strip Pogo says, "I have met the enemy and he is us". Something to that effect, anyhow, when I was teaching the very techniques I now condemn, indeed when I devoted a chapter in my first book on how to use Affective Memory, I truly believed I was doing something good for my students and for actors everywhere. The bad teachers were the other guys. These are hard truths and I don't condemn anyone. I am vigorous in presenting what I learned, because there is such complacency in the area of acting instruction. Complacency is really too kind; stagnation is a more appropriate word, and a very real decline in the Art has resulted from it. If, instead of defending the old ways, we all became aggressive in searching for new and better approaches, many would be discovered and acting would regain the vitality, power, and majesty that it deserves as a major art form. There were many psychiatrists that truly believed that lobotomies were the way to go, and in fact, there still are some that perform them, a few hundred a year; but just about every responsible member of that community has come to understand that there are better ways to deal with people. No disrespect to Stanislavski but guys; it really is time to move on.

Q) A director wanted to understand New School, in case he had to direct an actor trained in that approach. How he would have to change his work as a director, if he would have to talk in terms of a result, which would change from actor to actor, instead of talking about "Old School" terms like motivation, circumstance and relationship?

A) This is an important question. It is a vital part of what I am trying to accomplish and probably the most difficult for Directors to accept. The implications are more than likely the cause of much of the knee-jerking going on out there.

First of all, directors will never talk in terms of results. In fact, you will talk very little about anything, especially in the early stages of the work. You will make sure that the actors have a very clear understanding of the given circumstance. While Given Circumstance is considered a Method phase, the concept is as old as the craft. Greek, Roman, Shakespearean, and indeed any actor of worth, knew the absolute Rule of Given Circumstances, whatever they might have called them. Given Circumstance are a classic element of the actors craft and they provide the framework from which our art is launched.

As to relationships, they are discovered and shaped by the actors, and sharpened and penetrated further with the aid of the director.

As far as motivation, that is strictly an intellectual exercise, and while intellectual exercises and intellectualism are the cornerstone of old school acting, they still have a place in new school, however, as a priority, they move way down the list. They will be used, only after other more organic spontaneous techniques have been thoroughly investigated.

The actor/director relationship is radically altered, but it is highly unlikely to reach the ideal, at least not for some time. As a goal in NEW SCHOOL ACTING, the director becomes part of the ensemble, not in some condescending symbolic method, but in a very real way. Directors will have to conform to the actual spirit and law of ensemble; equal not above. You (directors) can influence a creative decision, but you will no longer be able to dictate one. If your ideas are good, they will be used, if not, they will be ignored. No more Art by decree.

In a final note to you and anyone else who might catch this post, I would be selling out a very powerful technique, useful to actors and directors, if out of the fear of being accused of self promotion, I failed to mention that one major tool in reaching a higher more creative level of acting is already available. The tape technique I created is truly an extremely effective tool. Designed to be used in the early stages of rehearsal, it will delight the genuinely artistic by the creativity it stimulates in actors, and the demands it makes on directors. I will send a file on how to use it to anyone that might care to look at it.

Q This director asserts that by re experiencing the tragic moments we use for affective memory, by confronting them, that they don't hurt us any more.

A) Either you never did this technique yourself or you are really shallow. I could not disagree more. First of all; Duh, if it didn't hurt anymore how could we use it to always make us cry.

Anyone who has suffered tragedy, hurts every time it comes to mind. It's true in my case and I would shudder if I thought that everybody else in the world was so callous, that they could just toss those feelings aside; if I truly believed that, it would kill me. Obviously that is not true, or actors could not continually mine that source, whenever they wished to create the verisimilitude of tragedy.

Q) Another says, it is necessary for actors to use their own emotions in training situations, so that actors can get in touch with their emotional well.

A) In response to the statement, that an actor digging into his own personal emotional nightmares opens him up to being able to access the characters, like priming a well.

I'm afraid if you took a hard look at the actor's emotional well, you will find it is not very deep and moreover, it is polluted and adorned by the actors own life experiences. I am not saying that actors are shallow; only so in as much as they are also part of the human race. (Some producers and directors might not agree) There is global ignorance on this subject. As a world we have never studied emotion; we have studied everything but emotions. Strange, as emotions are the very root of our humanity.

Q) Someone asks, how, after all these emotions are identified, labeled, defined, assigned colors and objects etc., how then do we access them?

A) The answer to that question is, we (Actors) access them the same way a painter accesses a color when she is at "the moment of creation", inspired to use it as an element of a work. Likewise, the way a musician accesses a note when he is, at "the moment of creation", inspired to use it as an element of a work.

Just for the record, the terms I prefer to use, and which were altered in the course of discussion by someone, are Emotional Vocabulary and Emotional Mobility, not emotional inventory. I can see why some old school type would change Emotional Vocabulary to emotional inventory. I don't know whether it was done by a sneaky guy trying to pervert the concept, or just by some hapless old school dupe, who has to look backward to see anything. Look at the words. Inventory, while it denotes a flexible quantity, connotes what you have on your shelf, it is in that regard, either static or diminishing. Vocabulary is a dynamic term that is perpetually expanding.

Q) Here a director says that emotions must be real; that's fine, but then says that the actor has to consciously go from his own emotions, to get to the character's and from my answer, (I can't find that file now) I guess he stated that everything else comes first and then the emotions.

A) My question is, if this is the goal, real emotion, and I wholeheartedly agree that it is, why not go directly to the characters emotions? Why take such a circuitous dangerous and unnecessary route? Do you truly believe that the actor is incapable of internalizing a character without using tricks? A ruse which ultimately, though the actor may get away with it, prevents him/her from ever achieving a truly original performance.

As far as plot and circumstance coming before emotion; once again, from the actors perspective, how they (as character) feel, is why they do what they do, who they see, where they go and everything else about their lives. It is the difference between a literary/intellectual approach and an emotional/organic one. To the literary/intellectual type actor, they see the different sets of circumstance that the character is placed in; that puts them outside the experience. The emotional/organic type actor is inside the experience, and the circumstance comes out of how she feels about what is going on at the moment. This actor doesn't care about the circumstance, she only cares about how she feels about it. Indeed, she doesn't even see it as circumstance, she feels a new emotion coming out of the prior emotion and how she physically reacted to it. Acting is going from emotion to emotion in a theatrical manner. Actors play feelings; they don't play circumstance.

If I were to rewrite your statement so as I could agree with it, it would read; the emotions will provide the true force behind the words the character says, the experiences the character has and the relationships the character encounters.

Q) Someone suggested, that the actor only use her own emotions to get in touch with that emotion on a personal level, to give her a reference point for it.

A) To me that is like saying, gee, I'm sorry I dropped your baby on it's head, but I won't do it again. The initial contact has been established by linking the actors limited emotional frame of reference to the character in the most powerful way possible. If the actor is ever able to break that bond, which I doubt, it will only be after a great deal of valuable time is wasted in the process.

Q) A guy thought I must have been tortured by directors and teachers because I am so adamant.

A) I have had wonderful teachers all over the world, and worked with some of the most creative and professional directors acting has had the joy to embrace. I have also worked with some real bums, people who should never be permitted anywhere near an actors psyche, especially a young one with stars in her eyes and the obedience level of a well trained attack dog. Anything the teacher says the actors on it with a vengeance, without regard to health or safety.

There are many kinds of acting teachers. The good ones, the bullies, the gurus, those that are well intentioned, but improperly trained or uninformed, and many who are completely untrained and incompetent, and who only see an easy dollar in it. I dislike the gurus more than the bullies. While both are contemptible, the bullies just want the actors body and mind, whereas the guru wants their soul as well. On occasion the bullies get results, as Confucius says "Those that cannot be made to listen will be made to feel." Still, I fail to see the satisfaction in it.

The guru's are worse and too many of them exist. They are self inflated little demi-gods who demand applause and blind obedience from their students. They make a religion out of it, putting themselves next to god and the only way you stupid acting students can talk to this god is through them, so kneel down, bend over or anything else they say or else, go to bad acting hell. If you're looking around for a teacher, and you see one that gives of the faintest odor of this garbage, run.

The last group, the misinformed, can be saved if they will find humility, however in a business rancid with ego not many turn that corner.

Q) Somebody said that he had not seen actors who had been hurt through the use of affective memory.

A) I would like to know where have you spent your time studying and teaching, that you have not seen the problem I'm trying to address, redress might be better put. As an actor, I spent 12 years in NYC, working and teaching and making the rounds. I spent another dozen in Hollywood, doing the LA version of the New York thing. Another 10 in various places around the world as actor director and teacher. From San Francisco to London, Chicago to Mexico, Orlando to Paris, etc. etc. I've worked with thousands of actors, directors, students and teachers; professionals and amateurs. In thirty four years as an actor/director, with fourteen of those years teaching in private workshops, professional schools, and college, I've dealt with actor's problems on a daily basis. As a teacher, there were times that I thought I was running a Mash unit; all these busted up kids coming in with horror stories about this teacher this, and that teacher that. Their love of acting and their determination to succeed at it got them that far; if from where ever you sit, it is easy to marginalize the problem, I think you're naively fortunate.

Q) Somebody who obviously never read my books, asked if the audience for my books was composed of those actors/directors who only work by dictating every tiny move and choice in a production, without input from anyone else?

No, the audience for my books are actors/directors who have gone beyond that point and are hungry for tools that will help them push exploration to the limits, while staying inside of professional demands. They are for actors who are not afraid of taking more of the responsibility for creating their character, and directors who revel in the sight of actors who take that responsibility. They are for directors who find their own creativity stimulated by that type of actor. They are also for people so completely numbed by and utterly bored with the Method, that in their desperation, they will try anything to get away from it. If you ever actually try that tape technique of mine, really do it the way it's written, no matter how egalitarian you think you are, you will find that you were in reality, a tyrant of sorts. Actors are Maseratis that are being driven at twenty miles an hour. The pity is that actors set themselves up for it and now we all pay the price. Viola Spolin, lead the charge that broke the steel cord of director dependence, one which bound and gagged actors for decade upon decade. The freedom her techniques demanded, for and from actors, is all still so new, that some actors are like slaves getting off a train in a northern city just after the emancipation, others are still hiding in Plato's cave and some are like wild beasts, let from a cage, ravenous for the creative freedom dimly perceived from a former life. My my my I do just rattle on now and then don't I, but it's all true.

Q) Two directors offered up the theory of actions, which was the focus of Stanislavski's last years. Late in his career, Stanislavski became convinced that the actions the actor performed generated the feelings he showed. Action came first, then the emotion.

A) Regarding the theory of actions, that theory does not work in acting, it may in sports. In acting, Given Circumstances define the intentions. As far as what actor A and actor B are doing to each other, we can SEE that. If that were it, silent movies would do. The "Why" is the impetus to action, allow me to explain.

There are only three possible moves an actor can make and they are dictated by the emotions. The emotional content of the line will, assuming that A speaks first:

Repel: Force A to move away from B.

Impel: Draw A closer to B

Compel: Force A to stay where she is in relation to B.

The emotional need is what creates action in almost every single case regarding plays or movies. People have, what I once referred to as a physical, intellectual and emotional memory. I no longer call them memories, I now refer to them as Physical, Intellectual and Emotional Networks, of which the memories are only a part. The concept that feelings follow actions may be true in instances when the Physical Network dominates, i.e. moments of great peril, such as when we are almost in a bad car accident, where we respond first and then get scared later, or in cases of serious sexual attraction; exemplified by the expression that suggests a man was following something other than reason when pursuing a woman. Woman have the same impulses, that response is just more obvious in a man. Stanislavski, in the early part of his work, dealt with the Intellectual Network, asking emotion to follow the thoughts of the character. In reality, the Intellectual Network dominates in business and other logical left brain functions. However, plays and movies are almost in every case, based on people in emotional, right brain situations. It is for that reason that the Emotional Network dominates in the actors art. While, as characters, we may be called upon to enter into those other networks at certain points in the script, practically everything, all movement and all thought, are predominantly motivated by the emotional content of the line.

Q) This director, responding to my idea of having the director as a coordinator without creative control, said he thought that the word coordinator gave the director a slight edge.

A) I suggest you look up the word: coordinate. My reference is <u>The New Shorter Oxford Dictionary</u>: A person or thing of equal rank or value. A person or thing of the same rank as another, an equal. Etc. etc. It lists as it's opposite: Subordinate.

Old school does tend to think of creativity as a top down process, although at times, and for affect, it likes to pose as egalitarian, what a hoot. Actually, I think the word director ought to be changed, it sounds too Orwellian to me. THE DIRECTOR WILL SEE YOU NOW; it's Kafka all over. While I'm at it, could somebody come up with a word to replace BLOCKING, block this, my hat that is. The word reverberates anti-art and the concept belongs in the domain of painters and photographers, not to an art form dealing with the fluid rhythms of a human being in motion or at rest. In formalistic or stylized productions tableaus can be very beautiful, and very effective, but in the main as working professionals, we deal with naturalistic themes.

Q) This person said that actors and a coordinator, if they all had a different way of looking at the piece, could never produce anything more that garbage and that chaos would ensue from the attempt.

A) He said, if 20 people are working on a production and have 20 different views of where it ought to go, chaos and garbage will result. I would have to ask, is it beyond comprehension that 20 dedicated professional actors and a director, working on equal footing, could create a unified and moving work?

I agreed with them initially, on the condition that they were taking an old school approach to the work, upon reflection, even in old school, that statement is really pregnant with potential conjecture:

A) Only an autocratic mind could conceive it.

B) Why did the director hire them?

C) It is a great opportunity to coordinate a group of talented opinionated artists by someone equal to the task.

D) Professionals, concerned about their next job, would keep their mouths shut.

E) Is "chaos and garbage" the only possible result?

In any event, try to think of the director as a friendly and creative third eye, it might help make the distinction between an autocrat and a coordinator.

Q) A director thought that I was being disrespectful to old schools contribution to acting .

A) You seem to think that I do not respect the work of those who have gone before, nothing could be further from the truth. My first book, <u>THE ABC'S OF ACTING ,</u> was dedicated to Lee Strasberg, and Viola Spolin". You say you think I need to be careful in terminology such as "old school" and "new school." You say my using the term old school doesn't give relevance to our history or tradition. Let me say this; my mother is old and I respect her, but I do recognize her limitations. We can't play the way we once did. She does not have the same vitality. She recognizes her limitations too and is extremely graceful in accepting them. Pity that others seem to have so much difficulty extending that to the realm of ideas and techniques. I use the terms old school and new school to distinguish between a new direction in acting and what has been the direction of acting for many decades. It is an important distinction, for it establishes a fixed point in time when we realized it was time to move on. It is a reference mark to young actors and directors coming into the field, that there actually is an option to Stanislavski and Stanislavski based work, which is what they will encounter in ninety percent or more of institutions and with most of the private teachers in this country.

Any system of acting will work, regardless of how clumsy it is, because the actor will find a way to make it work, that is part of the job. Unfortunately, a great deal of creative energy is burned up doing what often amounts to no more than busy work, concocted or adopted by people who haven't a clue as to how the actors creative process has been changing over the last forty plus years.

You decry blocking and then you say you want physical action that is not calculated, but then you say you look through the text for verbs that suggest or dictate physical action.

I have to ask, doesn't it take a certain amount of calculation to pull through a script rummaging for verbs, so that when the actor gets to that verb, she has an action to do? It sounds more as if you are scoring the script, so that we actors memorize the score, then in performance, we pop up or plunk down at those verbs, and that will make us feel something.

Avoiding for the moment, evaluation of any merit that might be derived from such deliberate manipulation of the actor, that proposal is simply blocking by another name and most certainly falls in the realm of "something to do." Blocking is any predetermined set of activities given by a director to an actor, and while distinguished technically from "business", in reality, they are the same.

I like Balanchine's' statement that, "In classical (dance), movement begets emotion; in modern (dance) emotion begets movement."

Q) A director was saying how important directors are, because they had to make sure the "stage picture" looked good.

The situation brings the emotion, the emotion brings the movement. It is my belief, that if the movements the actors find, are truly from character, the picture will be perfect and will not need adjustment. Actors make mistakes, a character can never make a mistake. If actors need adjustment for stage picture, then I know they are in their head and not playing the moment. I will go to work helping them find the truth of that moment, that done, the problem of picture is solved.

Q) A director suggests that there are many ways to tell a story; that only a director can pick one and make everybody else do it his way and then there is no confusion.

A) It might sound like Utopia, but I've seen it done. If the material is good, there is only one way to tell the story, and as a group you work to discover that way. If everyone is true to that, then nobody has to have a whip.

Q) A young director had a question in relation to upstaging.

A) My advice to actors; it's a cheap trick so don't let it happen to you.

I work with a technique that has the actors find their own movement and I insist on, and I hope inspire a commitment to the work, which would not allow that sort of selfish deviation. Still there are slime actors who will do it to you, especially in audition situations.

The way I teach actors to deal with it, is to counter (move to another position where you're again sharing stage or camera), if the upstaging actor adjusts, (moves further upstage) well then it's time to get physical. If the situation being played is friendly, just throw an arm over his shoulder and adjust him back. If the situation is adversarial, grab him and throw him downstage.

Q) I had brought up Learning styles and Split brain research as support for my techniques and theories , somebody asked me what they were. and where to find out more.

A) There is a very strong movement in education called Learning Styles Dunn and Dunn are at St. John's U., in New York; they created a Learning Styles Inventory. It all has to do with learning modalities, and 30 years of research has gone into them. If you like a little light reading try, "A Meta-Analytic Validation of the Dunn and Dunn Model of Learning-Style Preferences," by Bernard S. Goodman, at Nassau Community College with Rita Dunn, S. Griggs, J. Olson, and M. Beasly, from St. Johns University, New York. Also "What 4MAT Training Teaches Us About Staff Development" by Burnoose. There are tons of research papers on Learning Styles and Whole Brain Teaching. It is very interesting stuff and very useful to the actor and director. I've been working with it for ten years, even though I didn't know it. I had been aware that something like this was going on, but did not see the full connection until I got around to some hard research. I still have a great deal of research to do in the area.

Split brain research is the left brain right brain thing, only now they are referred to as hemispheres. Many researchers have been involved with this and you can find plenty of material in any decent library.

Q) I had mentioned a dissatisfaction with today's acting and today's actors. One of the directors got very indignant and demanded to know how I could berate my colleagues in such a manner.

A) My colleagues have been mislead and bullied by autocratic directors and teachers into giving up their birth right. They have let themselves be tossed around like beanbags by tableau obsessed directors and abused emotionally by non-licensed, ill equipped, imitation shrinks wearing the badge of Director/teacher.

Q) Somebody came in to the discussion late and didn't understand the distinction I was trying to make. between private and universal emotions. He also said that we had always studied emotions bringing up Freud and others psychiatrist.

A) What I'm talking about, is separating the actors own tainted, tinged, stained, or, decorated by their life experience emotions, from a universal and pure emotion, a universal awareness gained by objective and in depth study. Freud, Jung. Maslow, et al, were not your everyday actor on the street. I've found the book Emotional Intelligence is echoing, in many ways, what I've been teaching for 12 years now. Have you read it? Are you aware of that area of research? At this writing, Emotional Intelligence has been on the Best Seller list for 22 weeks. So, many people are interested, and those people are part of today's audience, get the hint. I think you'll find my argument about the general ignorance of emotions confirmed there. In that book, you will find around thirty pages of bibliography, in case you get interested in going further into the subject. If you've been following this discussion, you saw the references I've made to Whole Language, Learning Styles and Learning Modalities. You don't have too look to deep into those areas to see that we have obviously neglected emotions in our left hemisphere obsession.

The fact that individual emotional awareness is colored by individual life experience, should be a concept easy to grasp. The fact that an actor would bring some of his emotional baggage into the character, should be obvious and easily recognized as inappropriate. We need a pure universal awareness of emotions, if we are to truly allow the characters to express themselves, and their feelings through us as actors.

Q) What to do about performances that get stale.

A) One good way is to find out what research the actors have done and to find new areas for them to research. The most neglected word in the amateur actors vocabulary is research. Professionals know that you can't do a part without proper research. Find out what they did and then suggest other areas that they can research; that will bring new life to the work.

Q) Someone didn't want to know about Learning Styles, because they were just theories and there were too many of them.

A) While some of these theories differ, they all agree on the significant point that people definitely have different ways of learning, and that only one is in general usage. The educational system has always shown bias to that particular style and other type learners were ignored. Learning Styles go way beyond theory, these theories have generated many techniques which have been irrefutably proven to work. Hundreds of thousands of students got better grades using these techniques.

Q) More on the "problem" actor.

A) All the advice from the others is good sound advice regarding a problem actor, but my question is what is your directing style? It might be you. You may be overdirecting early and not giving the actor a chance to get a feel for the part before you start "directing". When an actor approaches a part, they need some time to get to know the character. Once they get that chance, they can respond to direction without feeling it is artistic or personal criticism. So if you like, give a quick breakdown of your directorial style and it will be much easier to see if the problem is with the actor or with you. You can post that or e-mail me.

Q) The director that was having trouble with the actor, responded to my question about her directorial style.

A) Well, after reading the description of how you work, I see a very normal old school style. Boredom is built into that approach, especially when you ask actors to read without emotion. I tell actors approaching a new script, don't work for anything but don't deny anything. Don't act, don't feel like you have to, but if something real happens, don't hurt yourself fighting it; just go with it and see where it takes you. Of course I don't have to deal with a second reading, because I audio taped that first read and the actors are on their feet as soon as they get done taping and are acting out the script to the playback. Aside from your use of the word "impose", I got a general sense that you feel the need to firmly control the rehearsal process. That is an old school disease and you sound too young to be bound to that. Guide the rehearsal process, don't be a control freak, that style is dead, loosen up have some fun and enjoy your actors creativity. You're stressing much too much. I tell people coming into the business, if it stops being fun stop doing it.

CHAPTER IX

THAT'S A WRAP

This work is very important, but simply because of its newness, it is going to meet with a great deal of resistance. It might be called the, "You call that music," syndrome. Actors surrogate parents, directors and teachers, are going to take the same attitude to this as your parents do to the music you listen to. Few of us have parents that understand our music, a few maybe, but not many. This work is going to have to go from you to another student or professional actor, and keep being passed on until it grows so big, that though they may not like it, they can't stop it. Over the years, I've gotten calls and letters from ex-students who had gone on to college or to doing professional shows; they tell me about trying to turn their teachers or directors on to the tape technique, and being ignored. Many have told me about sneaking off with other cast members or fellow students and teaching them the tape technique, so they could take advantage of the benefits in the show or class they were doing. We have shared a few laughs; they tell of teachers or directors feeling as if it was their own genius that had been the cause of the rapid improvement in the work.

This is the next step in the evolution of the art of acting, and you are right here at ground zero, so pass the word. Something better will come along, it always does, and in this age of instant international communication it will not take the hundred years it took us to get past Stanislavski. Until that happens, apply yourself diligently to the techniques you learned in this book and share the results. Speaking of instant international communication, as you see how good this stuff is, put it on the Web, and any local bulletin boards that have actors talking to actors. Fax it, E-mail it, post it on every web site that deals with acting. Hopefully, I'll have a home page by the time this book hits the street, and anybody who wants to find out more can hit it. One last shout on the subject of instant communication, take a look at INSTANT ACTING, I put some techniques and exercises in that book that you will find very useful.

It may not work, but try to turn directors and teachers you're working with on to these techniques, some might just love them, but if they don't, drop it, don't risk your job or grade. In my first book, THE ABC'S OF ACTING, I had a chapter called, "On Working with a Dumb Director," my publisher for that book cut it. The sum of it was, directors are still in a dictatorial position and they can hurt you; the only recourse we actors have is to overwhelm them with creativity. The beauty of creativity as a weapon is that those who oppose it, those who want to control it, don't have the imagination to see it coming until it smacks them in the head.

Ciao for now,

JEREMY

INDEX

—E—

—F—

—G—

Opening night actor, 59
opportunities to get lost are multiple, 49
Oprah, 1
"Formosa", 40
Organic movement from the character's sincerest emotional need., 20
Orwellian, 66
other art forms have already made this adjustment to the new world reality, 49
outline a first rehearsal with two actors doing a 3-4 page scene, 31
overdirecting early, 68
overwhelming emotional circumstance, 35
overwhelming script oriented world of film, TV or commercial theatre, 43

—P—

P = Prevents premature vocal characterization, 30
P = Prevents premature c, 37
parent has found themselves in jail for child abuse, 26
pause technique, 29
paused for a long time, it is possible to lose your concentration., 36
Pearlman, 47
Peele, Norman Vincent, 26
perfect example of a Whole Language learning technique, 28
performance will be noticeably richer, 9
performances that get stale, 68
physical health and the emotional state of the patient, 25
physical, intellectual and emotional memory, 66
Physical, Intellectual and Emotional Networks, 66
pick these big juicy moments, 36
PIE = Physical Memories, 37
Plato's cave, 65
Playboy of the Western World,, 46
Pogo, "I have met the enemy, and he is us", 63
pop up or plunk down, 67
population explosion, 40
Power words or power phrases, try them both, 25
predictability of the structure and the open-endedness of the materials, 28
prejudiced to the intellectual (left) side of your brain, 53
prima donna, shoot him, 59
primary distinction between Old School and New School, 13
Primary Emotions and Secondary Emotions., 9
primary motivations for children are fear and money, 48
Prince of Wales Theatre, London, 40, 41
problem actor, 59
problem is a clogged imagination, 11
problem spots, 29
problem that comes up using the chart, 11
professional actor's first obligation is to the text, 34
professional race car driver, 27
props create homes for these RIC's, a bar down left, might be the home for a repel, etc., 33
Pseudo-art, 62
psycho-intellectual based, 13
Psycho-Intellectual Age, 42
psycho-intellectual influence on acting, 42

pulling the emotion apart make it objective and universal, 55
pulls a gun, jumps the counter, blows the head off the cashier, 3
punished for expressing them, 26
push exploration to the limits, 65

—Q—

Quick test of emotional of awareness, 7
quick test of thesaurus technique, 9

—R—

rather see a traffic accident live on the news than a well written drama, 42
read without emotion, 68
real bums, 64
recognize the limitations of instruction you may have already received, 52
reference mark to young actors and directors, 67
relationships, 63
repeated physical gestures, 18
repelled, 30
Repels-Impels-Compels, 29
research into Learning Styles, 28
research possibilities are almost infinite from intellectual perspective, 20
research with integrated approach, 20
respond instantly upon hearing the emotion, with any physical motion/gesture, 23
responding to subtle shifts in emotional tone, 4
revolution in schools everywhere, 52
rhythms of a human being in motion, 66
RIC's, 30, 59
Richard Stockton College of New Jersey, 42
right hemisphere rules creative type functions, 52
right which deals with art/emotions, 26
Robertson, T.W., 40
rote memorization process, 37
Rule of Given Circumstances, 63
rules of baseball, 29
Russian School, 6, 41

—S—

same orchestra, same score, same conductor, different sound, 4
San Francisco City College, 46
say yes sir or yes ma'm, 45
scales are the cornerstones of music, 22
Schaal, Dick, 46
Schary, Dory, 29
script sets up boundaries, 3
script should be experienced emotionally, physically, and intellectually, from character, immediately, 31
scripts took on a more naturalistic speech and acting had to adjust, 40
Second City, 46
Seeing, Feeling , Hearing, or Audial, Visual, Tactile /Kinesthetic, 15
self absorbed display of personal intensity, 4
separating a cause from a symptom, 1

75

—T—

—U—

—V—

Dictionary of the Emotions

As the lead researcher and organizer of this section of the book, as well as a fellow actor, allow me to give you some background in how the *Dictionary* and *Thesaurus of the Emotions* were created.

Eliminating redundancies:

In compiling the *Thesaurus*, I came across many redundancies.   For example, in a general thesaurus you might find:

Eager: (as a main entry) with *Animated, Ebullient, Vehement, Zealous, Vivacious, Ardent, Exuberant, Agog, Enthusiastic, High-spirited, Impatient, Trenchant, Gusto* (as synonyms);

and then, later in the same thesaurus:

Zealous: *Verve, Earnest, Keen, Ardent, Enthusiastic, Eager, Exuberant, Ebullient, Ambitious, Vigorous, Impetuous, Ruthless, Gusto.*

Instead of listing these two primary emotions (Eager and Zealous) separately, and therefore, forcing the reader/actor to define many of the same words over and over, I combined them under one main primary emotion - in this example, Zealous. And so, the *Thesaurus* entry reads:

Zealous: *Verve, Earnest, Impatient, Keen, Trenchant, Ardent, Enthusiastic, Ambitious, Agog, Exuberant, High-spirited, Vivacious, Ebullient, Eager, Vigorous, Animated, Impetuous, Vehement, Ruthless, Gusto.*

In deciding which items could be combined, I relied on the secondary emotions (synonyms/ related words) as a guide. If there was a great deal of repetition, as in the above example, I combined them. In a regular, general thesaurus you'll get this kind of redundancy. However, for our purposes here, I didn't want there to be too much overlap since it is to be used as a workbook, too.

Note: There are, however, words that do appear more than once. This is due to those words having more than one meaning or usage. Each meaning will be found in the *Dictionary*.

A comprehensive thesaurus:

This workbook is quite extensive. However, it is possible that I have left out an emotion that you would have included. If this happens, just look it up in a general dictionary and add your emotion under the primary emotion you think it relates to. If you feel it's in a category by itself, then use a whole new blank sheet making your emotion the primary one. (Blank sheets can be found at the end of the *Thesaurus*.) Look up your word in a general thesaurus (you may have to check in more than one) and list the synonyms following the format here. Then proceed as you have with the rest of the workbook.

Research team:

Finally, I would like to express my deep appreciation to a few of Jeremy's other students for their time and support on this project, without whom it could not have been done. Thanks to all.

The Research Team: Laura Kelly, Lisa Marie Mascieri, Colleen J. McQuaide, Rob Rowand, and Roseanne Shaker.

-- Maura C. Kelly

Abandon	A thorough yielding to natural impulses, esp. Enthusiasm, exuberance—IMPASSIONED, p. 148]
Abandoned	Feeling, or the experience of being forsaken or cast off—[ABANDONED, p. 103]
Abashed	A feeling of shame or guilt; a feeling of inferiority—[HUMILIATED, p. 145]
Abhor	To regard with extreme disgust and hatred, detest utterly; loathe—[HATE, p. 143]
Abject	1) cast off, rejected; 2) feeling low in position, condition or status—[LONELY, p. 157]
Abominate	To utterly loathe or detest; abhor—[HATE, p. 143]
Absorbed	Totally mentally concentrated—[CHARMED, p. 123]
Abused	The experience of being violated, defiled—HUMILIATED, p. 145]
Acerbic	Bitter and sharp, esp. In speech, manner or temper—[BITTER, p. 121]
Ache	Suffer continuous or prolonged dull pain or mental distress—[SAD, p. 175]
Acid	Displaying a biting, severe and unpleasant disposition—[BITTER, p. 121]
Acquisitive	Keen to acquire things; acquiring—[RAPACIOUS, p. 174]
Acrimonious	Bitter and irritating in tone or manner—[BITTER, p. 121]
Adamant	Unshakable; refusing to yield to requests—[ADAMANT, p. 104]
Addled	To make or become muddled or confused—[CONFUSED, p. 125]
Admire	Feeling of pleasure, wonder and approval at—[ADMIRE, p. 105]
Adore	To regard with the utmost esteem, love and respect or affection; to honor—[LOVE, p. 158]
Adventurous	Disposed to take risks; bold, daring—[VALIANT, p. 187]
Affable	Pleasant and easy to approach or talk to—[KINDLY, p. 151]
Affectionate	Loving, fond (of a thing or person); expressing or indicating affection—[WARM-HEARTED, p. 189]
Affinity	1) having a particular attraction for another person, esp. of the opposite sex; 2) sympathy marked by a community of interest; kinship—[LIKE, p. 155; WARM-HEARTED, p. 189]
Afflicted	Beset by a feeling of distress and grief—[MOURNFUL, p. 162]
Affronted	Feeling confused or ashamed—[HUMILIATED, p. 145]
Afraid	1) filled with fear or apprehension; 2) filled with regret over an unwanted situation; 3) dislike for something—[AFRAID, p. 106]
Agape	Open mouthed with wonder or expectation—[SHOCKED, p. 180]
Aggravated	Displeasure or anger roused by usu. Persistent and often petty goading—[ANNOYED, p. 114,]
Aggressive	Disposed to attack others, self assertive, forceful—[ADAMANT, p. 104]
Aghast	Terrified; struck with amazement—[SHOCKED, p. 180]
Agitated	Excited and often troubled mind and feelings; disturbed—[AGITATED, p. 108]
Agnostic	Have disbelief, doubt and uncertainty about something, usually unless given concrete proof—[DOUBTFUL, p. 130]
Agog	In eager readiness, expectant—[ZEALOUS, p. 192]
Agonize	To suffer great distress—[SAD, p. 175]
Alarmed	Suddenly disturbed, excited; struck with fear—[ALARMED, p. 110]
Alienated	Caused to become unfriendly or hostile; estranged—[ANGRY, p. 111]
Allegiance	Loyalty or devotion toward something or someone or a party or government—[FAITH, p. 133]
Allured	Enticed by charm or attraction—[CHARMED, p. 123]
Alone	Feeling solitary; lonely—[LONELY, p. 157]
Aloof	Distant; detached, unsympathetic—[UNFEELING, p. 185]
Amazed	Feeling overwhelming surprise or wonder; astonishment—[SHOCKED, p. 180]
Ambitious	Having a desire to achieve a particular goal—[ZEALOUS, p. 192]
Amiable	Friendly, kind in action, having a friendly disposition that inspires friendliness in return—[KINDLY, p. 151]
Amity	Desiring or fostering friendship; friendly—[KINDLY, p. 151]
Amorous	1) strongly moved by love and esp. Sexual love; 2) being in love; enamored—[LOVE, p. 158]
Amused	Diverted from seriousness; stimulated to laugh or smile—[HAPPY, p. 140]
Angry	Feeling anger or resentment, enraged, extremely displeased; revealing or expressing anger—[ANGRY, p. 111]
Angst	1) anxiety, neurotic fear; 2) guilt, remorse—[AFRAID, 106; GUILTY, p. 139]
Anguished	Experiencing severe bodily or mental pain or intense suffering—[SAD, p. 175]
Animated	Feeling and behaving lively or vivacious—[ZEALOUS, p. 192]
Animosity	Violent and active hatred; strong dislike—[HATE, p. 143]
Annoyed	Bothered or irritated; perturbed—[ANNOYED, p. 114]
Antagonized	Rendered actively opposed by another—[ANNOYED, p. 114]
Anticipative	Feeling expectation; to foresee and act in advance of—[HOPEFUL, p. 144]
Antipathy	Feeling of dislike, hatred or aversion—[DISLIKE, p. 129]

Anxious	1) characterized by extreme uneasiness of mind or brooding fear about some contingency; worried; 2) ardently or earnestly wishing—[IMPASSIONED, p. 148; NERVOUS, p. 164]
Apathetic	Not feeling emotion, uninterested, indifferent (towards or about something)—[APATHETIC, p. 116]
Appalled	Overcome with horror or consternation; dismayed—[SHOCKED, p. 180]
Appreciate	1) sensitively aware; recognizing aesthetic values; 2) expressing admiration, approval or gratitude—[EMPATHETIC, p. 132; LIKE, p. 155]
Apprehensive	Experiencing suspicion or fear of future trouble or evil—[AFRAID, p. 106]
Approve	Be in sympathy or agreement; pronounce or consider to be good or satisfactory, commend—[LIKE, p. 155]
Ardent	Characterized by warmth of feeling typically expressed in eager zealous support or activity—[ZEALOUS, p. 192]
Ardor	1) an often restless or transitory warmth of feeling; 2) extreme vigor or energy; zeal; loyalty; 3) sexual excitement—[IMPASSIONED, p. 148]
Aroused	Stirred up into activity or emotions—[AROUSED, p. 118]
Arrogant	Overbearing and self-important—[PROUD, p. 170]
Ashamed	Affected, embarrassed or disconcerted by shame—[HUMILIATED, p. 145]
Asperity	Harshness or sharpness of temper esp. As displayed in tone or manner; bitterness; acrimony—[ANGRY, p. 111]
Assured	1) certain; confident; 2) made sure—[HOPEFUL, p. 144]
Astonished	Suddenly surprised or amazed; astounded—[SHOCKED, p. 180]
Astounded	Shocked with surprise or wonder, overwhelmed with amazement; greatly astonished—[SHOCKED, p. 180]
Atrabilious	Melancholy, hypochondriac; acrimonious, splenetic—[DEPRESSED, p. 126; QUARRELSOME, p. 172]
Attached	Affectionate, devoted; part of a sympathetic, friendly or romantic connection—[LIKE, p. 155]
Attracted	Drawn, enticed or allured by someone or something—[LIKE, p. 155]
Audacious	Bold or daring, usually with great confidence; intrepid—[VALIANT, p. 187]
Austere	Stern; solemn; rigorously self-disciplined—[UNFEELING, p. 185]
Avaricious	Greedy for wealth; grasping—[RAPACIOUS, p. 174]
Averse	Turned away in thought or feeling; opposed, disinclined—[DISLIKE, p. 129]
Avid	Desirous to the point of greed; urgently eager; characterized by enthusiasm and vigorous pursuit—[RAPACIOUS, p. 174; IMPASSIONED, p. 148]
Awe	A feeling of wonder and amazement mixed with reverence and dread—[AFRAID, p. 106; BEWILDERED, p. 119]
Baffled	1) bewildered, confused; reduced to perplexity, puzzled; 2) defeated in one's efforts, thwarted, foiled—[CONFUSED, p. 125]
Baleful	Full of woe, misery or sorrow—[MOURNFUL, p. 162]
Bashful	Easily embarrassed and diffident; shy, timid—[TIMID, p. 181]
Bathetic	Marked by feeling the lowest, deepest or bottom of emotion—[SAD, p. 175]
Beaten	Conquered, defeated, overcome, baffled, dejected—[OVERWHELMED, p. 168]
Beatific	In a state of being perfectly blessed or happy—[HAPPY, p. 140]
Bedazzled	Dazzled to a point of confusion or amazement—[BEWILDERED, p. 119]
Beguiled	Deceived by trickery or flattery; misled—[CHARMED, p. 123]
Believe in	Have confidence, faith or trust in something or someone—[FAITH, p. 133]
Belittled	The sense and feeling of others thinking less of one; disparaged—[HUMILIATED, p. 145]
Bellicose	Quarrelsome or hostile nature; eager to fight or quarrel—[BITTER, p. 121]
Belligerent	Carrying hostilities, pugnacious—[BITTER, p. 121]
Benevolent	Desirous of the good of others; of a kindly disposition; charitable—[EMPATHETIC, p. 132]
Benumbed	Feeling totally deadened or stupefied—[BEWILDERED, p. 119]
Berserk	Behaving or inclined to behave wild or frenzied—[IMPASSIONED, p. 148]
Betrayed	Feeling the pain from having been given up treacherously; feeling lead astray, deceived—[ABANDONED, p. 103]
Beware	Be cautious, take heed; take care; take notice—[DOUBTFUL, p. 130]
Bewildered	Having lost one's bearings; perplexed or confused esp. By a complexity, variety, or multitude of objects or considerations; mystified; dazed; confounded—[BEWILDERED, p. 119]
Bewitched	Enchanted; fascinated or captivated as by charm—[CHARMED, p. 123]
Bile	An experience of anger, peevishness—[FURIOUS, p. 137; QUARRELSOME, p. 172]
Bitter	Angered by a severe pain or suffering; grievous; full of affliction—[BITTER, p. 121]
Black	Pessimistic or dismal; sullen or hostile; gloomy—[MOURNFUL, p. 162; PESSIMISTIC, p. 169]

Blackguardly	Given to behaving villainous or scurrilous—[MISCHIEVOUS, p. 159]
Blasé	Cloyed with or tired of pleasure; bored or unimpressed by things from having seen or experienced them too often—[APATHETIC, p. 116]
Blissful	Reveling in complete and utter happiness and joy; ecstatic—[HAPPY, p. 140]
Blithe	Feeling or showing a carefree or gay disposition—[FESTIVE, p. 134]
Blocked	The state or condition of being obstructed; experiencing a sudden stoppage of speech or thought, usually caused by emotional tension—[TIMID, p. 181]
Blue	Depressed, low-spirited; dismayed, downcast—[DEPRESSED, p. 126]
Boggled	Overwhelmed or bewildered with amazement—[BEWILDERED, p. 119]
Boisterous	Noisily jolly or rowdy; clamorous; rough and noisy—[FESTIVE, p. 134]
Bold	To be brave, fearless, daring and courageous—[VALIANT, p. 187]
Bored	Made weary by tedious talk, dullness or monotony—[APATHETIC, p. 116]
Bothered	Annoyed esp. By provocation; irked; anxious or concerned—[AGITATED, p. 108; ANNOYED, p. 114]
Bouncy	Vivacious; spirited; resilient; exuberant—[FESTIVE, p. 134]
Brave	Fearless in the presence of danger; courageous—[VALIANT, p. 187]
Brazen	Behaving or feeling bold or impudent—[VALIANT, p. 187]
Breathless	Holding one's breath from emotion; stunned, thrilled; gasping—[SHOCKED, p. 180]
Broken	Crushed in health, strength, feelings, etc.; Exhausted, enfeebled; subdued, humbled—[OVERWHELMED, p. 168]
Brooding	Meditating in a moody or resentful way—[MOODY, p. 161]
Bugged	Annoyed or bothered—[ANNOYED, p. 114]
Bullheaded	Blindly stubborn—[ADAMANT, p. 104]
Buoyant	Having or showing lightness or resilience of spirit; cheerfulness—[HOPEFUL, p. 144]
Burdened	Encumbered and oppressed—[OPPRESSED, p. 166]
Callous	Lacking pity, mercy, etc.; Unfeeling; insensitive—[UNFEELING, p. 185]
Calm	Free from excitement or passion; still, tranquil, quiet, serene—[SERENE, p. 178]
Cantankerous	Quarrelsome; perverse; bad-tempered—[QUARRELSOME, p. 172]
Captivated	Charmed or fascinated by someone; enchanted—[CHARMED, p. 123]
Care (for)	Feel concern or interest—[LIKE, p. 155]
Caring	Compassionate, concerned, involved in caring for others—[WARM-HEARTED, p. 189]
Casual	Feeling or showing little concern—[APATHETIC, p. 116]
Censorious	Fault finding, severely critical; inclined to disapproval—[BITTER, p. 121]
Chafe	An irritation or annoyance—[ANNOYED, p. 114]
Chagrined	Feeling vexation, arising from disappointment or humiliation—[HUMILIATED, p. 145; SAD, p. 175]
Charmed	Attracted to or fascinated with; delighted and pleased—[CHARMED, p. 123]
Chaste	Abstaining from unlawful or immoral or all sexual intercourse; pure, virginal—[TIMID, p. 181]
Cheerful	In good spirits; merry; happy—[HAPPY, p. 140]
Cheerless	Gloomy, low in spirits; sad—[DEPRESSED, p. 126]
Cherish	1) value, hold dear, cling to (esp. Hopes, feelings, ideas, etc.); 2) treat or regard (a person) affectionately; make much of; fondle—[LOVE, p. 158]
Chivalrous	Courageous, courteous, honorable and gallant—[VALIANT, p. 187]
Choleric	Irascible, hot-tempered—[FURIOUS, p. 137]
Churlish	Boorish, ill-bred, surly; niggardly, grudging—[QUARRELSOME, p. 172]
Cocky	Arrogant, conceited; saucy, impertinent—[PROUD, p. 170]
Cold-hearted	Unfeeling; indifferent; not cordial or kind; gloomy—[UNFEELING, p. 185]
Comforted	Feeling solace or consolation; ease of the mind or body—[SERENE, p. 178]
Compassionate	Sympathetically conscious of other's distress together with a desire to alleviate it—[EMPATHETIC, p. 132]
Complacent	Content, self-satisfaction or security, often with an unawareness of danger or trouble—[SERENE, p. 178]
Composed	Calmed, pacified, tranquilized—[SERENE, p. 178]
Compunction	Anxiety arising from guilt—[GUILTY, p. 139]
Conceited	Having an exaggerated opinion of oneself, one's merits, etc.; Vain—[PROUD, p. 170]
Concerned	Interested, involved; troubled, anxious; showing concern—[NERVOUS, p. 164]
Concupiscent	Eagerly desirous; lustful—[LASCIVIOUS, p. 153]
Confidence in	Sure of something or someone else—[FAITH, p. 133; HOPEFUL, p. 144]
Confident	Sure of oneself or something; bold—[VALIANT, p. 187]
Confounded	Brought into confusion or bewilderment; perplexed—[BEWILDERED, p. 119]
Confused	A state of disorder or bewilderment; perplexed; disconcerted—[CONFUSED, p. 125]
Congenial	Friendly, sociable; agreeable—[KINDLY, p. 151]
Consecrated	Solemnly dedicated to a service or goal—[XENOPHOBIC, p. 190]
Consternated	Experiencing great fear, shock, amazement or dismay that makes one feel helpless, or

	hinders or throws into confusion—[SHOCKED, p. 180]
Contempt	The action of scorning or despising; the mental attitude in which something or someone is considered as worthless or of little account—[HATE, p. 143]
Content	To be pleased or satisfied with what is and no more; to feel at ease—[SERENE, p. 178]
Contrary	Opposite in nature or character; antagonistic or hostile; untoward or unfavorable—[ADAMANT, p. 104]
Contrite	Crushed or broken in spirit by a sense of wrongdoing; sincerely penitent—[GUILTY, p. 139]
Convivial	Sociable; jovial; merry, festive—[FESTIVE, p. 134]
Cool	Not affected by passion or emotion; undisturbed, calm—[SERENCE, p. 178]
Coquettish	Like (that of) a woman who trifles with men's affections or who is given to flirting—[FLIRTATIOUS, p. 136]
Cordial	Warm and sincere, courteous and friendly; hearty—[KINDLY, p. 151]
Courageous	Having and displaying the ability to face difficulty or danger with confidence; fearless, brave—[VALIANT, p. 187]
Covetous	Strongly desiring something belonging to another—[JEALOUS, p. 150]
Cowardly	Lacking courage, or having fear in face of danger—[TIMID, p. 181]
Coy	Displaying modest backwardness, shy; unresponsive to amorous advances, esp. In an affected or coquettish way—[FLIRTATIOUS, p. 136]
Crabby	Bad-tempered or morose—[QUARRELSOME, p. 172]
Cranky	Ill-tempered; grouchy; cross—[QUARRELSOME, p. 172]
Crave	Desire or long for intensely, urgently or abnormally—[YEARN, p. 191]
Crazed	1) insane; 2) to be made insane—[IMPASSIONED, p. 148]
Crazy.about	1) distracted with desire or excitement; 2) absurdly fond; infatuated; 3) passionately preoccupied; obsessed—[LOVE, p. 158]
Credence	Belief as to the truth of something—[FAITH, p. 133]
Crestfallen	Feeling shame or humiliation; dejected—[HUMILIATED, p. 145]
Cross	Annoyed, ill-tempered (at, with); expressing or showing annoyance or ill temper—[ANGRY, p. 111; ANNOYED, p. 114]
Crotchety	Peevish; having a perverse belief or preference, usu. About a trivial matter—[QUARRELSOME, p. 172]
Cruel	Intentionally causing pain, suffering or distress to others—[BITTER, p. 121]
Crush (on)	Be or become infatuated with—[LOVE, p. 158]
Crushed	Overwhelmed with confusion or humiliated—[HUMILIATED, p. 145]
Curious	Desire to learn or know about something; inquisitive—[RAPACIOUS, p. 174]
Cynical	1) believing that all human actions have selfish motives; 2) feeling or showing contempt for accepted standards of honesty or morality—[BITTER, p. 121; PESSIMISTIC, p. 169]
Cyprianic	Of or pertaining to a lewd person or prostitute—[LASCIVIOUS, p. 153]
Dander	Temper, anger or indignation—[ANGRY, p. 111]
Daring	1) willing to take risks; full of courage and audacity; 2) boldness—[VALIANT, p. 187]
Dashed	Depressed; daunted; confounded, abashed—[DEPRESSED, p. 126; HUMILIATED, p. 145]
Dastardly	1) sneaky and malicious; 2) cowardly and fearsome—[MISCHIEVOUS, p. 159; TIMID, p. 181]
Daunted	Discouraged, dispirited, intimidated—[AFRAID, p. 106]
Dazed	In a state of being or feeling stunned or bewildered—[BEWILDERED, p. 119]
Dazzled	Deeply impressed; overwhelmed, amazed, or bewildered—[BEWILDERED, p. 119]
Deadened	Deprived of vitality, force, etc.; Dulled, benumbed; made dead or insensible—[APATHETIC, p. 116]
Debased	The feeling or state of having had one's dignity or significance reduced; degraded—[HUMILIATED, p. 145]
Debauched	Dissolute, licentious; perverted from virtue or morality; corrupted, depraved esp. By intemperance or sensual indulgence—[LASCIVIOUS, p. 153]
Debilitated	Made weak or feeble; enervated—[OVERWHELMED, p. 168]
Deceived	Misled or caused to believe what is not true; deluded—[CHARMED, p. 123]
Dedicated	Wholly committed or devoted to a particular cause, goal, idea, etc.—[xenophobic, p. 190]
Defeated	Frustrated, baffled; caused to fail—[OVERWHELMED, p. 168]
Deferential	Characterized by or showing deference, respectful—[ADMIRE, p. 105]
Degraded	The feeling of having been reduced in status or reputation; the feeling of abasement—[HUMILIATED, p. 145]
Dejected	Low-spirited, downcast, depressed—[DEPRESSED, p. 126]
Delighted	In a state of feeling highly pleased—[HAPPY, p. 140]
Delirious	Experiencing violent emotion or excitement—[HAPPY, p. 140]
Deluded	Misled or deceived in the mind or judgment; beguiled—[CHARMED, p. 123]

Demanding	Hard to satisfy, exacting, difficult—[RAPACIOUS, p. 174]
Demeaned	The state or feeling of having had one's dignity or standing lowered; debased—[HUMILIATED, p. 145]
Demoralized	Lowered or destroyed morale or confidence; disheartened—[SAD, p. 175]
Demure	Affectedly or artificially quiet and serious; coy; decorous; calm, settled, still—[TIMID, p. 181]
Deprecated	Having been or feeling depreciated; belittled—[HUMILIATED, p. 145]
Depreciated	The feeling of having been reduced in value or worth; disparaged, degraded—[HUMILIATED, p. 145]
Depressed	Dejected or cast down; gloomy—[DEPRESSED, p. 126]
Deranged	Unable to function normally; mentally disturbed; unsettled, disordered—[NERVOUS, p. 164]
Deserted	Feeling as though one has been forsaken, abandoned, left desolate—[ABANDONED, p. 103]
Desire	To hope or wish for ardently; crave; to want in a sexual way—[YEARN, p. 191]
Desirous	Impelled or governed by desire—[RAPACIOUS, p. 174]
Desolate	Left alone, lonely; destitute of joy or comfort; forlorn, wretched—[LONELY, p. 157]
Despair	To lose or give up hope—[DEPRESSED, p. 126]
Despairing	Having given up all hope—[PESSIMISTIC, p. 169]
Desperate	1) having a great desire, need, etc.; 2) in despair; given up as hopeless; leaving little or no room for help—[YEARN, p. 191; PESSIMISTIC, p. 169]
Despise	Feeling contempt or scorn—[HATE, p. 143]
Despondent	Feeling or showing extreme discouragement, dejection or depression—[SAD, p. 175]
Determined	Having a firm or fixed purpose; resolute; decided—[ADAMANT, p. 104]
Detest	Dislike or hate intensely; abhor—[HATE, p. 143]
Devastated	Lay wasted, ravaged; made desolate or wretched—[OVERWHELMED, p. 168]
Devilish	1) wicked, fiendish; violent, terrible; 2) like the Devil or a devil—[MISCHIEVOUS, p. 159]
Devoted	Ardent in loyalty and dedication; concentrated—[XENOPHOBIC, p. 190]
Diffident	Lacking self-confidence or esteem; shy, timid—[TIMID, p. 181]
Dignified	Inherently noble; self-respected and feeling worthy—[PROUD, p. 170]
Dirgeful	Full of lamentation; mournful—[MOURNFUL, p. 162]
Disappointed	Feeling frustration due to the failure to satisfy to hope or expectations of—[SAD, p. 175]
Disapprobation	Disapproval due to lack of morals or principles; condemnation—[DISGUSTED, p. 128]
Disapproval	To reject or condemn someone or something; to refuse to accept—[DISGUSTED, p. 128]
Disbelieve	Refuse to accept something as being true or real—[DOUBTFUL, p. 130]
Discombobulated	In a state of being or feeling upset or confused—[AGITATED, p. 108; CONFUSED, p. 125]
Discomfited	Baffled, thwarted; thrown into confusion, disconcerted, embarrassed—[HUMILIATED, p. 145]
Discomfort	A feeling of uneasiness, pain and distress—[DEPRESSED, p. 126]
Discomposed	Disturbed, ruffled; agitated; thrown into confusion—[AGITATED, p. 108]
Disconcerted	Feeling ruffled, flustered—[AGITATED, p. 108]
Disconsolate	Without consolation or comfort; forlorn, inconsolable, unhappy disappointed—[SAD, p. 175]
Discouraged	Deprived of courage, confidence, hope or the will to proceed; disheartened, dejected—[DEPRESSED, p. 126]
Disdainful	Scornful, contemptuous; full of or showing disdain—[HATE, p. 143]
Disesteem	Lack of self-confidence or belief in oneself and abilities—[HUMILIATED, p. 145]
Disgraced	Shamed or dishonored; discredited—[HUMILIATED, p. 145]
Disgruntled	Feeling discontented or unsatisfied—[ANNOYED, p. 114]
Disgusted	Aversion, nausea and repugnance; loathing—[DISGUSTED, p. 128]
Disheartened	Having lost all courage, confidence and hope; depressed—DEPRESSED, p. 126]
Dishonored	Feeling disgraced, shamed or indignified—[HUMILIATED, p. 145]
Disillusioned	Disenchanted or freed from illusion—[SAD, p. 175]
Disinclined	Feeling dislike or aversion; reluctant, unwilling—[DISLIKE, p. 129]
Disinterested	Without self-interest or concern; indifferent—[APATHETIC, p. 116]
Dislike	To feel aversion or antipathy towards; distaste—[DISLIKE, p. 129]
Dismayed	Discouraged or depressed; feeling of apprehension and fear—[AFRAID, p. 106; DEPRESSED, p. 126]
Dispassionate	Free from the influence or effect of strong emotion; calm; impartial—[SERENE, p. 178]
Dispirited	1) deprived of essential quality or force; deprive of vigor, weaken; 2) lowered morale, despondent, disheartened—[DEPRESSED, p. 126]
Displeased	1) unsatisfied; 2) angry, annoyed or irritated; dislike—[ANGRY, p. 111; ANNOYED, p. 114]

Disquieted	Uneasy or restless in the mind; disturbed—[AGITATED, p. 108]
Disrelish	Experiencing distaste or aversion—[DISLIKE, p. 129]
Disreputed	Discredited or degraded; shamed—[HUMILIATED, p. 145]
Dissatisfied	Feeling discontented or displeased—[DISGUSTED, p. 128]
Dissolute	Relaxed, enfeebled, lacking firmness of temperament; having one's energies or attention relaxed; careless, negligent—[APATHETIC, p. 116]
Distaste	A dislike or aversion - usually of food—[DISLIKE, p. 129]
Distempered	Disordered, disturbed; made ill-humored, ill at ease, vexed or troubled—[ANGRY, p. 111]
Distracted	Mentally drawn in different directions; so confused or troubled that one hardly knows how to act; unable to settle because of worry, distress, etc.; Troubled, disturbed—[AGITATED, p. 108; CONFUSED, p. 125]
Distraught	Deeply agitated; mentally deranged; distracted; bewildered—[NERVOUS, p. 164]
Distressed	Suffering extreme mental, physical or emotional anguish or pain; suffering; needing immediate help—[AFRAID, p. 106; ALARMED, p. 110]
Distrust	Having no faith or belief in someone—[DOUBTFUL, p. 130]
Disturbed	Upset mentally or emotionally; disquieted or agitated—[AGITATED, p. 108; AROUSED, p. 118]
Diverted	Having had one's attention distracted—[CHARMED, p. 123]
Dizzy	Giddy; mentally confused or dazed—[CONFUSED, p. 125]
Docile	1) apt or willing to learn; 2) submissive to training or direction, not assertive—[TIMID, p. 181]
Doleful	Full of grief; expressing grief; sad—[MOURNFUL, p. 162]
Dolorous	Expressing grief or sadness; mournful—[MOURNFUL, p. 162]
Doting	Being infatuated, having or showing excessive affection—[LOVE, p. 158]
Doubtful	Feeling or admitting uncertainty; ambiguous—[DOUBTFUL, p. 130]
Doughty	Brave, fearless; valiant—[VALIANT, p. 187]
Dour	Severe, stern, relentless; fierce, bold—[VALIANT, p. 187]
Downcast	Depressed or downhearted; despondent—[DEPRESSED, p. 126]
Downhearted	Feeling downcast or dejected—[DEPRESSED, p. 126]
Downtrodden	Crushed by oppression or tyranny; oppressed, kept under—[OPPRESSED, p. 166]
Dread	A feeling of overwhelming apprehension; terror and awe—[AFRAID, 106]
Dreamy	Full of dreams; given to dreaming or fantasy—[SENTIMENTAL, p. 177]
Dreary	To be dismal or gloomy; downcast; monotonous; dull—[MOURNFUL, p. 162]
Dubious	Full of uncertainty and doubt; undecided—[DOUBTFUL, p. 130]
Dumbfounded	Struck dumb; confounded; nonplused—[CONFUSED, p. 125]
Eager	Marked by desire or yearning; earnest—[ZEALOUS, p. 192]
Earnest	A serious and sincere state of mind; zealous—[ZEALOUS, p. 192]
Ease	A state of rest or relaxation free from anxiety, worry, agitation concern, discomfort or effort; leisure—[SERENE, p. 178]
Easygoing	Fond of comfort; indolent, not strict, taking things as they come—[APATHETIC, p. 116]
Ebullient	Enthusiastically bursting with feeling; anxious—[ZEALOUS, p. 192]
Ecstatic	Experiencing intense joy or delight; feeling overpowering emotion or exaltation; experiencing a sudden, intense feeling—[HAPPY, p. 140]
Edgy	Feeling anxious or nervous; irritable—[NERVOUS, p. 164]
Effervescent	To show or feel in high spirits—[FESTIVE, p. 134]
Elated	To have high or enlivened spirits; proud—[HAPPY, p. 140; PROUD, p. 170]
Elegiac	Expressing sorrow or lamentation—[MOURNFUL, p. 162]
Embarrassed	Caused to be self-conscious or uncomfortable; abashed—[HUMILIATED, p. 145]
Embittered	Intensely hostile, bitter or discontented—[FURIOUS, p. 137]
Empathetic	Relating to and understanding the feelings of another—[EMPATHETIC, p. 132]
Enamored	1) inflamed with love; 2) fascinated—[CHARMED, p. 123]
Enchanted	1) influenced by or as if by charms and incantation; bewitched; deeply attracted and moved; 2) roused to ecstatic admiration—[CHARMED, p. 123]
Encumbered	Burdened with difficulty or obligation; impeded—[OPPRESSED, p. 166]
Enervated	Deprived of nerve, force or strength; vigor destroyed; weakened—[BEWILDERED, p. 119]
Enfeebled	Deprived of strength or weakened—[BEWILDERED, p. 119]
Enjoy	Take great delight or pleasure in; feel satisfied with—[HAPPY, p. 140]
Enlivened	Enhanced liveliness; happy or cheerful—[FESTIVE, p. 134]
Enmity	Ill-will, hatred; the feelings for an enemy—[HATE, p. 143]
Enraged	Made very angry or violent; exacerbated, inflamed—[FURIOUS, p. 137]
Enraptured	Filled with delight about something or someone—[CHARMED, p. 123]
Enslaved	Made complete subject to or dominated by habit, superstition, passion or the like—[OPPRESSED, p. 166]

Enthralled	Charmed, fascinated; enslaved—[CHARMED, p. 123]
Enthusiastic	Filled with or marked by enthusiasm—[ZEALOUS, p. 192]
Enticed	Attracted or lead on by aroused hope or craving; allured—[CHARMED, p. 123]
Entranced	Carried away with delight, wonder or rapture; put into a trance—[CHARMED, p. 123]
Envenomed	Embittered; morally corrupt, tainted—[TRUCULENT, p. 184]
Envious	Feeling resentment towards someone; jealous—[JEALOUS, p. 150]
Erotic	Of or pertaining to sexual love; amatory, esp. Tending to arouse sexual desire or excitement—[LASCIVIOUS, p. 153]
Esteem	To regard with admiration or respect—[ADMIRE, p. 105]
Estranged	Made unfriendly, hostile, unsympathetic or indifferent—[ANGRY, p. 111]
Euphoric	Feeling great happiness, well-being, confidence or elation—[HAPPY, p. 140]
Exalted	Elated with joy; ecstatic—[HAPPY, p. 140]
Exasperated	Feeling frustrated, irritated or angered—[ANNOYED, p. 114; FURIOUS, p. 137]
Excited	Roused or stimulated to strong emotion; agitated—[AROUSED, p. 118; IMPASSIONED, p. 148]
Exhilarated	Cheerful; excited; refreshed, stimulated—[HAPPY, p. 140]
Exposed	The sense of being laid open to danger, attack, harm, etc.—[ABANDONED, p. 103]
Exuberant	Joyously unrestrained and enthusiastic—[ZEALOUS, p. 192]
Faith	Confidence or trust in a person or thing—[FAITH, p. 133]
Famished	Suffering for lack of something necessary; starving to death—[YEARN, p. 191]
Fanatical	Actuated or characterized by extreme, uncritical enthusiasm or zeal—[IMPASSIONED, p. 148]
Fanciful	Marked by fancy or unrestrained imagination rather than by reason or experience; whimsical—[SENTIMENTAL, p. 177]
Fancy	1) to have a fancy for, like; 2) to visualize; imagine—[LIKE, p. 155]
Fascinated	Transfixed and held spellbound by an irresistible power—[CHARMED, p. 123]
Favor	Have a liking or preference for; approve—[LIKE, p. 155]
Fazed	Feeling disconcerted, perturbed—[AGITATED, p. 108]
Fearful	Full of a feeling of anxiety, reverence and dread, usually in the presence or nearness of danger, evil, pain - or the illusion of such—[AFRAID, p. 106]
Fearless	To be brave and courageous; without fear—[VALIANT, p. 187]
Fed up	Surfeited, disgusted, extremely bored or tired—[DISGUSTED, p. 128]
Feel	Sympathetic; kind or generous—[EMPATHETIC, p. 132]
Felicitous	Enjoying great happiness—[HAPPY, p. 140]
Ferocious	Savagely fierce or violently cruel—[TRUCULENT, p. 184]
Fervent	Intensely enthusiastic; ardent—[IMPASSIONED, p. 148]
Fervid	Feeling or behaving intense or impassioned—[IMPASSIONED, p. 148]
Festive	Feeling joyous or merry—[FESTIVE, p. 134]
Feverish	Behaving or acting in an excited or restless or hectic manner—[IMPASSIONED, p. 148]
Fidelity	Strict observances of promises, duties, etc.—[FAITH, p. 133]
Fidgety	Uneasy, restless, impatient; inclined to fidget—[NERVOUS, p. 164]
Fierce	1) experiencing a violent, uncontrolled quality or feeling; 2) intensely eager; ardent—[TRUCULENT, p. 184]
Flabbergasted	Overcome with amazement; dumbfounded—[BEWILDERED, p. 119]
Flirtatious	Given to behave in a superficially amorous manner—[FLIRTATIOUS, p. 136]
Flustered	Put into a state of nervous, agitated confusion; upset—[AGITATED, p. 108]
Fond	Of a person, an action or attribute: affectionate, doting; tender—[LIKE, p. 155]
Forlorn	Sad and lonely because of isolation or desertion; nearly hopeless—[LONELY, p. 157]
Forsaken	The experience of having been deserted, left solitary or desolate—[ABANDONED, p. 103]
Fractious	Hard to manage; peevish; irritable; cross; unruly—[QUARRELSOME, p. 172]
Frantic	Wild with anger, pain, worry—[NERVOUS, p. 164]
Frazzled	Completely fatigued, usu. By too much strain or nervous tension—[NERVOUS, p. 164]
Frenetic	Wildly excited, over enthusiastic, fanatical—[IMPASSIONED, p. 148]
Frenzied	A state of wild excitement or violent agitation—[IMPASSIONED, p. 148]
Fretful	Irritated, annoyed or querulous; vexed or peevish; worrisome—[NERVOUS, p. 164; QUARRELSOME, p. 172]
Friendless	Destitute of friends—[LONELY, p. 157]
Friendly	Favorably disposed; warm, helpful, kind or comforting—[KINDLY, p. 151]
Frightened	1) the state of having fear of something or someone; terrified or scared; 2) made to be afraid—[ALARMED, p. 110]
Frigid	Without warmth of feeling or manner; stiff and formal—[UNFEELING, p. 185]
Frivolous	Silly and light-minded; not properly serious or sensible—[FESTIVE, p. 134]
Frustrated	Discouraged or baffled; thwarted; disappointed—[SAD, p. 175]
Fuddled	1) stupefied, muddled, confused; 2) intoxicated, confused by drink or drug—

[BEWILDERED, p. 119]

Fulfilled	Having a completely satisfied appetite or desire; thoroughly enjoying having received what one wished for—[HAPPY, p. 140]
Fuming	Experiencing or expressing an outburst of anger, annoyance; etc.; Showing or giving way to such emotion—[FURIOUS, p. 137]
Funereal	1) sorrowful, mournful; 2) of or relating to a funeral; befitting or suggesting a funeral (as in solemnity)—[MOURNFUL, p. 162]
Furious	Uncontrollably and violently angered or enraged—[FURIOUS, p. 137]
Gallant	Noble in spirit or action; displaying heroic bravery or courage—[VALIANT, p. 187]
Galled	1) irritated, vexed; 2) made to feel bitter—[ANNOYED, p. 114; BITTER, p. 121]
Gay	Feeling and acting merry, bright and lively—[FESTIVE, p. 134]
Genial	Friendly and sympathetic; cordial and kindly; amiable; good humored—[KINDLY, p. 151]
Glad	1) experiencing pleasure, joy or delight; 2) made pleased, satisfied or grateful (often used with of)—[HAPPY, p. 140]
Gleeful	Demonstrating or feeling joy or exultation—[FESTIVE, p. 134]
Gloomy	To be dejected and dreary; despondent; pessimistic—[PESSIMISTIC, p. 169]
Glum	Sullen, frowning, silent and morose; looking or feeling dejected or displeased—[SAD, p. 175]
Goaded	Spurred, incited or tormented toward some disposition or action—[ANGRY, p. 111]
Goatish	Displaying a quite lecherous demeanor; animalistic—[LASCIVIOUS, p. 153]
Good-hearted	Feeling or behaving kindly or well meaning—[WARM-HEARTED, p. 189]
Gracious	Having or showing kindness, courtesy, charm, etc.; Merciful; compassionate—[KINDLY, p. 151]
Grateful	Deeply appreciative and thankful to someone—[HAPPY, p. 140]
Gratified	1) a feeling of pleasure or satisfaction; 2) to be made happy—[SERENE, p. 178]
Grave	Dignified and solemn or sedate in manner or mien; somber; dull—[MOURNFUL, p. 162]
Greedy	Having an intense desire or inordinate appetite for food or drink; voracious; eager for gain, wealth, etc.; Avaricious, covetous, rapacious—[RAPACIOUS, p. 174]
Grievous	Severe or serious; a grave wound or pain—[MOURNFUL, p. 162]
Groggy	Staggering or dazed, as from exhaustion or blows—[CONFUSED, p. 125]
Grouchy	Grumbling; sulky, irritable, bad-tempered—[QUARRELSOME, p. 172]
Groveling	Humbling oneself; behaving obsequiously esp. In seeking favor or forgiveness; lying or moving in a prone position with the face downward esp. In abject humility—[HUMILIATED, p. 145]
Grudging	1) unwilling, reluctant; 2) done, given or allowed unwillingly, reluctantly or sparingly—[UNFEELING, p. 185]
Grumpy	Behaving and/or feeling grouchy, bad-tempered—[QUARRELSOME, p. 172]
Guilty	Conscious of, or moved by, having willfully committed a crime or moral offense—[GUILTY, p. 139]
Gushy	Gushing over someone or something; over effusive—[SENTIMENTAL, p. 177]
Gusto	Keen enjoyment; relish, zest—[ZEALOUS, p. 192]
Half-hearted	Lacking interest, spirit or enthusiasm—[APATHETIC, p. 116]
Hanker	To have a strong or persistent desire; yearn—[YEARN, p. 191]
Happy	1) a state of well-being and contentment; joy; 2) pleasurable or satisfying—[HAPPY, p. 140]
Hard	Not easily moved; unfeeling; unfriendly; hostile—[ANGRY, p. 111]
Hate	An extreme disliking or aversion; to detest or abhor—[HATE, p. 143]
Haughty	Having or showing great pride in oneself and disdain, contempt or scorn for others; proud; arrogant—[PROUD, p. 170]
Hazy	Somewhat vague, obscure, confused or indefinite—[CONFUSED, p. 125]
Headstrong	Determined to have one's own way; willful; obstinate—[ADAMANT, p. 104]
Heart-broken	Affected by overwhelming sorrow or distress—[MOURNFUL, p. 162; SAD, p. 175]
Heartache	Distress of mind esp. From a disappointment in love—[SAD, p. 175]
Heartfelt	Deep or sincere in feeling—[KINDLY, p. 151]
Heartless	Lacking in spirit, courage or enthusiasm; lacking kindness or feeling; hard and pitiless—[UNFEELING, p. 185]
Heartsick	Very despondent; depressed—[SAD, p. 175]
Hearty	Expressed with or marked by exuberant warmth—[KINDLY, p. 151]
Heavy-hearted	Feeling sad, melancholy or doleful—[SAD, p. 175]
Helpless	Weak or dependent; unable to help oneself—[OPPRESSED, p. 166]
Hesitant	Hesitating, irresolute or undecided—[AFRAID, p. 106]
High	In an elated mood; merry or hilarious—[FESTIVE, p. 134]
High-spirited	Characterized by a bold or energetic spirit—[ZEALOUS, p. 192]
Honor	Regard with honor, respect highly, revere—[ADMIRE, p. 105]
Honored	Extremely appreciative or thankful for admiration, respect or a bestowed honor—

[PROUD, p. 170]

Hopeful	Expecting to get what one wants—[HOPEFUL, p. 144]
Hopeless	Having or feeling no hope; despairing—[PESSIMISTIC, p. 169]
Horrified	1) experiencing painful and intense fear, dread or dismay; 2) intensely averse or feeling repugnance—[ALARMED, p. 110; DISGUSTED, p. 128]
Hospitable	Feeling or displaying warmth and good will toward guests—[KINDLY, p. 151]
Hostile	Opposed in feeling, action or character; antagonistic—[QUARRELSOME, p. 172]
Hot	1) lustful, amorous, sexually aroused; 2) very angry, indignant—[AROUSED, p. 118; FURIOUS, p. 137]
Hot-tempered	Given to behaving impulsively angry; short-tempered—[QUARRELSOME, p. 172]
Huff	A sudden rush of anger or arrogance; a fit of pique or offended dignity—[ANGRY, p. 111]
Huffy	Quick to take offense or go into a huff; touchy—[QUARRELSOME, p. 172]
Humane	Kind; benevolent; respecting life—[EMPATHETIC, p. 132]
Humble	Having a low estimate of one's own importance; lacking assertion; deferential—[TIMID, p. 181]
Humbled	Made to feel insignificant or inferior—[HUMILIATED, p. 145]
Humiliated	The feeling of having lost all pride and dignity; humbled—[HUMILIATED, p. 145]
Hung-up	Emotionally disturbed (by); neurotic, repressed, etc.—[TIMID, p. 181]
Hunger	Having a strong desire or craving spec. Eager for money, profits, etc.—[YEARN, p. 191]
Hurt	Feeling or suffering mental or physical pain—[SAD, p. 175]
Hysterical	Exhibiting an uncontrollable outburst of emotion or fear, often characterized by irrationality, laughter, weeping, etc.—[NERVOUS, p. 164]
Idolize	Adore or love to excess, make an idol of, worship idolatrously—[ADMIRE, p. 105]
Ignominy	Extreme disgrace, dishonor and humility—[HUMILIATED, p. 145]
Ill-humored	Bad-tempered, sullen; given to bad moods—[ANGRY, p. 111]
Ill-tempered	Having a bad temper; irritable—[ANGRY, p. 111]
Impassioned	Filled with passion, deeply moved or excited; passionate, ardent—[IMPASSIONED, p. 148]
Impassive	Calm; serene; not subject to suffering—[SERENE, p. 178]
Impatient	1) not patient; restless or short of temper esp. Under irritation, delay or opposition; intolerant; 2) eagerly desirous; anxious—[ANGRY, p. 111; ZEALOUS, p. 192]
Impetuous	Impulsive; doing things suddenly, with very little thought—[ZEALOUS, p. 192]
Incensed	Utterly angry, enraged or exasperated—[FURIOUS, p. 137]
Incited	Stimulated, usu. To a fit of anger; given an incentive, spur or exciting stimulus—[ANGRY, p. 111]
Inclined	Favorably disposed toward; having a mental propensity—[LIKE, p. 155]
Inconsolable	Unable to be consoled or comforted; disconsolate—[DEPRESSED, p. 126]
Incredulity	State of disbelief or doubt; uncertainty—[DOUBTFUL, p. 130]
Indifferent	Being disinterested and without concern; uninterested; apathetic—[APATHETIC, p. 116]
Indignant	Feeling angry due to some injustice—[BITTER, p. 121]
Indisposed	Rather disinclined towards something or someone—[DISLIKE, p. 129]
Indolent	Averse to work or exertion; self indulgent, lazy, idle—[APATHETIC, p. 116]
Infatuated	Foolish; deprived of sound judgment; inspired with a foolish or extravagant love or admiration—[CHARMED, p. 123]
Inflamed	Having one's passion and anger stirred up—[FURIOUS, p. 137]
Infuriated	Provoked to fury, made mad with rage—[FURIOUS, p. 137]
Inhibited	Restrained, curbed; held back or kept from some action, feeling, etc.—[TIMID, p. 181]
Inhuman	Destitute of natural human sympathy for others; monstrous—[BITTER, p. 121]
Inquisitive	Unduly curious and eager for knowledge—[RAPACIOUS, p. 174]
Insecure	Unsure and uncertain, usually in oneself or abilities; doubtful—[TIMID, p. 181]
Insensitive	Lacking sensibility or feeling; without physical sensation or feeling—[BITTER, p. 121]
Insistent	Dwelling firmly on something; assertive; demanding—[ADAMANT, p. 104]
Insolent	Proud, disdainful, arrogant, overbearing; offensively contemptuous of the rights of others—[PROUD, p. 170]
Insouciant	Behaving or feeling carefree or undisturbed—[SERENCE, p. 178]
Inspired	Moved the intellectually or emotionally—[AROUSED, p. 118]
Insulted	Having had one's modesty or self-respect offended—[ANGRY, p. 111]
Interested	Affected; involved; characterized by a feeling of interest; having an interest, share or concern in something—[LIKE, p. 155; RAPACIOUS, p. 174]
Intimidated	Terrified, overawed, cowed; forced to or deterred from some action by threats or violence from another—[AFRAID, p. 106]
Intoxicated	In a state of feeling strongly excited or elated—[HAPPY, p. 140]
Intrepid	Resolutely fearless and courageous; dauntless—[VALIANT, p. 187]
Invigorated	Given life and energy; animated; stimulated—[AROUSED, p. 118]

Irascible	Easily provoked to anger or resentment; prone to anger—[ANGRY, p. 111]
Irate	Feeling angry, incensed or enraged—[FURIOUS, p. 137]
Ireful	Full of anger or wrath—[FURIOUS, p. 137]
Irked	Weary, bored, irritated, annoyed; disgusted—[ANNOYED, p. 114]
Irritable	To be easily annoyed or bothered; ill-tempered; abnormally sensitive or responsive to stimuli—[QUARRELSOME, p. 172]
Irritated	Aggravated, excited, provoked; excited to an impatient or angry feeling—[AGITATED, p. 108; ANNOYED, p. 114]
Jaunty	Having an easy confidence; gay and carefree; sprightly; perky—[FESTIVE, p. 134]
Jealous	Feeling resentment or bitterness towards someone due to possession or characteristic; envious—[JEALOUS, p. 150]
Jilted	The resulting feelings from having been deceived, cheated, tricked; abruptly rejected or abandoned—[ABANDONED, p. 103]
Jolly	Full of high spirits and good humor—[FESTIVE, p. 134]
Jovial	Seeming or feeling cheerful and convivial—[FESTIVE, p. 134]
Joyless	Being without joy, cheerless or sad—[SAD, p. 175]
Joyous	Full of joy; happy; gay; glad—[HAPPY, p. 140]
Jubilant	In an exultant mood—[HAPPY, p. 140]
Jumpy	Characterized by sudden involuntary movement caused by nervous excitement; nervous, easily startled—[NERVOUS, p. 164]
Keen	1) feeling eagerness or desire; characterized by intense interest; 2) sharp or biting in speech or manner—[ZEALOUS, p. 192; QUARRELSOME, p. 172]
Kindly	Having a friendly or warm-hearted disposition; generous or benevolent in character—[KINDLY, p. 151]
Kittenish	1) a feeling of joy or affected playfulness; 2) resembling a kitten—[FLIRTATIOUS, p. 136]
Knavish	Being or given to behaving in a dishonest or unprincipled way—[MISCHIEVOUS, p. 159]
Lackadaisical	Feebly sentimental, affectedly languishing; dreamily idle, listless, unconcerned, unenthusiastic—[APATHETIC, p. 116]
Lament	Express or feel profound grief; mourn passionately—[MOURNFUL, p. 162]
Lascivious	Inclined to lust, lustful, lecherous, wanton—[LASCIVIOUS, p. 153]
Lecherous	Sexually provocative; characterized by indulgence of sexual lust—[LASCIVIOUS, p. 153]
Lethargic	Affected with a condition of torpor, inertness or apathy or lack of vitality; of or pertaining to a pathological state of sleepiness or deep unresponsiveness and inactivity—[APATHETIC, p. 116]
Lewd	Indecent, treating sexual matters in a vulgar way—[LASCIVIOUS, p. 153]
Libertine	Characterized by habitual disregard of morality, esp. With regard to sexual relations; licentious, dissolute—[LASCIVIOUS, p. 153]
Libidinous	Given to, full of, or characterized by lust or lewdness; lustful, lecherous, lewd—[LASCIVIOUS, p. 153]
Licentious	Lawless, lax, immoral (usu. Immoral or promiscuous in sexual relations); disregarding commonly accepted rules or conventions—[LASCIVIOUS, p. 153]
Lighthearted	Cheerful, without cares; not treating something seriously; blithe, gay—[FESTIVE, p. 134]
Like	To be attracted to or pleased by—[LIKE, p. 155]
Listless	Characterized by unwillingness to move, act or make any exertion; marked by languid indifference—[APATHETIC, p. 116]
Liverish	Seeming or acting bilious; peevish, glum; irritable—[QUARRELSOME, p. 172]
Livid	Furiously angry, as if pale with rage—[ANGRY, p. 111]
Loathe	To feel great hatred and disgust for—[DISGUSTED, p. 128; HATE, p. 143]
Lofty	Behaving or feeling overproud or arrogant—[PROUD, p. 170]
Lonely	Sad because one lacks friends or companions; unhappy as a result of being alone—[LONELY, p. 157]
Lonesome	Lonely; being in a state of loneliness—[LONELY, p. 157]
Long	To have an earnest or strong craving or desire—[YEARN, p. 191]
Lost	Gone astray or bewildered; distraught—[BEWILDERED, p. 119]
Love	1) intense affection or fondness; strong feeling of attraction; 2) to feel affection for; to feel a passion, devotion or tenderness for; to cherish or foster with divine love or mercy; to delight in—[LOVE, p. 158]
Lovelorn	1) suffering because of love; 2) forsaken by one's lover—[ABANDONED, p. 103]
Lovesome	In a state of feeling loving, friendly or amorous—[LOVE, p. 158]
Low	Emotionally depressed; lacking in vigor; abased, humbled, dejected—[DEPRESSED, p. 29; HUMILIATED, p. 145]
Low-spirited	Feeling dejected or depressed—[DEPRESSED, p. 126]
Loyal	1) faithful and committed to a certain person or cause; dedicated, devoted 2) true or faithful to the obligations of duty, love, friendship, etc.—[XENOPHOBIC, p. 190]

Lubricious	Lewd, wanton, licentious; shifty, unstable, fickle, elusive—[LASCIVIOUS, p. 153]
Lugubrious	Mournful; esp.: Exaggeratedly or affectedly mournful—[MOURNFUL, p. 162]
Lustful	Characterized by an intense longing or desire—[LASCIVIOUS, p. 153]
Mad	1) carried away by intense anger; furious; 2) carried away by intense enthusiasm or desire; 3) intensely excited; frantic—[FURIOUS, p. 137; IMPASSIONED, p. 148]
Malaise	Vague sense of mental or moral ill being, or uneasiness—[DEPRESSED, p. 126]
Malevolent	Wishing harm or ill-will to others; malicious—[BITTER, p. 121]
Malicious	Intending or desiring to do evil or harm to others, or to tease; desiring to see others suffer usually through doing something unlawful or otherwise unjustified—[MISCHIEVOUS, p. 159]
Maligning	Showing malice; evil in nature or intent; having intense, viscous ill will; intensely hostile; taking pleasure in the suffering of others—[BITTER, p. 121]
Marveling	Filled with wonder or astonishment; struck with surprise—[CHARMED, p. 123]
Maudlin	Weakly or tearfully sentimental because of drunkenness; drunk enough to be emotionally silly—[SENTIMENTAL, p. 177]
Mawkish	Sentimental in a sickly way; falsely sentimental—[SENTIMENTAL, p. 177]
Meek	Enduring injury without resentment; difficient in spirit and courage; gentle in nature; humble and submissive—[TIMID, p. 181]
Melancholy	A pensive sadness; mental depression; depression of the spirits; gloom—[DEPRESSED, p. 126]
Mellow	Relaxed and at ease; slightly and pleasantly intoxicated; pleasantly convivial—[SERENCE, p. 178]
Mercurial	Given to volatile or changeable moods or dispositions—[MOODY, p. 161]
Merry	1) cheerful and lively; full of high spirits; 2) elated with drink—[FESTIVE, p. 134]
Mesmerized	Fascinated or charmed; hypnotized—[CHARMED, p. 123]
Miffed	Having taken offense; put out of humor; offended, irritated—[ANGRY, p. 111]
Mirth	Merriment, laughter, gaiety or enjoyment—[FESTIVE, p. 134]
Mirthless	Feeling utterly joyless, sad or dismal—[DEPRESSED, p. 126]
Mischievous	Having a spirit of Irresponsible fun or playfulness—[MISCHIEVOUS, p. 159]
Miserable	Wretchedly unhappy or uncomfortable; existing in a state of extreme poverty or unhappiness; discontented, disagreeable—[SAD, p. 175]
Misgiving	A feeling of mistrust, apprehension or loss of confidence—[DOUBTFUL, p. 130]
Mistrust	A lack of confidence; distrust; suspicion, doubt—[DOUBTFUL, p. 130]
Modest	1) having a moderate or humble estimate of one's own abilities or merits; unassuming, diffident, bashful; not bold or forward; 2) reserved in sexual matters—[TIMID, p. 181]
Monomaniacal	An exaggerated zeal for or interest in a single thing, idea, subject, etc.; Obsessive—[IMPASSIONED, p. 148]
Moody	Subject to or indulging in moods of bad temper, depression, etc.; Sullen, melancholy—[MOODY, p. 161]
Mopy	Given to or characterized by remaining in a listless, apathetic condition without making any effort to rouse oneself; gloomily dejected; sulking—[DEPRESSED, p. 126]
Mordant	1) expressing incisive sarcasm; 2) caustic—[BITTER, p. 121]
Morose	Sullenly melancholy, gloomy, unsocial—[SAD, p. 175]
Mortified	Deeply embarrassed, shamed; deeply wounded pride—[HUMILIATED, p. 145]
Mournful	Feeling or expressing grief or lamentation, usually due to loss; sad, doleful, sorrowful—[MOURNFUL, p. 162]
Moved	1) affected by tender emotion; 2) stirred—[AROUSED, p. 118]
Mulish	Behaving or feeling quite sullen; very stubborn—[ADAMANT, p. 104]
Mushy	Feebly sentimental; excessively tender or emotional—[SENTIMENTAL, p. 177]
Narcissistic	Marked by excessive self-love—[LOVE, p. 158]
Naughty	Morally bad, wicked; wayward, disobedient, badly behaved—[MISCHIEVOUS, p. 159]
Nauseated	Feeling disgust, loathing or aversion strongly—[DISGUSTED, p. 128]
Neglected	Feeling disregarded, slighted; feeling unattended to, uncared for—[ABANDONED, p. 103]
Nervous	Easily agitated and excited; timid as a result of anxiety; jittery, having delicate or disordered nerves; high strung; acting unsteady; irregular—[NERVOUS, p. 164]
Nervy	Confident, assured, cool; audacious, impudent—[VALIANT, p. 187]
Nettled	Irritated, vexed, provoked, annoyed; incited, roused—[ANGRY, p. 111]
Nihilism	Extreme skepticism and disbelief; doubtfulness—[DOUBTFUL, p. 130]
Nonchalant	Calm and casual; unmoved, not feeling anxiety or excitement—[APATHETIC, p. 116]
Numb	Devoid of emotion; deprived of feeling the power of motion; stunned or paralyzed from shock or strong emotion—[UNFEELING, p. 185]
Nymphomaniac	Person (usu. A woman) experiencing excessive abnormally strong and uncontrollable sexual desire—[LASCIVIOUS, p. 153]
Object	State or have an objection; express or feel opposition, disapproval or reluctance—

	[DISGUSTED, p. 128]
Obsessed	1) worrying persistently usu. About someone or something in particular; 2) preoccupied; haunted as with an obsession—[IMPASSIONED, p. 148]
Offended	Displeased, annoyed, resentful, wounded in the feelings; affronted—[ANGRY, p. 111]
Oppressed	Weighed down heavily with cares or unhappiness; be burdened spiritually or mentally as if by pressure—[OPPRESSED, p. 166]
Optimistic	Anticipating the best, often to an unwise extent—[HAPPY, p. 140]
Ornery	Of a stubborn and mean spirited nature, unpleasant; having a touchy disposition—[QUARRELSOME, p. 172]
Outcast	Feeling rejected, despised, discarded; homeless; the experience of being banished, forsaken—[ABANDONED, p. 103]
Outraged	Having had a fierce anger, resentment or indignation aroused by something regarded as an injustice or insult; deeply offended—[FURIOUS, p. 137]
Overburdened	To feel excessively burdened; to be burdened with too much work—[OVERWHELMED, p. 168]
Overcome	Overwhelmed by a sudden attack or shock—[OVERWHELMED, p. 168]
Overexcited	Feeling excessive excitement—[AROUSED, p. 118]
Overjoyed	Feeling great joy; delighted—[HAPPY, p. 140]
Overpowered	Overcome by superior power or force; reduced to submission; overwhelmed—[OVERWHELMED, p. 168]
Overwhelmed	1) overpowered by thought or feeling; 2) overcome by superior force or numbers—[OVERWHELMED, p. 168]
Overwrought	Overexcited, nervous, distraught, agitated; in a state of nervous agitation through overexcitement—[NERVOUS, p. 164]
Pain	1) mental distress or trouble esp. Grief or sorrow; 2) the state or condition of consciousness arising from mental or physical suffering; an unpleasurable feeling or effect—[SAD, p. 175]
Panic	A sudden overpowering fright that produces hysterical or irrational behavior; esp.: A sudden unreasoning terror often accompanied by mass flight—[ALARMED, p. 110]
Panicky	Feeling or experiencing a sudden, unreasoning, hysterical fear often spreading quickly—[NERVOUS, p. 164]
Paralyzed	Unable to move as from fear; scared stiff—[AFRAID, p. 106]
Partial	Favoring a particular person or thing excessively; favorably disposed; inclined beforehand to favor one party in a cause, or one side of a question; more than the other; prejudiced; biased—[LIKE, p. 155]
Passionate	Affected with or easily moved by a strong emotion spec. Intense sexual love or desire—[IMPASSIONED, p. 148]
Passive	Not reacting visibly to something that might be expected to produce an emotion or feeling; inactive; inert; quiescent—[APATHETIC, p. 116]
Patriotic	Devoted to the well-being or interest of one's country—[XENOPHOBIC, p. 190]
Peevish	Querulous, irritable, childishly fretful; spiteful—[QUARRELSOME, p. 172]
Penitent	Repenting with serious desire and intention to amend a sin or wrongdoing —[GUILTY, p. 139]
Pensive	Thoughtful, meditative, musing; reflective; sadly or sorrowfully thoughtful; gloomy, brooding, melancholy—[DEPRESSED, p. 126]
Perplexed	Filled with uncertainty—[CONFUSED, p. 125]
Perturbed	Disturbed greatly in mind; thrown into confusion; agitated—[AGITATED, p. 108; CONFUSED, p. 125]
Perverse	Willfully determined not to do what is expected or desired; contrary—[QUARRELSOME, p. 172]
Pessimistic	Tending to take a gloomy view of circumstances or prospects; hopeless about the future—[PESSIMISTIC, p. 169]
Petrified	Motionless or rigid with fear; astonished—[ALARMED, p. 110]
Petulant	Impatient or irritable esp. Over a petty annoyance; peevish—[QUARRELSOME, p. 172]
Pining	Yearning intensely and persistently esp. For something unattainable—[YEARN, p. 191]
Piqued	1) stimulated to action or emotion esp. By aroused jealousy; 2) having one's curiosity, interest, etc. Aroused—[ANGRY, p. 111]
Pitiless	Lacking sympathy or understanding for another; merciless—[BITTER, p. 121]
Pity	Having sympathy and compassion for another's misfortune—[EMPATHETIC, p. 132]
Platonic (love)	Of a purely spiritual or intellectual character; not sexual; detached; dispassionate—[LOVE, p. 158]
Playful	Fond of play, inclined to play; pleasantly humorous or jocular—[FLIRTATIOUS, p. 136; MISCHIEVOUS, p. 159]
Pleased	Given pleasure or satisfaction; happy—[HAPPY, p. 140]
Poltroonery	State of being extremely cowardly and fearsome—[AFRAID, p. 106]

Pompous	Feeling or behaving self-important; ostentatious—[PROUD, p. 170]
Powerless	Helpless; unable to produce any effect—[OVERWHELMED, p. 168]
Predatory	Given to or living by plunder or marauding; ruthlessly acquisitive at the expense of others, rapacious, exploitative; unfairly competitive or aggressive in business—[RAPACIOUS, p. 174]
Predilection	A mental preference or partiality; a favorable predisposition—[LIKE, p. 155]
Prefer	Favor one person or thing in preference to another; like better—[LIKE, p. 155]
Pressed	Feeling pushed or driven toward something—[OPPRESSED, p. 166]
Pretentious	Making excessive or unwarranted claim to merit or importance; making an exaggerated outward show, ostentatious—[PROUD, p. 170]
Preyed upon	Seized and killed as prey; made a victim of—[OPPRESSED, p. 166]
Profligate	Abandoned to vice or indulgence; recklessly licentious, dissolute; recklessly extravagant—[LASCIVIOUS, p. 153]
Proud	Feeling self-respect, worth or esteem; dignified—[PROUD, p. 170]
Provoked	Irritated, angry, annoyed; having received provocation—[ANGRY, p. 111]
Prowess	Superior strength, courage or bravery; exceptional valor esp. In combat or battle—[VALIANT, p. 187]
Prurient	Having or characterized by an unhealthy concern with sexual matters; encouraging such a concern—[LASCIVIOUS, p. 153]
Puckish	Mischievous in a childlike way—[MISCHIEVOUS, p. 159]
Pusillanimous	Lacking courage; timidity, cowardice—[TIMID, p. 181]
Puzzled	Presented with a problem difficult to solve or a situation difficult to resolve; mentally challenged—[CONFUSED, p. 125]
Quarrelsome	In a mood to quarrel; inclined to quarrel; given to quarreling—[QUARRELSOME, p. 172]
Rabid	Furious or raging; violently intense—[TRUCULENT, p. 184]
Rancorous	Hating or feeling ill will bitterly and continuously—[HATE, p. 143]
Randy	1) lustful, lewd, sexually promiscuous; eager for sexual gratification; 2) boisterous, riotous, disorderly; unruly, unmanageable—[LASCIVIOUS, p. 153]
Rapacious	Grasping; excessively or violently greedy—[RAPACIOUS, p. 174]
Rapturous	Experiencing extreme joy or exaltation; elation—[HAPPY, p. 140]
Rattled	Stirred up; roused, flustered, nervous, agitated, alarmed, frightened—[AGITATED, p. 108; ALARMED, p. 110]
Raving	Delirious; frenzied; irrational; wildly extravagant—[NERVOUS, p. 164]
Ravished	1) transported by the strength of some emotion; filled with ecstasy or delight; 2) violently seized; raped, violated—[HAPPY, p. 140; HUMILIATED, p. 145]
Recreant	Feeling or behaving cowardly or craven—[AFRAID, 106]
Regard	Respect, affection or esteem towards someone—[LIKE, p. 155]
Regret	Feeling sorry, distressed or disappointed about something—[GUILTY, p. 139]
Rejected	Feeling or emotion of not being accepted or denied; discord; belittle—[LONELY, p. 157]
Rejoicing	The feeling or expression of joy—[FESTIVE, p. 134]
Relentless	Pitiless; insistent and uncompromising—[ADAMANT, p. 104]
Reliant	Trusting that someone or something can be relied upon—[FAITH, p. 133]
Relief	Alleviation from anxiety, pain or distress; easiness—[SERENCE, p. 178]
Relinquished	Feeling as though one has been deserted, abandoned, left behind—[ABANDONED, p. 103]
Relish	To be pleased or gratified by; enjoy; to appreciate with taste and discernment—[LIKE, p. 155]
Reluctant	1) unwilling, adverse, disinclined; 3) holding back—[APATHETIC, p. 116; TIMID, p. 181]
Remorseful	Affected with deep regret and repentance—[GUILTY, p. 139]
Repentant	Regretful for past sins; penitent—[GUILTY, p. 139]
Repudiate	Reject, disown or disavow something or someone—[HATE, p. 143]
Repugnance	A feeling of aversion and disgust—[DISGUSTED, p. 128]
Repulsed	Feeling a strong aversion or utter repugnance; quite disgusted—[DISGUSTED, p. 128]
Resent	To feel anger or indignation towards—[ANGRY, p. 111; JEALOUS, p. 150]
Reserved	Marked by self-restraint or diffidence; timid; distant, cold—[UNFEELING, p. 185]
Resolute	Firm and determined; set in purpose or opinion—[ADAMANT, p. 104]
Respect	Treat or regard with deferential esteem; feel or show deferential or polite attention for—[ADMIRE, p. 105]
Restless	Lacking or denying rest; uneasy—[NERVOUS, p. 164]
Restrained	Held back from action; kept in check or under control; repressed—[TIMID, p. 181]
Reticent	Disinclined to speak freely; reserved—[TIMID, p. 181]
Retiring	Feeling unassertive, reserved or shy, or given to such behavior—[TIMID, p. 181]
Reveling	Experiencing and expressing boisterous festivity—[FESTIVE, p. 134]
Revere	Hold in or regard with deep respect or veneration; be reverent—[ADMIRE, p. 105]
Revolted	Feeling disgust or loathing towards someone or something—[DISGUSTED, p. 128]

Revulsion	Repugnance or abhorrence; hatred—[DISGUSTED, p. 128]
Rigid	Strictly unapproachable, not friendly; not bending or flexible; unyielding—[ADAMANT, p. 104; UNFEELING, p. 185]
Riled	To be excited, irritated or made angry—[ANGRY, p. 111]
Roguish	Given to behaving or feeling playfully mischievous—[MISCHIEVOUS, p. 159]
Romantic	Of, characterized by or suggestive of, an idealized, fantastic or sentimental view of life, love or reality; inclined towards sentimental or idealized love; readily influenced by the imagination; imaginative, idealistic—[LOVE, p. 158; SENTIMENTAL, p. 177]
Roused	Started out of a state of inactivity, security, etc.; Provoked to activity; excited—[ALARMED, p. 110]
Rueful	Feeling deeply mournful or regretful—[MOURNFUL, p. 162; GUILTY, p. 139]
Ruffled	Stirred up to indignation; annoyed, vexed, discomposed, disturbed, made angry, irritated, etc.—[ANGRY, p. 111; ANNOYED, p. 114]
Ruthless	Without pity or compassion; cruel; merciless—[ZEALOUS, p. 192]
Ruttish	Displaying lustful or lascivious behavior or thoughts—[LASCIVIOUS, p. 153]
Sad	Feeling or expressing sorrow or grief; unhappy—[SAD, p. 175]
Salacious	Lustful, lecherous; erotic, lewd—[LASCIVIOUS, p. 153]
Sanguine	Cheerful and confident; optimistic—[HOPEFUL, p. 144]
Sarcastic	Given to the use of sarcasm; bitterly cutting or ironic—[BITTER, p. 121]
Sardonic	Characterized by or exhibiting bitterness, scorn or mockery—[BITTER, p. 121]
Satisfied	Feeling fulfilled or gratified—[SERENE, p. 178]
Saturnine	Of a cold, sluggish and gloomy temperament—[MOODY, p. 161]
Satyrlike	Lustful, sensual; characteristic of a satyr—[LASCIVIOUS, p. 153]
Savage	1) enraged or furiously angry; 2) an uncivilized human being; a fierce, brutal or cruel person —[TRUCULENT, p. 184]
Scared	Filled with fear or terror; suddenly frightened or startled—[AFRAID, p. 106; ALARMED, p. 110]
Scorn	Hold in disdain or strong contempt; despise; reject contemptuously—[HATE, p. 143]
Scoundrelly	Of, belonging to, or characteristic of, an unscrupulous villain or a rogue—[MISCHIEVOUS, p. 159]
Seductive	Alluring, enticing; tending to seduce a person—[FLIRTATIOUS, p. 136]
Seething	Agitated; full of unexpressed anger—[FURIOUS, p. 137]
Self-conscious	Unduly aware of oneself as an object of observation by others; embarrassed, shy—[TIMID, p. 181]
Self-esteemed	Having a high regard for oneself—[PROUD, p. 170]
Self-reproachful	Full of excess disapproval of oneself—[GUILTY, p. 139]
Self-respectful	Feeling respect for oneself; having proper concern for the way one behaves or is treated—[PROUD, p. 170]
Sensationless	Without strong stimulation or powerful emotion—[UNFEELING, p. 185]
Sensitive	1) very responsive or susceptible to emotional, artistic, etc. Impressions; 2) possessing delicate or tender feelings; easily offended or emotionally hurt, touchy; 3) naturally perceptive of the feelings, etc. Of others—[NERVOUS, p. 164]
Sensual	Given or excessively devoted to the pursuit of physical pleasures or the gratification of the senses, spec self-indulgent sexually or with regard to food or drink—[LASCIVIOUS, p. 153]
Sentimental	Affected by or showing emotion rather than reason; exaggeratedly or superficially sensitive or emotional; excessively prone to emotional or tender feelings—[SENTIMENTAL, p. 177]
Serene	Calm, peaceful and tranquil—[SERENE, p. 178]
Sexual	Deriving from or relating to desire for sex or for carnal pleasure—[LASCIVIOUS, p. 153]
Sexy	Sexually aroused; sexually attractive—[AROUSED, p. 118]
Shaken	Feeling as though one has just (or having just) shook with emotion—usu. fear or shock—[ALARMED, p. 110]
Shamed	Made to feel guilty or having had done something wrong, usually through dishonor or disgrace—[HUMILIATED, p. 145]
Shameful	Modest, shamefaced; having a feeling or appearance of shame, full of shame, ashamed—[GUILTY, p. 139]
Sheepish	Excessively submissive, fearful or cowardly; poor-spirited; bashful, shy, reticent; diffident, feeling or showing embarrassment—[TIMID, p. 181]
Shiftless	Lacking resourcefulness, initiative or ambition; lazy, inefficient, incompetent—[APATHETIC, p. 116]
Shock	(In shock) having experienced a sudden and disturbing effect on the mind or feelings, esp. As causing depression or distress—[OVERWHELMED, p. 168]
Shocked	Startled by a surprise, excitement, etc.—[SHOCKED, p. 180]
Short-tempered	Quick to lose one's temper—[MOODY, p. 161]

Shy	Easily startled; diffident, timid or reserved—[TIMID, p. 181]
Sickened	Feeling nausea, loathing or disgust—[DISGUSTED, p. 128]
Sincere	Earnest or honest; free of deceit, falseness or hypocrisy; genuine—[KINDLY, p. 151]
Skeptical	Given to doubting, disbelieving and distrusting—[DOUBTFUL, p. 130]
Sleepless	Unceasingly active; not able to sleep due to anxiety—[NERVOUS, p. 164]
Slothful	Given to inactive, lazy or sluggish behavior or moods—[APATHETIC, p. 116]
Sly	Skillful, clever, dexterous; possessing practical skill, wisdom or ability; characterized by artifice, craft or cunning, practicing secrecy or stealth; guileful, wily—[MISCHIEVOUS, p. 159]
Smitten	Inspired or inflamed with love; enamored—[CHARMED, p. 123]
Smug	Feeling confident or satisfied with one's ability or situation; complacent, content—[SERENE, p. 178]
Social	Desirous of the pleasant society or companionship of others; inclined to friendly interaction or companionship; sociable—[KINDLY, p. 151]
Soft-hearted	Tender, compassionate or easily moved—[WARM-HEARTED, p. 189]
Solaced	Partially or greatly relieved from grief, loneliness, discomfort, etc.—[HAPPY, p. 140]
Solemn	Feeling or seeming deeply ardent and serious—[MOURNFUL, p. 162]
Somber	Gloomy or melancholy—[MOURNFUL, p. 162]
Sore	In a state of being irritated, angry or resentful—[ANGRY, p. 111]
Sorrowful	Full of mental distress caused by bereavement, suffering, disappointment, etc.; Grief, deep sadness—[MOURNFUL, p. 162]
Sorry	Regretful, penitent; pained, distressed, sad—[GUILTY, p. 139; SAD, p. 175]
Sour	Harsh, sullen, morose, discontented, embittered—[JEALOUS, p. 150]
Spellbound	Enchanted or fascinated by or as by a spell—[CHARMED, p. 123]
Spirited	Lively; vigorous; energetic; animated—FESTIVE, p. 134]
Spiritless	Lacking courage, vigor or animation; low-spirited, depressed, dejected—[APATHETIC, p. 116]
Spiteful	Full of a mean or evil feeling toward another, characterized by the inclination to hurt, humiliate, annoy, frustrate. Etc.—[BITTER, p. 121; MISCHIEVOUS, p. 159]
Splenetic	Peevish, ill-humored; irritable, ill-tempered, testy—[QUARRELSOME, p. 172]
Spooked	In a frightened, nervy or excited state—[NERVOUS, p. 164]
Sportive	1) inclined to jesting or levity; playful, frolicsome; 2) lustful, amorous, sexually aroused or active—[FLIRTATIOUS, p. 136]
Spurn	Reject with contempt or disdain; treat contemptuously; scorn, despise—[HATE, p. 143]
Squeamish	1) reserved, cold, coy; bashful, diffident; easily shocked or offended by immodesty or indecency, prudish; 2) easily turned sick or faint, readily affected with nausea—[TIMID, p. 181]
Startled	Having been surprised; feel suddenly astonished, frightened or shocked; awakened with a start—[SHOCKED, p. 180]
Stew	To fret, fume or worry; to be vexed or troubled—[ANGRY, p. 111]
Stimulated	Aroused or affected by a stimulant (as a drug)—[AROUSED, p. 118]
Strained	Showing signs of nervous tension—[NERVOUS, p. 164]
Stressed	Affected by or showing signs of stress or strain—[NERVOUS, p. 164]
Stubborn	Unreasonably obstinate; obstinately perverse—[ADAMANT, p. 104]
Stunned	Dazed, astonished, astounded, or stupefied—[BEWILDERED, p. 119]
Stupefied	Overwhelmed with amazement or shock—[BEWILDERED, p. 119; SHOCKED, p. 180]
Stuporous	Dazed, torpid; affected with or characterized by insensibility or unconsciousness, admiring wonder or amazement—[BEWILDERED, p. 119]
Subdued	Reduced or lacking in intensity, force or vividness; restrained, soft, quiet—[OPPRESSED, p. 166]
Subjugated	Brought into subjection, vanquished, subdued; made subservient or dependent—[OPPRESSED, p. 166]
Submissive	Characterized by or displaying submission; yielding to power or authority; humble, obedient—[TIMID, p. 181]
Suffering	The bearing or undergoing of pain, hardship, etc.; A painful condition; a pain or hardship suffered—[SAD, p. 175]
Sulk	Keep aloof from others in moody silence; indulge in sullen ill-humor; move or respond sluggishly or inadequately—[MOODY, p. 161]
Sullen	Averse to company, disinclined to be social; characterized by gloomy ill-humor; morose, resentful—[MOODY, p. 161]
Sunny	Behaving and feeling bright and cheerful—[FESTIVE, p. 134]
Suppressed	Having a feeling, reaction, etc. Prevented from being expressed or displayed; restrained, stifled, subdued—[OPPRESSED, p. 166]
Surprised	Feeling wonder or amazement resulting from something unexpected or unanticipated—[SHOCKED, p. 180]

Suspicious	Suspecting something wrong without proof or on slight evidence; mistrusting; mental uneasiness and uncertainty—[DOUBTFUL, p. 130]
Sympathetic	Feeling sympathy; sharing, responsive to, or affected by the feelings of another or others; compassionate; inclined to favor, give support to or approve—[EMPATHETIC, p. 132]
Tantalized	Tormented, teased or fascinated by the sight, promise or expectation of something which is out of reach; having hopes raised and then disappointed—[ANNOYED, p. 114]
Taxed	Burdened by an oppressive obligation, duty or heavy demand—[OPPRESSED, p. 166]
Tearful	Crying or inclined to cry; shedding tears—[SENTIMENTAL, p. 177]
Tender	1) sensitive to or easily affected by external physical forces, impressions; sensitive to pain and emotional influences; easily hurt or offended; 2) gentle or sensitive for or about others; loving, mild, affectionate—[TIMID, p. 181; WARM-HEARTED,p. 98]
Tense	Feeling or showing nervous tension—[NERVOUS, p. 164]
Tentative	Feeling hesitant or uncertain—[DOUBTFUL, p. 130]
Terrified	Having extreme fear of something or someone; greatly scared or frightened—[AFRAID, 106; ALARMED, p. 110]
Testy	Irritable; impatient of being thwarted; irascible, short-tempered; peevish, touchy, aggressive, contentious—[QUARRELSOME, p. 172]
Thankful	Feeling or expressing gratitude or appreciation—[HAPPY, p. 140]
Thrilled	Experiencing a sudden sharp feeling of excitement; having a shivering or tingling sensation—[HAPPY, p. 140]
Thunderstruck	Struck with sudden amazement, terror, etc.; Extremely startled, astonished or terrified—[SHOCKED, p. 180]
Timid	Lacking self-confidence; reserved, shy—[TIMID, p. 181]
Timorous	Feeling fear; frightened, apprehensive, afraid; subject to fear; easily frightened, timid—[AFRAID, 106]
Tormented	1) feeling great bodily or mental suffering; agonizing; miserable; 2) worrying or annoyed excessively—[SAD, p. 175]
Torpid	Inactive, apathetic; sluggish, slow; dull—[APATHETIC, p. 116]
Tortured	Having been subjected to severe physical or mental suffering, anguish, agony or torment—[SAD, p. 175]
Touchy	Easily moved to anger; apt to take offense on slight cause; irascible, irritable—[QUARRELSOME, p. 172]
Transported	Affected strongly with emotion; exalted, ecstatic, enraptured; stimulated or inspired to imagine oneself in a different place or time—[HAPPY, p. 140]
Trenchant	Vigorous and clear; incisive; effective, energetic—[ZEALOUS, p. 192]
Trepidation	Timorous, uncertain agitation; apprehension; tremulous fear, alarm or agitation; perturbation—[ALARMED, p. 110]
Troubled	Mentally agitated; distressed or anxious—[AGITATED, p. 108; NERVOUS, p. 164]
Truculent	Fierce, savage; pugnacious, aggressive; aggressively defiant; mean, mercenary—[TRUCULENT, p. 184]
Trust	Confident expectation of something; hope—[FAITH, p. 133]
Tyrannized	Being subjected to excessive or cruel behavior from another; ruled; oppressed—[OPPRESSED, p. 166]
Unaggressive	Not aggressive; retiring—[TIMID, p. 181]
Unassured	Being uncertain or insecure about something; doubtful—[TIMID, p. 181]
Uncaring	Not caring or compassionate; disinterested, unconcerned—[UNFEELING, p. 185]
Uncertain	Being or feeling of insecurity and unassurance; lacking confidence—[DOUBTFUL, p. 130]
Uncompromising	Unwilling to compromise; unyielding, stubborn; relentless—[ADAMANT, p. 104]
Unconcerned	Without care or interest; indifferent—[APATHETIC, p. 116]
Unconfident	Without confidence or certainty in oneself; insecure—[TIMID, p. 181]
Undaunted	Courageously resolute esp. In the face of danger or difficulty; not discouraged—[VALIANT, p. 187]
Understanding	To realize and empathize with the feelings of another—[EMPATHETIC, p. 132]
Uneasy	Apprehensive, worried; restless, unquiet—[NERVOUS, p. 164]
Unemotional	Impassive; not feeling particularly emotional at all—[UNFEELING, p. 185]
Unenthusiastic	Not enthusiastic; blasé; nonchalant—[APATHETIC, p. 116]
Unexcited	Not mentally excited or stirred; not affected by outside influenced—[APATHETIC, p. 116]
Unfeeling	Unsympathetic; callous; not feeling—[UNFEELING, p. 185]
Unhappy	Not happy with one's circumstances; miserable, wretched; dissatisfied, not pleased—[DEPRESSED, p. 126]
Unhinged	In an unstable, unsettled or disrupted state—[AGITATED, p. 108]
Unimpressed	Not impressed; having no impression made—[APATHETIC, p. 116]

Uninspired	Not inspired; not particularly motivated toward or away from action, creativity, feeling, etc.—[APATHETIC, p. 116]
Unmoved	Unaffected; not particularly moved toward an emotion—[UNFEELING, p. 185]
Unnerved	Deprived of resolution or courage; disquieted, disturbed—[AGITATED, p. 108]
Unostentatious	Not ostentatious or showy; discreet, unpretentious—[TIMID, p. 181]
Unpretentious	Not pretentious; modest, simple—[TIMID, p. 181]
Unsettled	Disturbed in thought or feeling; disconcerted. Discomposed; nervous—[NERVOUS, p. 164]
Unsure	Marked or characterized by uncertainty, lack of sureness; faltering, irresolute, doubtful—[AFRAID, 106]
Upset	1) emotionally disturbed or agitated; 2) a nervous, irritable state of mind—[AGITATED, p. 108; NERVOUS, p. 164]
Vague	Not clear or definite in thought, perception or understanding—[CONFUSED, p. 125]
Vain	Delighting in or desirous of attracting the admiration of others; conceited, proud—[PROUD, p. 170]
Valiant	Showing bravery and valor; boldly courageous, heroic—[VALIANT, p. 187]
Valor	Boldness or confidence in danger; heroic courage or bravery—[VALIANT, p. 187]
Vehement	Vigorously impetuous; violent; furious—[ZEALOUS, p. 192]
Venerate	To respect deeply; to honor—[ADMIRE, p. 105]
Venery	The practice or pursuit of sexual pleasures, sexual indulgence—[LASCIVIOUS, p. 153]
Vengeful	Vindictive; desiring or seeking vengeance—[BITTER, p. 121]
Venturesome	Disposed to take risks or face danger; daring—[VALIANT, p. 187]
Verve	Enthusiasm, vigor or spirit esp. In artistic or literary work, or in sport; style, energy—[ZEALOUS, p. 192]
Vexed	Troubled, distressed, grieved; annoyed, irritated; tormented, worried—[ANGRY, p. 111; ANNOYED, p. 114]
Vicious	1) characterized by vice or immorality; depraved; profligate; 2) malignantly bitter or severe; malicious, spiteful, violent—[MISCHIEVOUS, p. 159]
Victimized	Made a victim of; caused to suffer inconvenience, discomfort, harm, etc.; Cheated, fallen prey to fraud—[OPPRESSED, p. 166]
Vigorous	Feeling intensely energetic and eager—[ZEALOUS, p. 192]
Villainous	Like that of a depraved, wicked criminal—[MISCHIEVOUS, p. 159]
Vindictive	Tending to seek revenge; vengeful, spiteful—[BITTER, p. 121]
Violent	Expressing or acting with great force or strength of feeling, conduct or expression—[TRUCULENT, p. 184]
Virulent	Violently bitter or rancorous; full of acrimony or hostility—[TRUCULENT, p. 184]
Vitalized	Endowed with vitality; animated—[FESTIVE, p. 134]
Vivacious	Lively in temper, conduct or spirit; sprightly—[ZEALOUS, p. 192]
Volatile	Readily changing from one interest or mood to another; flighty, fickle; characterized by unpredictable changes of emotion—[MOODY, p. 161]
Voracious	Having a huge appetite; excessively eager—[RAPACIOUS, p. 174]
Wallow	To indulge oneself in a state of mind or way of life—[PESSIMISTIC, p. 169]
Want	To desire or need greatly; wish—[YEARN, p. 191]
Wanton	1) insolent in triumph or prosperity; reckless; merciless; 2) lewd, lascivious, sexually promiscuous—[LASCIVIOUS, p. 153]
Warm	To become friendly, kindly, affectionate or sympathetic (to or toward)—[WARM-HEARTED, p. 189]
Warm-hearted	Feeling generous and affectionate; hearty; cordial—[WARM-HEARTED, p. 189]
Wary	Habitually on one's guard; cautious; careful; circumspect—[DOUBTFUL, p. 130]
Weak-kneed	Lacking resolution or determination—[TIMID, p. 181]
Weary	Depressed; dispirited; exhausted by strong (usually painful) emotions—[DEPRESSED, p. 126]
Weepy	In a weeping or mournful state—[MOURNFUL, p. 162]
Weighed upon	Depressed; oppressed; the experience of having something or someone laying heavily on one—[OPPRESSED, p. 166]
Well meaning	Having or based on good intentions but freq. Ineffective or ill-advised—[KINDLY, p. 151]
Wicked	1) spiteful, malicious, ill-tempered; disposed to serious and willful wrong doing (freq. Cruel and injurious acts); morally depraved; shamefully extravagant or sensuous; 2) playfully mischievous, roguish—[LASCIVIOUS, p. 153; MISCHIEVOUS, p. 159]
Wild	1) uncivilized, barbarous, rebellious; uncontrolled, unrestrained, taking or disposed to taking one's way; acting or moving unrestrictedly; 2) yielding to sexual desire; licentious, dissolute; distracted, distraught—[IMPASSIONED, p. 148]
Wish	Have or feel a wish, desire or aspiration for; hope for; request, ask; require—[YEARN, p. 191]
Wistful	Mournfully or yearningly expectant or wishful—[MOURNFUL, p. 162]

Withdrawn	Detached from others and from one's own emotions—[APATHETIC, p. 116]
Woeful	Afflicted with sorrow, distress or misfortune; sorrowful, mournful—[MOURNFUL, p. 162]
Wonder	1) rapt attention or astonishment at something awesomely mysterious or new to one's experience; 2) a feeling of doubt or uncertainty—[CHARMED, p. 123; DOUBTFUL, p. 130]
Worried	Feeling anxious or distressed about something—[NERVOUS, p. 164]
Worship	Regard with extreme respect, devotion or love; idolize—[ADMIRE, p. 105]
Wrathful	Full of violent anger, rage, or fury; indignant—[TRUCULENT, p. 184]
Wretched	1) deeply affected, dejected, or distressed in body or mind—[SAD, p. 175]
Xenophobic	Affected with a deep antipathy to foreigners or to foreign things—[XENOPHOBIC, p. 190]
Yearn	To have an earnest desire or strong craving for—[YEARN, p. 191]
Yen	1) a craving, a yearning, a longing for; 2) the craving of a drug addict for a drug—[YEARN, p. 191]
Zealous	Full of intense interest; eagerness; ardently active, devoted or diligent—[ZEALOUS, p. 192]
Zestful	Full of enthusiasm, excitement—[IMPASSIONED, p. 148]

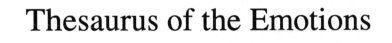

Thesaurus of the Emotions

Introduction to Thesaurus Workbook

I don't believe that anyone would be foolish enough to argue against the fact that emotions are the core of the actors art and that the more an actor knows about emotions, the better actor he or she will be. So how can anybody not see that these charts would be helpful in getting an emotions education? Yet, I'm constantly challenged to defend this work. Generally these challenges come from old school types trying to hold onto their turf, but occasionally they come from people who, though genuine, have trouble understanding the concept. To those people, I would suggest that your learning style may necessitate testing the idea by doing; you will quickly see that it works.

This entire book is dedicated to convincing you that this work is vital to actors and acting, I know it's very different from anything anyone has ever proposed and therefore suspect; however in every learning situation an element of trust must exist between the teacher and the student in order for it to be successful. I have promised you that you will get positive results in a short period of time. I have offered you a Quick test that should lead you to see that this workbook will make you a better actor. It always astounds me that students will pay teachers to teach them and then not follow the teacher's instruction; I've had students that did that, every teacher has. Some of you will buy this book and never fill out one column of these charts. To those actors, I'll make another promise; you are going to sit there and watch actors who do fill out these columns, consistently beat you out at auditions and they will also receive higher artistic recognition than you. For those who are ready to get to work, let me do a quick recap of how to use this section of the book.

The mechanics of the workbook are simple and have been explained clearly and repeatedly in prior sections of this book. On pages 10 and 11 you will find a full explanation but in case you're browsing, I've cut and pasted a small piece of that example. It should help you understand.

The first step in using the chart is to look over the synonyms in column one.

Emotions Chart: Example (not actual size-see workbook)

Primary Emotion:	Definition	Emotion (rearrange in order of descending intensity)	Color (descending intensity)	Weight (arbitrary, in order of descending intensity)	Smell	Taste	Sound	Feel (physical texture)	Physical Object
GRIEF									
Secondary Emotions:									
affliction									
agony									
anguish									
bemoaning									
bereavement									
bewailing									
care									
dejection									
* Since this is previously shown; I cut the example very short.									

In column 2 define each word, using The Dictionary of the Emotions. (contained in this book)

In column 3, Intensity, rearrange the secondary emotions from the strongest intensity to the weakest intensity as distinguished by the definition in column 2. For instance, in this very abbreviated example, if I were filling it out "agony" would certainly come higher on the list than "dejection."

In column 4, select one specific color that represents that emotion to you. Go to a paint store and get those color strips that they give out. Get every shade of your emotion's color possible and then cut them down to size and paste them into column 4 in the appropriate place; remember the strongest to the weakest. You can also go to an artist supply store and get a set of artist pencils that are all that color's intensities and color them in, but that can be expensive.

Column 5 is an arbitrary weight you assign to each level of that emotion, it too is in a highest to lowest mode.

The rest is pure imagination, but imagination is a muscle too little exercised. Artists have to work that muscle the same as body builders work their muscles. This should help, but for a fuller explanation please go to pages 10 and 11.

EMOTIONS	DEFINITION	EMOTIONS REARRANGED (in descending order of intensity)	COLOR	WEIGHT (arbitrary numerical - descending order)	SMELL	TASTE	SOUND	FEEL (physical texture)	PHYSICAL OBJECT
Primary-									
ABANDONED									
Secondary-									
Deserted									
Forsaken									
Jilted									
Neglected									
Relinquished									
Exposed									
Outcast									
Lovelorn									
Betrayed									

NEW SCHOOL ACTING   by Jeremy Whelan   © 1996

EMOTIONS	DEFINITION	EMOTIONS REARRANGED (in descending order of intensity)	COLOR	WEIGHT (arbitrary numerical - descending order)	SMELL	TASTE	SOUND	FEEL (physical texture)	PHYSICAL OBJECT
Primary-									
ADAMANT									
Secondary-									
Aggressive									
Insistent									
Relentless									
Resolute									
Rigid									
Stubborn									
Uncompromising									
Determined									
Headstrong									
Mulish									
Contrary									
Bull-headed									
Willful									

NEW SCHOOL ACTING   by Jeremy Whelan   ©1996

EMOTIONS	DEFINITION	EMOTIONS REARRANGED (in descending order of intensity)	COLOR	WEIGHT (arbitrary numerical - descending order)	SMELL	TASTE	SOUND	FEEL (physical texture)	PHYSICAL OBJECT
Primary-									
ADMIRE									
Secondary-									
Deferential									
Honor									
Venerate									
Idolize									
Worship									
Revere									
Esteem									
Respect									

NEW SCHOOL ACTING   by Jeremy Whelan   © 1996

EMOTIONS	DEFINITION	EMOTIONS REARRANGED (in descending order of intensity)	COLOR	WEIGHT (arbitrary numerical - descending order)	SMELL	TASTE	SOUND	FEEL (physical texture)	PHYSICAL OBJECT
Primary-									
AFRAID									
Secondary-									
Apprehensive									
Daunted									
Distressed									
Fearful									
Paralyzed									
Awe									
Intimidated									
Dismayed									
Hesitant									
Scared									
Poltroonery									
Recreant									
Unsure									

EMOTIONS	DEFINITION	EMOTIONS REARRANGED (in descending order of intensity)	COLOR	WEIGHT (arbitrary numerical - descending order)	SMELL	TASTE	SOUND	FEEL (physical texture)	PHYSICAL OBJECT
Primary-									
AFRAID cont.									
Secondary-									
Terrified									
Timorous									
Dread									
Angst									

NEW SCHOOL ACTING   by Jeremy Whelan   © 1996

EMOTIONS	DEFINITION	EMOTIONS REARRANGED (in descending order of intensity)	COLOR	WEIGHT (arbitrary numerical - descending order)	SMELL	TASTE	SOUND	FEEL (physical texture)	PHYSICAL OBJECT
Primary-									
AGITATED									
Secondary-									
Disconcerted									
Discomposed									
Unnerved									
Flustered									
Bothered									
Perturbed									
Irritated									
Troubled									
Disturbed									
Rattled									
Disquieted									
Discombobulated									
Distracted									

NEW SCHOOL ACTING   by Jeremy Whelan   © 1996

EMOTIONS	DEFINITION	EMOTIONS REARRANGED (in descending order of intensity)	COLOR	WEIGHT (arbitrary numerical - descending order)	SMELL	TASTE	SOUND	FEEL (physical texture)	PHYSICAL OBJECT
Primary-									
AGITATED									
Secondary-									
Unhinged									
Upset									
Fazed									

NEW SCHOOL ACTING   by Jeremy Whelan   © 1996

EMOTIONS	DEFINITION	EMOTIONS REARRANGED (in descending order of intensity)	COLOR	WEIGHT (arbitrary numerical - descending order)	SMELL	TASTE	SOUND	FEEL (physical texture)	PHYSICAL OBJECT
Primary-									
ALARMED									
Secondary-									
Distressed									
Trepidation									
Horrified									
Roused									
Panic									
Scared									
Frightened									
Shaken									
Terrified									
Rattled									
Petrified									

EMOTIONS	DEFINITION	EMOTIONS REARRANGED (in descending order of intensity)	COLOR	WEIGHT (arbitrary numerical - descending order)	SMELL	TASTE	SOUND	FEEL (physical texture)	PHYSICAL OBJECT
Primary-									
ANGRY									
Secondary-									
Livid									
Offended									
Piqued									
Stew									
Cross									
Asperity									
Estranged									
Goaded									
Dander									
Nettled									
Hard									
Displeased									
Distempered									

NEW SCHOOL ACTING   by Jeremy Whelan   © 1996

EMOTIONS	DEFINITION	EMOTIONS REARRANGED (in descending order of intensity)	COLOR	WEIGHT (arbitrary numerical - descending order)	SMELL	TASTE	SOUND	FEEL (physical texture)	PHYSICAL OBJECT
Primary-									
ANGRY cont.									
Secondary-									
Ill-humored									
Irascible									
Huff									
Miffed									
Ill-tempered									
Vexed									
Impatient									
Alienated									
Provoked									
Resent									
Riled									
Ruffled									
Sore									

EMOTIONS	DEFINITION	EMOTIONS REARRANGED (in descending order of intensity)	COLOR	WEIGHT (arbitrary numerical - descending order)	SMELL	TASTE	SOUND	FEEL (physical texture)	PHYSICAL OBJECT
Primary-									
ANGRY cont.									
Secondary-									
Insulted									
Incited									

NEW SCHOOL ACTING   by Jeremy Whelan   © 1996

EMOTIONS	DEFINITION	EMOTIONS REARRANGED (in descending order of intensity)	COLOR	WEIGHT (arbitrary numerical - descending order)	SMELL	TASTE	SOUND	FEEL (physical texture)	PHYSICAL OBJECT
Primary-									
ANNOYED									
Secondary-									
Irritated									
Exasperated									
Aggravated									
Antagonized									
Ruffled									
Cross									
Bothered									
Irked									
Bugged									
Chafe									
Galled									
Vexed									
Disgruntled									

EMOTIONS	DEFINITION	EMOTIONS REARRANGED (in descending order of intensity)	COLOR	WEIGHT (arbitrary numerical - descending order)	SMELL	TASTE	SOUND	FEEL (physical texture)	PHYSICAL OBJECT
Primary-									
ANNOYED cont.									
Secondary-									
Displeased									
Tantalized									

NEW SCHOOL ACTING   by Jeremy Whelan   © 1996

EMOTIONS	DEFINITION	EMOTIONS REARRANGED (in descending order of intensity)	COLOR	WEIGHT (arbitrary numerical - descending order)	SMELL	TASTE	SOUND	FEEL (physical texture)	PHYSICAL OBJECT
Primary-									
APATHETIC									
Secondary-									
Slothful									
Indolent									
Shiftless									
Listless									
Easygoing									
Lackadaisical									
Lethargic									
Spiritless									
Casual									
Bored									
Unconcerned									
Indifferent									
Unenthusiastic									

116

EMOTIONS	DEFINITION	EMOTIONS REARRANGED (in descending order of intensity)	COLOR	WEIGHT (arbitrary numerical - descending order)	SMELL	TASTE	SOUND	FEEL (physical texture)	PHYSICAL OBJECT
Primary-									
APATHETIC cont.									
Secondary-									
Unexcited									
Dissolute									
Unimpressed									
Withdrawn									
Passive									
Disinterested									
Reluctant									
Blasé									
Nonchalant									
Half-hearted									
Torpid									
Uninspired									
Deadened									

NEW SCHOOL ACTING   by Jeremy Whelan   © 1996

EMOTIONS	DEFINITION	EMOTIONS REARRANGED (in descending order of intensity)	COLOR	WEIGHT (arbitrary numerical - descending order)	SMELL	TASTE	SOUND	FEEL (physical texture)	PHYSICAL OBJECT
Primary-									
AROUSED									
Secondary-									
Excited									
Disturbed									
Hot									
Moved									
Sexy									
Inspired									
Invigorated									
Stimulated									
Overexcited									

NEW SCHOOL ACTING   by Jeremy Whelan   © 1996

EMOTIONS	DEFINITION	EMOTIONS REARRANGED (in descending order of intensity)	COLOR	WEIGHT (arbitrary numerical - descending order)	SMELL	TASTE	SOUND	FEEL (physical texture)	PHYSICAL OBJECT
Primary-									
BEWILDERED									
Secondary-									
Stupefied									
Enervated									
Enfeebled									
Dazed									
Awe									
Dazzled									
Fuddled									
Bedazzled									
Confounded									
Boggled									
Flabbergasted									
Stuporous									
Benumbed									

119

NEW SCHOOL ACTING   by Jeremy Whelan   © 1996

EMOTIONS	DEFINITION	EMOTIONS REARRANGED (in descending order of intensity)	COLOR	WEIGHT (arbitrary numerical - descending order)	SMELL	TASTE	SOUND	FEEL (physical texture)	PHYSICAL OBJECT
Primary-									
BEWILDERED cont.									
Secondary-									
Stunned									
Lost									

EMOTIONS	DEFINITION	EMOTIONS REARRANGED (in descending order of intensity)	COLOR	WEIGHT (arbitrary numerical - descending order)	SMELL	TASTE	SOUND	FEEL (physical texture)	PHYSICAL OBJECT
Primary-									
BITTER									
Secondary-									
Acerbic									
Acid									
Cynical									
Belligerent									
Acrimonious									
Censorious									
Indignant									
Malevolent									
Cruel									
Mordant									
Spiteful									
Pitiless									
Vengeful									

NEW SCHOOL ACTING   by Jeremy Whelan   © 1996

EMOTIONS	DEFINITION	EMOTIONS REARRANGED (in descending order of intensity)	COLOR	WEIGHT (arbitrary numerical - descending order)	SMELL	TASTE	SOUND	FEEL (physical texture)	PHYSICAL OBJECT
Primary-									
BITTER cont.									
Secondary-									
Sardonic									
Bellicose									
Sarcastic									
Inhuman									
Insensitive									
Vindictive									
Galled									
Maligning									

EMOTIONS	DEFINITION	EMOTIONS REARRANGED (in descending order of intensity)	COLOR	WEIGHT (arbitrary numerical - descending order)	SMELL	TASTE	SOUND	FEEL (physical texture)	PHYSICAL OBJECT
Primary-									
CHARMED									
Secondary-									
Wonder									
Enticed									
Captivated									
Entranced									
Allured									
Enchanted									
Beguiled									
Deluded									
Deceived									
Diverted									
Enamored									
Absorbed									
Enthralled									

EMOTIONS	DEFINITION	EMOTIONS REARRANGED (in descending order of intensity)	COLOR	WEIGHT (arbitrary numerical - descending order)	SMELL	TASTE	SOUND	FEEL (physical texture)	PHYSICAL OBJECT
Primary-									
CHARMED cont.									
Secondary-									
Bewitched									
Spellbound									
Mesmerized									
Marveling									
Fascinated									
Infatuated									
Smitten									
Enraptured									

NEW SCHOOL ACTING   by Jeremy Whelan   © 1996

EMOTIONS	DEFINITION	EMOTIONS REARRANGED (in descending order of intensity)	COLOR	WEIGHT (arbitrary numerical - descending order)	SMELL	TASTE	SOUND	FEEL (physical texture)	PHYSICAL OBJECT
Primary-									
CONFUSED									
Secondary-									
Puzzled									
Perplexed									
Dumbfounded									
Vague									
Groggy									
Discombobulated									
Dizzy									
Hazy									
Perturbed									
Distracted									
Addled									
Baffled									

NEW SCHOOL ACTING   by Jeremy Whelan   © 1996

EMOTIONS	DEFINITION	EMOTIONS REARRANGED (in descending order of intensity)	COLOR	WEIGHT (arbitrary numerical - descending order)	SMELL	TASTE	SOUND	FEEL (physical texture)	PHYSICAL OBJECT
Primary-									
DEPRESSED									
Secondary-									
Weary									
Malaise									
Low-spirited									
Discomfort									
Despair									
Mirthless									
Inconsolable									
Cheerless									
Pensive									
Disheartened									
Mopy									
Atrabilious									
Melancholy									

126

NEW SCHOOL ACTING   by Jeremy Whelan   © 1996

EMOTIONS	DEFINITION	EMOTIONS REARRANGED (in descending order of intensity)	COLOR	WEIGHT (arbitrary numerical - descending order)	SMELL	TASTE	SOUND	FEEL (physical texture)	PHYSICAL OBJECT
Primary-									
DEPRESSED cont.									
Secondary-									
Dispirited									
Downhearted									
Unhappy									
Blue									
Discouraged									
Downcast									
Dejected									
Dashed									
Dismayed									
Low									

127

NEW SCHOOL ACTING   by Jeremy Whelan   © 1996

EMOTIONS	DEFINITION	EMOTIONS REARRANGED (in descending order of intensity)	COLOR	WEIGHT (arbitrary numerical - descending order)	SMELL	TASTE	SOUND	FEEL (physical texture)	PHYSICAL OBJECT
Primary-									
DISGUSTED									
Secondary-									
Repulsed									
Revulsion									
Revolted									
Dissatisfied									
Loathe									
Object									
Nauseated									
Sickened									
Horrified									
Disapprobation									
Repugnance									
Disapproval									
Fed up									

128

EMOTIONS	DEFINITION	EMOTIONS REARRANGED (in descending order of intensity)	COLOR	WEIGHT (arbitrary numerical - descending order)	SMELL	TASTE	SOUND	FEEL (physical texture)	PHYSICAL OBJECT
Primary-									
DISLIKE									
Secondary-									
Disrelish									
Indisposed									
Disinclined									
Distaste									
Antipathy									
Averse									

NEW SCHOOL ACTING   by Jeremy Whelan   © 1996

EMOTIONS	DEFINITION	EMOTIONS REARRANGED (in descending order of intensity)	COLOR	WEIGHT (arbitrary numerical - descending order)	SMELL	TASTE	SOUND	FEEL (physical texture)	PHYSICAL OBJECT
Primary-									
DOUBTFUL									
Secondary-									
Dubious									
Disbelieve									
Suspicious									
Distrust									
Uncertain									
Mistrust									
Wonder									
Beware									
Wary									
Agnostic									
Skeptical									
Misgiving									
Incredulity									

130

EMOTIONS	DEFINITION	EMOTIONS REARRANGED (in descending order of intensity)	COLOR	WEIGHT (arbitrary numerical - descending order)	SMELL	TASTE	SOUND	FEEL (physical texture)	PHYSICAL OBJECT
Primary-									
DOUBTFUL cont.									
Secondary-									
Nihilism									
Tentative									

NEW SCHOOL ACTING   by Jeremy Whelan   © 1996

EMOTIONS	DEFINITION	EMOTIONS REARRANGED (in descending order of intensity)	COLOR	WEIGHT (arbitrary numerical - descending order)	SMELL	TASTE	SOUND	FEEL (physical texture)	PHYSICAL OBJECT
Primary-									
EMPATHETIC									
Secondary-									
Understanding									
Pity									
Compassionate									
Benevolent									
Feel									
Sympathetic									
Humane									
Appreciate									

NEW SCHOOL ACTING   by Jeremy Whelan   © 1996

EMOTIONS	DEFINITION	EMOTIONS REARRANGED (in descending order of intensity)	COLOR	WEIGHT (arbitrary numerical - descending order)	SMELL	TASTE	SOUND	FEEL (physical texture)	PHYSICAL OBJECT
Primary-									
FAITH									
Secondary-									
Believe in									
Credence									
Confidence in									
Trust									
Allegiance									
Fidelity									
Reliant									

NEW SCHOOL ACTING   by Jeremy Whelan   © 1996

EMOTIONS	DEFINITION	EMOTIONS REARRANGED (in descending order of intensity)	COLOR	WEIGHT (arbitrary numerical - descending order)	SMELL	TASTE	SOUND	FEEL (physical texture)	PHYSICAL OBJECT
Primary-									
FESTIVE									
Secondary-									
Gay									
Gleeful									
Enlivened									
Merry									
Mirth									
Rejoicing									
Reveling									
Bouncy									
Boisterous									
Jaunty									
Frivolous									
Jolly									
Spirited									

NEW SCHOOL ACTING   by Jeremy Whelan   © 1996

EMOTIONS	DEFINITION	EMOTIONS REARRANGED (in descending order of intensity)	COLOR	WEIGHT (arbitrary numerical - descending order)	SMELL	TASTE	SOUND	FEEL (physical texture)	PHYSICAL OBJECT
Primary-									
FESTIVE cont.									
Secondary-									
Sunny									
Blithe									
Effervescent									
High									
Convivial									
Jovial									
Vitalized									
Lighthearted									

NEW SCHOOL ACTING   by Jeremy Whelan   © 1996

EMOTIONS	DEFINITION	EMOTIONS REARRANGED (in descending order of intensity)	COLOR	WEIGHT (arbitrary numerical - descending order)	SMELL	TASTE	SOUND	FEEL (physical texture)	PHYSICAL OBJECT
Primary-									
FLIRTATIOUS									
Secondary-									
Coy									
Seductive									
Kittenish									
Coquettish									
Sportive									
Playful									

EMOTIONS	DEFINITION	EMOTIONS REARRANGED (in descending order of intensity)	COLOR	WEIGHT (arbitrary numerical - descending order)	SMELL	TASTE	SOUND	FEEL (physical texture)	PHYSICAL OBJECT
Primary-									
FURIOUS									
Secondary-									
Enraged									
Hot									
Choleric									
Embittered									
Bile									
Outraged									
Inflamed									
Fuming									
Incensed									
Exasperated									
Infuriated									
Ireful									
Irate									

NEW SCHOOL ACTING   by Jeremy Whelan   © 1996

EMOTIONS	DEFINITION	EMOTIONS REARRANGED (in descending order of intensity)	COLOR	WEIGHT (arbitrary numerical - descending order)	SMELL	TASTE	SOUND	FEEL (physical texture)	PHYSICAL OBJECT
Primary-									
FURIOUS cont.									
Secondary-									
Mad									
Seething									

EMOTIONS	DEFINITION	EMOTIONS REARRANGED (in descending order of intensity)	COLOR	WEIGHT (arbitrary numerical - descending order)	SMELL	TASTE	SOUND	FEEL (physical texture)	PHYSICAL OBJECT
Primary-									
GUILTY									
Secondary-									
Contrite									
Regret									
Repentant									
Penitent									
Compunction									
Sorry									
Rueful									
Shameful									
Self-reproachful									
Angst									
Remorseful									

NEW SCHOOL ACTING   by Jeremy Whelan   © 1996

EMOTIONS	DEFINITION	EMOTIONS REARRANGED (in descending order of intensity)	COLOR	WEIGHT (arbitrary numerical - descending order)	SMELL	TASTE	SOUND	FEEL (physical texture)	PHYSICAL OBJECT
Primary-									
HAPPY									
Secondary-									
Euphoric									
Cheerful									
Enjoy									
Ravished									
Ecstatic									
Rapturous									
Joyous									
Blissful									
Exalted									
Felicitous									
Glad									
Intoxicated									
Elated									

NEW SCHOOL ACTING   by Jeremy Whelan   © 1996

EMOTIONS	DEFINITION	EMOTIONS REARRANGED (in descending order of intensity)	COLOR	WEIGHT (arbitrary numerical - descending order)	SMELL	TASTE	SOUND	FEEL (physical texture)	PHYSICAL OBJECT
Primary-									
HAPPY cont.									
Secondary-									
Delighted									
Thrilled									
Jubilant									
Pleased									
Overjoyed									
Exhilarated									
Optimistic									
Solaced									
Delirious									
Fulfilled									
Amused									
Transported									
Beatific									

NEW SCHOOL ACTING   by Jeremy Whelan   © 1996

EMOTIONS	DEFINITION	EMOTIONS REARRANGED (in descending order of intensity)	COLOR	WEIGHT (arbitrary numerical - descending order)	SMELL	TASTE	SOUND	FEEL (physical texture)	PHYSICAL OBJECT
Primary-									
HAPPY cont.									
Secondary-									
Grateful									
Thankful									

142

NEW SCHOOL ACTING   by Jeremy Whelan   © 1996

EMOTIONS	DEFINITION	EMOTIONS REARRANGED (in descending order of intensity)	COLOR	WEIGHT (arbitrary numerical - descending order)	SMELL	TASTE	SOUND	FEEL (physical texture)	PHYSICAL OBJECT
Primary-									
HATE									
Secondary-									
Loathe									
Detest									
Despise									
Repudiate									
Spurn									
Rancorous									
Animosity									
Abhor									
Disdainful									
Enmity									
Contempt									
Abominate									
Scorn									

NEW SCHOOL ACTING   by Jeremy Whelan   © 1996

EMOTIONS	DEFINITION	EMOTIONS REARRANGED (in descending order of intensity)	COLOR	WEIGHT (arbitrary numerical - descending order)	SMELL	TASTE	SOUND	FEEL (physical texture)	PHYSICAL OBJECT
Primary-									
HOPEFUL									
Secondary-									
Anticipative									
Assured									
Buoyant									
Confidence in									
Sanguine									

144

NEW SCHOOL ACTING   by Jeremy Whelan   © 1996

EMOTIONS	DEFINITION	EMOTIONS REARRANGED (in descending order of intensity)	COLOR	WEIGHT (arbitrary numerical - descending order)	SMELL	TASTE	SMELL	SOUND	FEEL (physical texture)	PHYSICAL OBJECT
Primary-										
HUMILIATED										
Secondary-										
Humbled										
Demeaned										
Degraded										
Dishonored										
Ashamed										
Belittled										
Debased										
Disgraced										
Abased										
Mortified										
Embarrassed										
Crushed										
Affronted										

145

NEW SCHOOL ACTING   by Jeremy Whelan   © 1996

EMOTIONS	DEFINITION	EMOTIONS REARRANGED (in descending order of intensity)	COLOR	WEIGHT (arbitrary numerical - descending order)	SMELL	TASTE	SOUND	FEEL (physical texture)	PHYSICAL OBJECT
Primary-									
HUMILIATED cont.									
Secondary-									
Chagrined									
Abashed									
Crestfallen									
Ravished									
Groveling									
Depreciated									
Discomfited									
Ignominy									
Disesteem									
Deprecated									
Shamed									
Disreputed									
Abused									

EMOTIONS	DEFINITION	EMOTIONS REARRANGED (in descending order of intensity)	COLOR	WEIGHT (arbitrary numerical - descending order)	SMELL	TASTE	SOUND	FEEL (physical texture)	PHYSICAL OBJECT
Primary-									
HUMILIATED cont.									
Secondary-									
Low									
Dashed									

NEW SCHOOL ACTING   by Jeremy Whelan   © 1996

EMOTIONS	DEFINITION	EMOTIONS REARRANGED (in descending order of intensity)	COLOR	WEIGHT (arbitrary numerical - descending order)	SMELL	TASTE	SOUND	FEEL (physical texture)	PHYSICAL OBJECT
Primary-									
IMPASSIONED									
Secondary-									
Fervent									
Zestful									
Anxious									
Avid									
Crazed									
Monomaniacal									
Frenzied									
Abandon									
Fanatical									
Obsessed									
Feverish									
Fervid									
Passionate									

NEW SCHOOL ACTING   by Jeremy Whelan   © 1996

EMOTIONS	DEFINITION	EMOTIONS REARRANGED (in descending order of intensity)	COLOR	WEIGHT (arbitrary numerical - descending order)	SMELL	TASTE	SOUND	FEEL (physical texture)	PHYSICAL OBJECT
Primary-									
IMPASSIONED cont.									
Secondary-									
Mad									
Wild									
Berserk									
Ardor									
Frenetic									
Excited									

149

NEW SCHOOL ACTING   by Jeremy Whelan   © 1996

EMOTIONS	DEFINITION	EMOTIONS REARRANGED (in descending order of intensity)	COLOR	WEIGHT (arbitrary numerical - descending order)	SMELL	TASTE	SOUND	FEEL (physical texture)	PHYSICAL OBJECT
Primary-									
JEALOUS									
Secondary-									
Envious									
Covetous									
Resent									
Sour									

NEW SCHOOL ACTING   by Jeremy Whelan   © 1996

EMOTIONS	DEFINITION	EMOTIONS REARRANGED (in descending order of intensity)	COLOR	WEIGHT (arbitrary numerical - descending order)	SMELL	TASTE	SOUND	FEEL (physical texture)	PHYSICAL OBJECT
Primary-									
KINDLY									
Secondary-									
Sincere									
Heartfelt									
Hearty									
Genial									
Cordial									
Amiable									
Friendly									
Gracious									
Affable									
Well-meaning									
Amity									
Congenial									
Hospitable									

151

EMOTIONS	DEFINITION	EMOTIONS REARRANGED (in descending order of intensity)	COLOR	WEIGHT (arbitrary numerical - descending order)	SMELL	TASTE	SOUND	FEEL (physical texture)	PHYSICAL OBJECT
Primary-									
KINDLY cont.									
Secondary-									
Social									

EMOTIONS	DEFINITION	EMOTIONS REARRANGED (in descending order of intensity)	COLOR	WEIGHT (arbitrary numerical - descending order)	SMELL	TASTE	SOUND	FEEL (physical texture)	PHYSICAL OBJECT
Primary-									
LASCIVIOUS									
Secondary-									
Lustful									
Randy									
Lecherous									
Licentious									
Lewd									
Prurient									
Salacious									
Libidinous									
Erotic									
Sensual									
Lubricious									
Ruttish									
Goatish									

NEW SCHOOL ACTING   by Jeremy Whelan   © 1996

EMOTIONS	DEFINITION	EMOTIONS REARRANGED (in descending order of intensity)	COLOR	WEIGHT (arbitrary numerical - descending order)	SMELL	TASTE	SOUND	FEEL (physical texture)	PHYSICAL OBJECT
Primary-									
LASCIVIOUS cont.									
Secondary-									
Satyrlike									
Wanton									
Cyprianic									
Debauched									
Profligate									
Libertine									
Concupiscent									
Venery									
Wicked									
Nymphomaniac									
Sexual									

EMOTIONS	DEFINITION	EMOTIONS REARRANGED (in descending order of intensity)	COLOR	WEIGHT (arbitrary numerical - descending order)	SMELL	TASTE	SOUND	FEEL (physical texture)	PHYSICAL OBJECT
Primary-									
LIKE									
Secondary-									
Relish									
Fond									
Affinity									
Care for									
Attracted									
Prefer									
Appreciate									
Interested									
Partial									
Predilection									
Inclined									
Attached									
Approve									

EMOTIONS	DEFINITION	EMOTIONS REARRANGED (in descending order of intensity)	COLOR	WEIGHT (arbitrary numerical - descending order)	SMELL	TASTE	SOUND	FEEL (physical texture)	PHYSICAL OBJECT
Primary-									
LIKE cont.									
Secondary-									
Fancy									
Regard									
Favor									

NEW SCHOOL ACTING   by Jeremy Whelan   © 1996

EMOTIONS	DEFINITION	EMOTIONS REARRANGED (in descending order of intensity)	COLOR	WEIGHT (arbitrary numerical - descending order)	SMELL	TASTE	SOUND	FEEL (physical texture)	PHYSICAL OBJECT
Primary-									
LONELY									
Secondary-									
Lonesome									
Desolate									
Forlorn									
Alone									
Abject									
Friendless									
Rejected									

EMOTIONS	DEFINITION	EMOTIONS REARRANGED (in descending order of intensity)	COLOR	WEIGHT (arbitrary numerical - descending order)	SMELL	TASTE	SOUND	FEEL (physical texture)	PHYSICAL OBJECT
Primary-									
LOVE									
Secondary-									
Romantic									
Amorous									
Lovesome									
Crush									
Adore									
Doting									
Cherish									
Narcissistic									
Platonic love									
Crazy about									

NEW SCHOOL ACTING   by Jeremy Whelan   © 1996

EMOTIONS	DEFINITION	EMOTIONS REARRANGED (in descending order of intensity)	COLOR	WEIGHT (arbitrary numerical - descending order)	SMELL	TASTE	SOUND	FEEL (physical texture)	PHYSICAL OBJECT
Primary-									
MISCHIEVOUS									
Secondary-									
Roguish									
Dastardly									
Knavish									
Devilish									
Naughty									
Puckish									
Sly									
Playful									
Spiteful									
Malicious									
Vicious									
Wicked									
Scoundrelly									

159

EMOTIONS	DEFINITION	EMOTIONS REARRANGED (in descending order of intensity)	COLOR	WEIGHT (arbitrary numerical - descending order)	SMELL	TASTE	SOUND	FEEL (physical texture)	PHYSICAL OBJECT
Primary-									
MISCHIEVOUS cont.									
Secondary-									
Blackguardly									
Villainous									

NEW SCHOOL ACTING   by Jeremy Whelan   © 1996

EMOTIONS	DEFINITION	EMOTIONS REARRANGED (in descending order of intensity)	COLOR	WEIGHT (arbitrary numerical - descending order)	SMELL	TASTE	SOUND	FEEL (physical texture)	PHYSICAL OBJECT
Primary-									
MOODY									
Secondary-									
Sullen									
Sulk									
Brooding									
Short-tempered									
Saturnine									
Volatile									
Mercurial									

NEW SCHOOL ACTING   by Jeremy Whelan   © 1996

EMOTIONS	DEFINITION	EMOTIONS REARRANGED (in descending order of intensity)	COLOR	WEIGHT (arbitrary numerical - descending order)	SMELL	TASTE	SOUND	FEEL (physical texture)	PHYSICAL OBJECT
Primary-									
MOURNFUL									
Secondary-									
Lament									
Elegiac									
Somber									
Dirgeful									
Funereal									
Dolorous									
Grievous									
Dreary									
Doleful									
Sorrowful									
Rueful									
Lugubrious									
Wistful									

162

NEW SCHOOL ACTING   by Jeremy Whelan   © 1996

EMOTIONS	DEFINITION	EMOTIONS REARRANGED (in descending order of intensity)	COLOR	WEIGHT (arbitrary numerical - descending order)	SMELL	TASTE	SOUND	FEEL (physical texture)	PHYSICAL OBJECT
Primary-									
MOURNFUL cont.									
Secondary-									
Grave									
Baleful									
Black									
Solemn									
Afflicted									
Woeful									
Weepy									
Heart-broken									

NEW SCHOOL ACTING   by Jeremy Whelan   © 1996

EMOTIONS	DEFINITION	EMOTIONS REARRANGED (in descending order of intensity)	COLOR	WEIGHT (arbitrary numerical - descending order)	SMELL	TASTE	SOUND	FEEL (physical texture)	PHYSICAL OBJECT
Primary-									
NERVOUS									
Secondary-									
Sensitive									
Strained									
Upset									
Fretful									
Uneasy									
Hysterical									
Edgy									
Fidgety									
Tense									
Restless									
Worried									
Concerned									
Sleepless									

164

NEW SCHOOL ACTING   by Jeremy Whelan   © 1996

EMOTIONS	DEFINITION	EMOTIONS REARRANGED (in descending order of intensity)	COLOR	WEIGHT (arbitrary numerical - descending order)	SMELL	TASTE	SOUND	FEEL (physical texture)	PHYSICAL OBJECT
Primary-									
NERVOUS cont.									
Secondary-									
Panicky									
Deranged									
Troubled									
Anxious									
Raving									
Frantic									
Stressed									
Frazzled									
Unsettled									
Distraught									
Jumpy									
Overwrought									
Spooked									

165

NEW SCHOOL ACTING   by Jeremy Whelan   © 1996

EMOTIONS	DEFINITION	EMOTIONS REARRANGED (in descending order of intensity)	COLOR	WEIGHT (arbitrary numerical - descending order)	SMELL	TASTE	SOUND	FEEL (physical texture)	PHYSICAL OBJECT
Primary-									
OPPRESSED									
Secondary-									
Preyed upon									
Taxed									
Weighed upon									
Tyrannized									
Burdened									
Encumbered									
Pressed									
Helpless									
Downtrodden									
Victimized									
Subdued									
Subjugated									
Enslaved									

NEW SCHOOL ACTING   by Jeremy Whelan   © 1996

EMOTIONS	DEFINITION	EMOTIONS REARRANGED (in descending order of intensity)	COLOR	WEIGHT (arbitrary numerical - descending order)	SMELL	TASTE	SOUND	FEEL (physical texture)	PHYSICAL OBJECT
Primary-									
OPPRESSED cont.									
Secondary-									
Suppressed									

NEW SCHOOL ACTING   by Jeremy Whelan   © 1996

EMOTIONS	DEFINITION	EMOTIONS REARRANGED (in descending order of intensity)	COLOR	WEIGHT (arbitrary numerical - descending order)	SMELL	TASTE	SOUND	FEEL (physical texture)	PHYSICAL OBJECT
Primary-									
OVERWHELMED									
Secondary-									
Overcome									
Shock									
Overpowered									
Devastated									
Defeated									
Beaten									
Powerless									
Broken									
Debilitated									
Overburdened									

NEW SCHOOL ACTING   by Jeremy Whelan   © 1996

EMOTIONS	DEFINITION	EMOTIONS REARRANGED (in descending order of intensity)	COLOR	WEIGHT (arbitrary numerical - descending order)	SMELL	TASTE	SOUND	FEEL (physical texture)	PHYSICAL OBJECT
Primary-									
PESSIMISTIC									
Secondary-									
Gloomy									
Black									
Despairing									
Hopeless									
Wallow									
Cynical									
Desperate									

NEW SCHOOL ACTING by Jeremy Whelan © 1996

EMOTIONS	DEFINITION	EMOTIONS REARRANGED (in descending order of intensity)	COLOR	WEIGHT (arbitrary numerical - descending order)	SMELL	TASTE	SOUND	FEEL (physical texture)	PHYSICAL OBJECT
Primary-									
PROUD									
Secondary-									
Honored									
Self-esteemed									
Self-respectful									
Dignified									
Conceited									
Arrogant									
Elated									
Lofty									
Pompous									
Cocky									
Vain									
Haughty									
Insolent									

EMOTIONS	DEFINITION	EMOTIONS REARRANGED (in descending order of intensity)	COLOR	WEIGHT (arbitrary numerical - descending order)	SMELL	TASTE	SOUND	FEEL (physical texture)	PHYSICAL OBJECT
Primary-									
PROUD cont.									
Secondary-									
Pretentious									

NEW SCHOOL ACTING   by Jeremy Whelan   © 1996

EMOTIONS	DEFINITION	EMOTIONS REARRANGED (in descending order of intensity)	COLOR	WEIGHT (arbitrary numerical - descending order)	SMELL	TASTE	SOUND	FEEL (physical texture)	PHYSICAL OBJECT
Primary-									
QUARRELSOME									
Secondary-									
Grumpy									
Petulant									
Fretful									
Hostile									
Touchy									
Hot-tempered									
Keen									
Crabby									
Atrabilious									
Huffy									
Perverse									
Crotchety									
Cantankerous									

NEW SCHOOL ACTING   by Jeremy Whelan   © 1996

EMOTIONS	DEFINITION	EMOTIONS REARRANGED (in descending order of intensity)	COLOR	WEIGHT (arbitrary numerical - descending order)	SMELL	TASTE	SOUND	FEEL (physical texture)	PHYSICAL OBJECT
Primary-									
QUARRELSOME cont.									
Secondary-									
Grouchy									
Bile									
Testy									
Splenetic									
Cranky									
Churlish									
Fractious									
Irritable									
Liverish									
Ornery									
Peevish									

NEW SCHOOL ACTING   by Jeremy Whelan   © 1996

EMOTIONS	DEFINITION	EMOTIONS REARRANGED (in descending order of intensity)	COLOR	WEIGHT (arbitrary numerical - descending order)	SMELL	TASTE	SOUND	FEEL (physical texture)	PHYSICAL OBJECT
Primary-									
RAPACIOUS									
Secondary-									
Avaricious									
Avid									
Curious									
Demanding									
Desirous									
Acquisitive									
Predatory									
Greedy									
Inquisitive									
Interested									
Voracious									

174

NEW SCHOOL ACTING   by Jeremy Whelan   © 1996

EMOTIONS	DEFINITION	EMOTIONS REARRANGED (in descending order of intensity)	COLOR	WEIGHT (arbitrary numerical - descending order)	SMELL	TASTE	SOUND	FEEL (physical texture)	PHYSICAL OBJECT
Primary-									
SAD									
Secondary-									
Hurt									
Joyless									
Heartache									
Anguished									
Miserable									
Tortured									
Glum									
Heartbroken									
Heartsick									
Ache									
Disconsolate									
Despondent									
Agonize									

175

NEW SCHOOL ACTING   by Jeremy Whelan   © 1996

EMOTIONS	DEFINITION	EMOTIONS REARRANGED (in descending order of intensity)	COLOR	WEIGHT (arbitrary numerical - descending order)	SMELL	TASTE	SOUND	FEEL (physical texture)	PHYSICAL OBJECT
Primary-									
SAD cont.									
Secondary-									
Wretched									
Tormented									
Pain									
Suffering									
Morose									
Bathetic									
Demoralized									
Heavy-hearted									
Sorry									
Disappointed									
Chagrined									
Frustrated									
Disillusioned									

NEW SCHOOL ACTING   by Jeremy Whelan   © 1996

EMOTIONS	DEFINITION	EMOTIONS REARRANGED (in descending order of intensity)	COLOR	WEIGHT (arbitrary numerical - descending order)	SMELL	TASTE	SOUND	FEEL (physical texture)	PHYSICAL OBJECT
Primary-									
SENTIMENTAL									
Secondary-									
Maudlin									
Mawkish									
Romantic									
Fanciful									
Tearful									
Gushy									
Mushy									
Dreamy									

NEW SCHOOL ACTING   by Jeremy Whelan   © 1996

EMOTIONS	DEFINITION	EMOTIONS REARRANGED (in descending order of intensity)	COLOR	WEIGHT (arbitrary numerical - descending order)	SMELL	TASTE	SOUND	FEEL (physical texture)	PHYSICAL OBJECT
Primary-									
SERENE									
Secondary-									
Complacent									
Satisfied									
Ease									
Comforted									
Gratified									
Smug									
Content									
Impassive									
Dispassionate									
Calm									
Composed									
Cool									
Insouciant									

EMOTIONS	DEFINITION	EMOTIONS REARRANGED (in descending order of intensity)	COLOR	WEIGHT (arbitrary numerical - descending order)	SMELL	TASTE	SOUND	FEEL (physical texture)	PHYSICAL OBJECT
Primary-									
SERENE cont.									
Secondary-									
Mellow									
Relief									

NEW SCHOOL ACTING   by Jeremy Whelan   © 1996

EMOTIONS	DEFINITION	EMOTIONS REARRANGED (in descending order of intensity)	COLOR	WEIGHT (arbitrary numerical - descending order)	SMELL	TASTE	SOUND	FEEL (physical texture)	PHYSICAL OBJECT
Primary-									
SHOCKED									
Secondary-									
Appalled									
Astonished									
Surprised									
Amazed									
Stupefied									
Consternated									
Breathless									
Startled									
Aghast									
Agape									
Thunderstruck									
Astounded									

EMOTIONS	DEFINITION	EMOTIONS REARRANGED (in descending order of intensity)	COLOR	WEIGHT (arbitrary numerical - descending order)	SMELL	TASTE	SOUND	FEEL (physical texture)	PHYSICAL OBJECT
Primary-									
TIMID									
Secondary-									
Bashful									
Diffident									
Shy									
Restrained									
Inhibited									
Cowardly									
Pusillanimous									
Squeamish									
Modest									
Reluctant									
Insecure									
Unconfident									
Unassured									

181

NEW SCHOOL ACTING   by Jeremy Whelan   © 1996

EMOTIONS	DEFINITION	EMOTIONS REARRANGED (in descending order of intensity)	COLOR	WEIGHT (arbitrary numerical - descending order)	SMELL	TASTE	SOUND	FEEL (physical texture)	PHYSICAL OBJECT
Primary-									
TIMID cont.									
Secondary-									
Reticent									
Self-conscious									
Tender									
Hung-up									
Blocked									
Humble									
Weak-kneed									
Demure									
Chaste									
Unostentatious									
Unpretentious									
Sheepish									
Unaggressive									

NEW SCHOOL ACTING   by Jeremy Whelan   © 1996

EMOTIONS	DEFINITION	EMOTIONS REARRANGED (in descending order of intensity)	COLOR	WEIGHT (arbitrary numerical - descending order)	SMELL	TASTE	SOUND	FEEL (physical texture)	PHYSICAL OBJECT
Primary-									
TIMID cont.									
Secondary-									
Submissive									
Docile									
Meek									
Retiring									
Dastardly									

EMOTIONS	DEFINITION	EMOTIONS REARRANGED (in descending order of intensity)	COLOR	WEIGHT (arbitrary numerical - descending order)	SMELL	TASTE	SOUND	FEEL (physical texture)	PHYSICAL OBJECT
Primary-									
TRUCULENT									
Secondary-									
Envenomed									
Savage									
Rabid									
Violent									
Fierce									
Virulent									
Wrathful									
Ferocious									

EMOTIONS	DEFINITION	EMOTIONS REARRANGED (in descending order of intensity)	COLOR	WEIGHT (arbitrary numerical - descending order)	SMELL	TASTE	SOUND	FEEL (physical texture)	PHYSICAL OBJECT
Primary-									
UNFEELING									
Secondary-									
Aloof									
Austere									
Cold-hearted									
Rigid									
Reserved									
Heartless									
Callous									
Frigid									
Uncaring									
Grudging									
Numb									
Sensationless									
Unemotional									

EMOTIONS	DEFINITION	EMOTIONS REARRANGED (in descending order of intensity)	COLOR	WEIGHT (arbitrary numerical - descending order)	SMELL	TASTE	SOUND	FEEL (physical texture)	PHYSICAL OBJECT
Primary-									
UNFEELING cont.									
Secondary-									
Unmoved									

EMOTIONS	DEFINITION	EMOTIONS REARRANGED (in descending order of intensity)	COLOR	WEIGHT (arbitrary numerical - descending order)	SMELL	TASTE	SOUND	FEEL (physical texture)	PHYSICAL OBJECT
Primary-									
VALIANT									
Secondary-									
Courageous									
Valor									
Bold									
Gallant									
Nervy									
Intrepid									
Audacious									
Brazen									
Chivalrous									
Prowess									
Fearless									
Brave									
Adventurous									

NEW SCHOOL ACTING   by Jeremy Whelan   © 1996

EMOTIONS	DEFINITION	EMOTIONS REARRANGED (in descending order of intensity)	COLOR	WEIGHT (arbitrary numerical - descending order)	SMELL	TASTE	SOUND	FEEL (physical texture)	PHYSICAL OBJECT
Primary-									
VALIANT cont.									
Secondary-									
Daring									
Dour									
Doughty									
Undaunted									
Venturesome									
Confident									

NEW SCHOOL ACTING   by Jeremy Whelan   © 1996

EMOTIONS	DEFINITION	EMOTIONS REARRANGED (in descending order of intensity)	COLOR	WEIGHT (arbitrary numerical - descending order)	SMELL	TASTE	SOUND	FEEL (physical texture)	PHYSICAL OBJECT
Primary-									
WARM-HEARTED									
Secondary-									
Tender									
Affectionate									
Affinity									
Caring									
Soft-hearted									
Warm									
Good-hearted									

EMOTIONS	DEFINITION	EMOTIONS REARRANGED (in descending order of intensity)	COLOR	WEIGHT (arbitrary numerical - descending order)	SMELL	TASTE	SOUND	FEEL (physical texture)	PHYSICAL OBJECT
Primary-									
XENOPHOBIC									
Secondary-									
Patriotic									
Loyal									
Devoted									
Consecrated									
Dedicated									

EMOTIONS	DEFINITION	EMOTIONS REARRANGED (in descending order of intensity)	COLOR	WEIGHT (arbitrary numerical - descending order)	SMELL	TASTE	SOUND	FEEL (physical texture)	PHYSICAL OBJECT
Primary-									
YEARN									
Secondary-									
Crave									
Desire									
Hanker									
Want									
Long									
Pining									
Wish									
Hunger									
Famished									
Yen									
Desperate									

EMOTIONS	DEFINITION	EMOTIONS REARRANGED (in descending order of intensity)	COLOR	WEIGHT (arbitrary numerical - descending order)	SMELL	TASTE	SOUND	FEEL (physical texture)	PHYSICAL OBJECT
Primary-									
ZEALOUS									
Secondary-									
Verve									
Earnest									
Impatient									
Keen									
Trenchant									
Ardent									
Enthusiastic									
Ambitious									
Agog									
Exuberant									
High-spirited									
Vivacious									
Ebullient									

NEW SCHOOL ACTING   by Jeremy Whelan   © 1996

EMOTIONS	DEFINITION	EMOTIONS REARRANGED (in descending order of intensity)	COLOR	WEIGHT (arbitrary numerical - descending order)	SMELL	TASTE	SOUND	FEEL (physical texture)	PHYSICAL OBJECT
Primary-									
ZEALOUS cont.									
Secondary-									
Eager									
Vigorous									
Animated									
Impetuous									
Vehement									
Ruthless									
Gusto									

NEW SCHOOL ACTING   by Jeremy Whelan   © 1996

EMOTIONS	DEFINITION	EMOTIONS REARRANGED (in descending order of intensity)	COLOR	WEIGHT (arbitrary numerical - descending order)	SMELL	TASTE	SOUND	FEEL (physical texture)	PHYSICAL OBJECT
Primary-									
Secondary-									

NEW SCHOOL ACTING   by Jeremy Whelan   © 1996

EMOTIONS	DEFINITION	EMOTIONS REARRANGED (in descending order of intensity)	COLOR	WEIGHT (arbitrary numerical - descending order)	SMELL	TASTE	SOUND	FEEL (physical texture)	PHYSICAL OBJECT
Primary-									
Secondary-									

NEW SCHOOL ACTING   by Jeremy Whelan   © 1996

EMOTIONS	DEFINITION	EMOTIONS REARRANGED (in descending order of intensity)	COLOR	WEIGHT (arbitrary numerical - descending order)	SMELL	TASTE	SOUND	FEEL (physical texture)	PHYSICAL OBJECT
Primary-									
Secondary-									

NEW SCHOOL ACTING   by Jeremy Whelan   © 1996

EMOTIONS	DEFINITION	EMOTIONS REARRANGED (in descending order of intensity)	COLOR	WEIGHT (arbitrary numerical - descending order)	SMELL	TASTE	SOUND	FEEL (physical texture)	PHYSICAL OBJECT
Primary-									
Secondary-									

NEW SCHOOL ACTING   by Jeremy Whelan   © 1996

EMOTIONS	DEFINITION	EMOTIONS REARRANGED (in descending order of intensity)	COLOR	WEIGHT (arbitrary numerical - descending order)	SMELL	TASTE	SOUND	FEEL (physical texture)	PHYSICAL OBJECT
Primary-									
Secondary-									

EMOTIONS	DEFINITION	EMOTIONS REARRANGED (in descending order of intensity)	COLOR	WEIGHT (arbitrary numerical - descending order)	SMELL	TASTE	SOUND	FEEL (physical texture)	PHYSICAL OBJECT
Primary-									
Secondary-									

NEW SCHOOL ACTING by Jeremy Whelan © 1996

EMOTIONS	DEFINITION	EMOTIONS REARRANGED (in descending order of intensity)	COLOR	WEIGHT (arbitrary numerical - descending order)	SMELL	TASTE	SOUND	FEEL (physical texture)	PHYSICAL OBJECT
Primary-									
Secondary-									